To Bea,
Many thanks,
Love
Russell

WALTER KERR

THE

THEATER

IN SPITE OF ITSELF

SIMON AND SCHUSTER · NEW YORK · 1963

First Printing

"*The Thirty-Year Itch*" *originally appeared as* "*What Ails the Theater*" *in the* Saturday Evening Post.

"*Speculation*" *originally appeared as* "*Cheers for the Uninhibited U.S. Theater*" *in* Life Magazine.

"*The Ambiguity of the Theater of the Absurd*" *appeared as* "*Making a Cult of Confusion*"; "*Tug of War*" *as* "*The Theater of Form and Anti-Form*"; "*And Television*" *as* "*What Good Is Television?*"; *and* "*Angle of Vision*" *as* "*The Theater Breaks Out of Belasco's Box*" *in* Horizon Magazine.

LIBRARY OF CONGRESS CATALOG CARD NUMBER: 63–11143
MANUFACTURED IN THE UNITED STATES OF AMERICA
BY H. WOLFF BOOK MFG. CO., INC., NEW YORK

For Josephine

CONTENTS

CONTENTS

NOTE

THE AMERICAN THEATER of our time—perhaps this is true of most theaters at most times—is two-faced: complacent and alarmed; entrenched and on its last legs; a creature of habit and a habit-breaker; grossly commercial and given to the stupidest sort of risk; aimed at buyers on expense accounts and frequently enraging to buyers on expense accounts; loyal to favorite sons and daughters—sacred cows, they are sometimes called—and quick to brush old-timers aside in the rush to acclaim the latest young writer who has written one mildly interesting play or to star the freshest young actress who has acted well once; sluggish and always on the move; mindless and ready to produce any man who will charge it with mindlessness; eager to entertain and constantly raiding Paris of its latest prophets of pain; awash in costly musicals and proud of having done *The Caretaker;* conniving and incredibly innocent, noisy and walking on tiptoe, formally committed to formula and behaving as though it couldn't care less.

The spectacle is confusing, most of all to those who are responsible for it. If I have tried to sort the following first-night reviews, Sunday pieces, and magazine articles into groups which may be labeled it is not really with any hope of trying to impose order on a disorderly scene but in an effort, rather, to suggest the contrary energies that do clash by night. Going to the theater night in and night out may well make a man's head spin, for one night he is watching George Abbott at work and the next night Eugene Ionesco; one night he is in the world of stable domestic comedy and the next night the world—the whole world—dissolves. It is surprising that these two contradictory thrusts do not kill one another, or the viewer. But they do not. The fact of the matter is that they help to keep one another alive, each becoming its own form of protest. Avant-garde theater, kicking out at an optimism it regards as old-hat, does not hold a monopoly on the act of protesting; *The Sound of Music* is a kind of protest, too, certainly for the theatergoer who has hated *The Caretaker* and hurried in rebellion to a show that would assure him all was not tartness and dark. In Edward Albee's *Who's Afraid of Virginia Woolf?* a wife accuses her husband of making their marriage one long laceration. "You married me for it," replies the husband, and you know that she did. The theater, too, likes to marry its spurs, sometimes with the sly intention of taming them, sometimes because it is the only way it can hope to keep awake.

It is often said these days that the theater is asleep; if so, it is certainly having nightmares. At the same time, it can often be caught smiling—in its sleep and in its nightmares. The following pieces, written during the six years from 1957 to 1962, span a time during which a new, abrasive concept of what the theater might become was effectively challenging every conventional practice without in the least disturbing the three-year run of *The Sound of Music*. There is schizophrenia in that, beyond doubt. But there is also vigor in it, on both sides: in the bitter-enders, and in the bitter beginners. If something of that vigor is not recorded here, in passing, that is my fault.

There are some separations I have not bothered to make. For instance, I haven't isolated Broadway from off-Broadway. Though these are different areas of work, and though off-Broadway must be credited with offering work to the unemployed more swiftly than Broadway does, the distinction between them is one that tends to dissolve with time. Temperamentally, they are capable of the same sort of unpredictable behavior; though each has a character, each behaves uncharacteristically with astonishing frequency: it is Broadway that introduces us to the work of Samuel Beckett and Harold Pinter and off-Broadway that chooses to revive *White Cargo* and *Tobacco Road*. But even when off-Broadway is being thanked for what it most particularly does—which is to discover untried playwrights and performers—the thanks are scarcely cool on the lips before Broadway has called hello. It is generally a matter of two or three years between the time that a Jack Richardson or an Edward Albee, a Geraldine Page or a Jason Robards, Jr., appears in a small house and then moves to a large one, and in a collection that covers five or six such years the sense of interchange becomes stronger than the sense of separation. Off-Broadway is indeed influential; but, Broadway being so greedy, its influence is very quickly felt.

Nor have I tried to indicate precisely to whom—on Broadway or off, in vogue or out—I think the future belongs. Opinions I have, evening by evening and month by month. But they are opinions about the shape of materials which often proclaim themselves as tentative. It is early for prophecy, let alone photo-finishes. What we are making our way through just now, trying neither to stub our toes too violently nor to hang back too self-protectively, is a series of contrary experiences which have not yet come into even precarious balance. We don't know how far, or even exactly where, the newest impulse is going; in our ignorance, we cannot be certain what adjustments the tried-and-true, or the tried-and-not-quite-true, will be prepared to make. No doubt the confrontation will end in the rout of convention by some form of the unconventional, which will then become the next convention needing to be routed. At the moment, I doubt that we are even in the middle of things; the stand-patters are still pretty strong, and the wildness, sometimes the gayety, of the rebels is the damn-your-hide exuberance that is at its most extravagant in skirmishes.

One more waiver: I don't think the theater should always be taken seriously. Nine-tenths of the time the theater does not even take itself seriously, a fact which is often held against it. But we must not press it too hard. It has a conviction of its own that it was born slightly lightheaded, no matter what challenges it has had to sober itself to from time to time, and this is a conviction that is shared by a large number of the people who go to it; an unblinking glance at its long history might support its instinct for giddiness more than we like to think. In any case, we should not be so foolish as to approach its perennial foolishness in a constant state of agony; we will only get ulcers that way.

"Off with the show" is what we are too quick to say nowadays. Most of the shows I shall be mentioning are indeed off, now. But there was a time, very recently, when they were quick with energy of one kind or another: with the spurious energy of the ephemeral, or with the groping energy of the plant-finger feeling its way toward a fissure. The latter energy is still with us, if only we can recognize it; it is the energy that cracks open the future. As for the other, while it lasted, wasn't it sometimes fun?

SHOW BUSINESS

SPECULATION

REALISTICALLY SPEAKING, everything that is done on Broadway, whether it is as experimental as *The Caretaker* or as traditionally tooled as a Norman Krasna farce, comes under the general heading of show business—for the simple reason that it must be financed if it is to get there and must compete for customers if it is to stay there. It first appears, in short, as a commercial enterprise, as part of that hit-or-miss activity that is an eternal gamble, an eternal disgrace, and—no matter how much one may wish to deny the fact—an eternal romance. Romantically speaking, one of the virtues of this commercial theater is that it never knows what it is doing.

It tries hard to know, of course. A genuinely intelligent producer will sit back at the end of an exhausting and possibly unprofitable season, assess what he has done "wrong" and what he has "guessed right" about, analyze his competitors' obvious gaffes and inexplicable lucky strikes, and try to sniff out the winds that are apt to prevail in another eight months. He goes through this little intellectual exercise for two reasons: if his vision of the theatrical future is correct, if he *knows* what he is doing when he buys his next script, he will become rich enough to pay his taxes; he is also eager, all popular superstition to the contrary, to place himself in the esthetic vanguard, to prod the theater along a bit in its eternal quest for perfection.

Critics are even more eager to reduce the frantic activity that passes for professional theater in this country to some sort of manageable formula. Since the reviewers are the *only* people who see *all* of the shows produced in a given year (it is surprising how rarely theater people get to the theater), they are obviously in the best position to decide what elusive, faintly wriggling undercurrents are beginning to reveal themselves beneath the sloppy, self-contradictory surface currents of Broadway. When *Variety,* or some other palpitating journal with a stake in the theater, asks the critics at the end of a season, "What new developments do you detect, where and how far are we going?" reviewers leap to the bait like a cat to the icebox. The air is always full of indications; listen carefully each May or June, and you will learn what they are.

Playwrights like to speculate, too. Is the nostalgic midwestern family play in or out? Dare I examine my adolescence once more? Do Beckett, Ionesco, and Duerrenmatt constitute the shape of things to come? The hacks need to know because their work is always, quite literally, cut out for them by the stencil that is coming into fashion; and the serious playwright, lonely and nervous, cannot help but wonder whether he is still in touch.

Luckily, the producer, reviewer, or dramatist who engages in this sort of prenatal woolgathering will always wind up looking a little sheepish and explaining that that wasn't exactly what he meant. I speak with some authority, having carefully analyzed an especially successful season not long ago, announced a reflective trend that promised us three or four fat years before the trend died down, and then spent the next eight months wondering what everybody else was doing wrong.

But reviewers are not the only prophets without honor in the theater. Take a small example. For the past ten years it has been the considered, and eminently sensible, opinion of all hands in the field of production that the musical revue was, for all practical purposes, washed up. The reasons given were excellent—irrefutable, really. In today's economy, the costs of mounting any kind of musical are terrifying to contemplate. The chances of recouping these costs are promptly cut in half when the musical elects to get along without a "book," a narrative line. (The last time my wife saw a revue in New York she was seated behind a woman who confided to her companion, "If I'd known there wasn't a plot, I wouldn't of come.") The British theater may have managed to keep the form flourishing by playing it cozy, putting intimate companies into intimate houses and letting an intimate orchestra, or perhaps two pianos, make a limited din; but Broadway must think big in order to survive, and intelligent vaudeville was clearly out of the question.

It was out of the question, that is, until a group of visiting Frenchmen, unfamiliar with the uncertainties of the American theater, opened a multiscened, substantially staffed revue with a patently uncommercial title, *La Plume de Ma Tante*. (It should be reported that one ashen backer sold out his interest twenty-four hours before curtain time.) The first-night audience collapsed with joy, the next-morning notices were unanimously ecstatic (the only other venture to catch all of the critics in so responsive a mood during that particular season had been Eugene O'Neill's *A Touch of the Poet*), and the man at the box office counted two hundred people in line as he opened his window for the day. All those people who were so passionate about plot had developed a quick, unreasonable affection for baritone solos on horseback, sopranos who grew an additional two inches with each new high note, and tonsured monks swooping through a belfry in jazz abandon.

Take a medium-sized example. Along about the mid-fifties most observers of theatrical progress decided, sorrowfully, that all the new television writers who were straying toward the theater weren't going to do the legitimate drama much good. Eight or ten TV craftsmen had tried to make the shift; the work of all eight or ten had been carted away on their respective Saturday nights. Theories were evolved to explain the recurring disaster: the successful television writer's vision had been so narrowed by that small screen, that limited time span, and those hushed close-ups that it was ever there-

17

after bound to the suppressed psychology and the subdued climaxes of a fragmentary form; how could such a man be expected to take a deep enough breath to make himself heard in a Forty-fourth Street barn?

This satisfactory resolution of the formal problem was arrived at just in time to be demolished by the arrival of Paddy Chayefsky's *Middle of the Night* and William Gibson's *Two for the Seesaw* (two characters only, just enough for a small screen—and for 750 performances on Broadway).

Take an example that may yet inundate us all. In the spring of 1958, and as a result of a running discussion at theatrical round tables, broad-stroke farce was buried with solemn rites. Comedies of any kind were difficult to come by; comedies in which anybody got hit over the head or pushed through a window were not only missing, they were unmourned. Only once, in late April of that year, did an irresponsible dramatist dare a preposterous gesture (he allowed his drugged college professor to mistake the basement of the Empire State Building for an enemy submarine and send it to the bottom with every steampipe hissing); the gesture was greeted with mixed feelings and did not survive the summer.

I remember discussing the play's failure with one of our most distinguished producers (I had enjoyed the nonsense, and was feeling depressed). The producer considered the matter for a moment and echoed the conclusion that was on everyone's lips: "There just may not be room in our theater any more for an inconsequential 'show'—only the movies can get away with it." This had become a firm conviction among the more astute managers: the movement of the theater toward greater and greater seriousness, toward the "responsibility" demanded of it as an art form, even toward the "importance" so expensive an occasion must assume in the eyes of customers, had cut adrift all of the lighter and lower forms: farce, melodrama, the theater of casual and conscious contrivance. "B" movies could take care of the demand for lightweight manufacture; the stage, shooting high, must narrow its course.

Naturally, the very next season opened with a series of seven entertainments which made it clear that while the soothsayers were busy writing an epitaph for farce, the writers were busy writing nothing but farces.

The catalogue of happy fallibility could be extended: the moment we were sure that "thrillers" were a thing of the past an entire season was saved from financial and critical despair by three of them; by the time we'd concluded that Hollywood screenwriters were too immersed in banality to be of use to the theater Ketti Frings dramatized *Look Homeward, Angel* and Dore Schary arrived in town with *Sunrise at Campobello*. We are always telling the theater to stand still and behave itself, so that we can establish its identity, take its proper measurements, and dress it suitably for the future we have in mind; it keeps twitching.

What is so cheerful about the theater's refusal to be bound by the good intentions of very good men? The moment we succeed in consciously patterning our theater, in making it do precisely what we think it ought to be doing, we are apt to paralyze it. Don't think this hasn't happened. Responsible scholars took over the destiny of the Italian theater in the sixteenth century: certain forms were decreed acceptable in a drama ruled by intelligence and taste, certain others were abandoned as vulgar. Similarly earnest minds attempted to lead the French theater of the seventeenth century by the hand, with knuckles rapped for any and all violations of precept. The British theater of the eighteenth century was given a "rational" basis by men who knew what was proper and profitable for a playgoer to see. In each case, the deliberately shaped experience became an experience of boredom, and what had been outlawed as vulgar proved to be embarrassingly vital.

The vitality of any theater pretty much depends on its ability to stuff itself—more or less indiscriminately—with goodies

19

of all kinds and from all tables, including the nickel candy counter. No one ever knows from what merely circusy frolic —or, for that matter, from what studiously intellectual experiment in abstraction—the next burst of energy is coming. Shakespeare probably drew more heavily upon the cheap theatrics of the money-minded marketplace than he did upon the carefully tooled conceits of the Elizabethan avant-garde; but he drew from both, because he hadn't decided that either source was off limits.

The second-greatest danger any theater faces is that of making up its mind that any one method, or any one manner, is the "right" method or manner for all right-thinking men. And the greatest danger is that, in arriving at this clear and responsible vision, everything that is lowest will be lopped off first.

There has been, for instance, a tendency in recent years to make a sharper and sharper distinction between the "art of the theater" and the follies of "show biz," as though the former could be produced in an almost puritanical isolation and the latter could be tolerated—as any amiable human weakness is tolerated—only if a sufficiently demeaning tag were put on it. (You can traffic with "show business" if you want to, but don't pretend that you belong to the club.)

In this view, "show business"—with all of its allure and perhaps because of its allure—is the enemy of art, the glittering, simple-minded, distracting dead weight that keeps the foolish content and drags the aspiring down. But show business has never been the enemy of art; it is, on the contrary, its line of supply.

The man who bathes himself in Marcel Marceau and murmurs "It's Bach" when he is at last able to speak is too often the man who feels himself contaminated in the presence of anything that runs longer than three weeks and turns a profit; he has generally not examined Marceau's sources, which, as the artist has repeatedly explained, lie in the movies when the movies were at their most vulgar. The man who admires Gian-Carlo Menotti's labors toward an idiomatic opera likes to forget that the idiomatic phrasing serves, and in return draws strength from, a kind of plotting that has long since been dismissed as ten-twent'-thirt': plotting that embraces crippled children, witching-hour clairvoyants, and the secret police. If *Waiting for Godot* is deliberate "art," where did the man who played it best—Bert Lahr—come from? (I have had a letter explaining to me that Mr. Lahr "destroyed the purity" of the work by his warm, funny, and moving presence, and I suppose this is possible in a work meant to be cold, neutral, and empty; I can only report that without Mr. Lahr the play did not seem richer.) Eugene O'Neill consciously repudiated the bravura melodrama of situation that dominated his father's theater; it is, most probably, the ghostly echo of all that fury that enables us to overlook those failures of thought and of language that every O'Neill fan acknowledges. Is an actor's ability to play a sound *Oedipus* a sign of artistic growth? If so, we must express our gratitude not to the serious theater of the past ten years but to a medium—television, which gave Christopher Plummer his first opportunity to tear out his eyes—that is dominated by westerns and identified with trivia.

These are random examples, and they barely suggest the profit an elevated and ambitious theater can squeeze from the practice of tolerating, and taking friendly notice of, the poor relatives on its threshold. Perhaps a better, because more literary, example might be Jean Anouilh's *The Waltz of the Toreadors*. This exacerbating study of the romantic sex-dream seems to me as close to "art" as almost anything written for the stage in our time; and a part of its achievement consists in the perfection of its form. The form, as it happens, is the form of mistaken-identity farce, which provides an arbitrary framework for an interior that is much more desperately real and sadly savage, in something of the same way that the

21

rhyme scheme and line limitations of a rondeau create an artifice inside which a truth can be expressed. If, however, the French theater in which M. Anouilh works had no living tradition of mathematical farce, and if the rest of us had no living memory of it, the form would be unavailable to the writer and unintelligible to the rest of us, as it would have been unavailable to Shakespeare, and unintelligible to his audiences, when he arrived at *Twelfth Night*. (The line between *The Comedy of Errors* and *Twelfth Night* is a direct one; the first use of the mechanics is primitive and believing, the second is sophisticated and indifferent to belief.) We should have lost in both cases the joy of irony, the deep pleasure that comes from the juxtaposition of dimensional content and sassy shape, if we had insisted upon sophistication too early —if we had killed off the joke when it was only a joke. The seeds of great work come all too often from the slums.

I think we cannot ever afford to divide the theater into the acceptable and the unacceptable, or even to make an a priori distinction between higher and lower forms. It is all right afterwards to say that a writer has written a "mere melodrama"; but you had better not say it before he has begun writing.

Art, I suspect, is not a lean fellow; he has a paunch, from overindulgence. The natural appetite of the audience for a wide, constantly changing, unpredictable menu—and don't eliminate the sweets—is not quite the menace to theatrical security and esthetic progress that well-meaning managers, critics, and playwrights sometimes imagine it to be; it is, rather, a sign of simple joy in the medium, a restless reassertion of primitive values that are also root values, a guarantee of an ultimate harvest that depends just now on cross-fertilization and the constant rotation of crops.

To switch metaphors once or twice more, art is a city that needs all of its suburbs, a language that arrives at perfection through a sifting of many dialects. If there is one strain that the American theater *is* neglecting at the moment it is the tough, knotted thread of earlier perfection, the lifeline of the theater's "classics," that W. H. Auden has described as our continuing conversation with the past. But even the major successes of history ought not to be produced merely because it is virtuous to produce them, or because their perfection may be thought to guide us toward a final purity. They have a curious light to shed on what we suppose to be our own special difficulty: Does a theater arrive at Molière without an experience of folk farce? (Does one even arrive at Chekhov without the preliminary horseplay of *The Boor* and *The Marriage Proposal?*) Can we arrive at opera, as Leonard Bernstein has asked, without an experience of *singspiel*, or something very like musical comedy? Does Hamlet spring full-blown from the head of Dionysus or does he owe a little something to the Elizabethan equivalent of horror fiction?

When we try to be precise and proper about the shape the theater ought to assume, we generally wind up being not so much accurate as arbitrary: there is no room in the innyard, we say, before we have quite guessed the identity of the buffoon begging admission. It is always wisest to leave the doors —perhaps especially the back doors—slightly ajar.

THE FANTASTIC, LIGHT AND HEAVY

WHEN SHOW BUSINESS is thinking big, it thinks musicals, a habit which can end in anything from the stunning mishaps of *Portofino* to the crisp discoveries of *West Side Story*, with various samplings of the tough mind and the tender heart lodged between.

Portofino

I don't know why people say actors are temperamental. Actors are lambs. They are loyal. They are prompt. They are dutiful. They are obedient. They will do anything they are told to do. They will walk right out on a stage and play *Portofino*.

Consider, if you will, the case of Helen Gallagher. In *Portofino* Miss Gallagher came through a couple of French doors onto a noticeably wobbling Italian balcony, rubbed her right hip up and down against the corner of the building to indicate what the authors conceived to be sex, blinked her big pretty eyes, opened her steam-whistle mouth, and clearly spoke the line, "When I think of him kissing me, I don't know whether to fall down, sit down, or Miltown."

She didn't cringe, or shudder, or hide her head under her wing. She didn't hand in her notice, effective at the first-act intermission (this would, in any case, have been difficult, because the first-act intermission didn't take place until the middle of the second act, a situation I am not even going to try to explain to you). She didn't go home to Mother. She stood there—*stood* there—with her happy eyelashes fluttering, her brave little heart beating proudly, and steadied herself for the next idiotic musical number, which was going to take place in spite of the fact that the spotlight that was supposed to be following her was flickering out, the men who were supposed to be operating it were engaged in loud, heated conversation in the booth, and the dress that was supposed to be so dazzling was ripping rapidly up the back. Good girl.

And a good boy, Georges Guetary. Mr. Guetary didn't seem to mind at all the fact that practically every time he opened his metallic larynx to sing a song a bevy of small creatures wearing domino masks and a great many pompons (I swear I saw Bessie McCoy, the Yama-Yama girl, among them) crept out of the wings, slithered across the floor, and crawled all over him. The idea was that this was "Festa" time, and they were mad for him. Anyway, he didn't brush them off, or hit them, or anything; he just waited until they were gone, straightened his shoulders under his bright red sweater, and turned to face the next invasion. Mr. Guetary, gentleman that he is, may have performed a further kindness for all of us in singing some of the lyrics indistinctly.

I did wish that Webb Tilton, who played a sudden inn-keeper (that is to say, he became an innkeeper just in time to sing an innkeeper's song in the second act) had been as thoughtful. Mr. Tilton commanded a large, clear voice, he did his duty as he saw it, and he made it perfectly possible for all of the customers (including two clever people who arrived in row B one hour and twenty minutes after the curtain went up) to hear a lyric offering the beautiful thought that "the word, when made flesh, was hardly heard" before it turned out there was "too little time for love." You earned your pay, Mr. Tilton, and I can't believe librettist-lyricist Richard Ney ever thanked you for it.

I will not say that *Portofino* was the worst musical *ever* produced, because I've only been seeing musicals since 1919.

Gypsy

Before coming to town in *Gypsy*, Ethel Merman had let it be known that, for the first time in her long and kindly career, she was acting. You needn't have told us, Ethel. We'd have noticed.

The acting was not easy. This "Mama" Rose, "Mama" to a teen-age Gypsy Rose Lee, bolted down the aisle of a theater to blackmail a harried producer and to hurtle her children into the nearest available spotlight. She hid behind telephone poles while the kids hitched rides, and then climbed in. She stole Boy Scouts for the "act," slept her charges six in a room, made their clothes out of hotel blankets, and screamed that the manager had attacked her when he had merely asked for the rent.

She was, in short, a brassy, brazen witch on a mortgaged broomstick, a steamroller with cleats, the very mastodon of all stage mothers. And you loved her. What Miss Merman had remembered is that the mastodon was one of the most innocent of all creatures, a simple soul with simple appetites and a strong, direct, quite admirable way of going about getting exactly what it needed.

The mastodon, of course, is extinct now—and therein lay the special secret of Miss Merman's triumph. Behind all of her backstage clamor, her shouting to the men in the spot booth, her wrangling with jealous burlesque strippers, her soaring ascents into confident song, there lurked a worrying sense of doom—a foreboding that she would be deserted, that she never would fulfill her dream of stardom for her girls because it was really a dream of stardom for herself. There was always a faint chill around those warm and glowing alley doors—and "Mama" gave us the warmth and the chill in every roaring, unforgettable bleat.

She brought us, too, to the only finale that was ever possible for this "fable." She stood alone in a garish nightmare of neon, still stomping out fresh confidence that couldn't help but break in the middle of a syllable, kingpin of a world that had vanished beneath her feet. If you didn't cry, don't speak to me.

How to Succeed in Business Without Really Trying

The principal figures in this cool-as-brass entertainment seemed always to be putting their hands to their hearts. Robert Morse did it, dancing about on his inner-spring feet, as he gave thirty seconds' thought to the girl he was nobly neglecting while he soared ever higher in the world of all-American industry. Rudy Vallee did it, looking exactly as soulful as the Spirit of Bicarbonate of Soda, while he raised his eyes as much as he could beneath his tent-shaped eyebrows and inquired plaintively, "Where will I find that treasure of treasures, the love from a heart of gold?" (His treasure was actually standing right next to him, with hips like parentheses and eyes like asterisks.) And Mr. Morse and Mr. Vallee took time to do it together, in lock-step, strutting to stage right and then, after a perfect pivot, strutting to stage left in a nostalgic tribute to a school one of them had never attended, "Grand Old Ivy." Whence came all this clasping of hand to heart? I think they were checking to see if they had any.

As it happened, not a sincere line was spoken in the Abe Burrows-Frank Loesser musical, and what a relief that turned out to be. It became clear to me on the instant that what has been killing musical comedy is sincerity.

Even the orchestral arrangements were dishonest. When a redheaded goldfish in a V-necked slipcover was discovered palpitating beneath a slithering sheath of silver fox, the great chords that greeted her from the pit had not the least trace of sex in them. They sounded like the sighs of pilgrims arriving at Valhalla. When an office boy on the rise made his first breathless entrance into the office of the company's president, the strains that swept him into the headquarters of the World Wide Wickets Corporation sounded as though they had been composed by Tennyson, just after he'd crossed the bar. A board meeting assembled to chapel music, with larceny coming right after Lauds.

And then there was what must be regarded as a juicy evening's most jaundiced Valentine (and also its most satisfying number), "I Believe in You." This rhapsody was, in point of fact, rather sentimental. The hero was sentimental about the hero. Mr. Morse, as the dashing young go-getter who had risen to the heights simply by getting on the elevator and calling all floors, spent this particular moment in the men's room, along with the hard-working colleagues he had beamingly left behind. The other fellows, hissing their secret thoughts into the mirrors as they washed up (to music), were after Mr. Morse's scalp, with his head attached. "Gotta get that man" was the way the underbeat went.

Mr. Morse, though, was all warmth. "Ah, there's that face," he sighed, looking with love into the glass that showed him his tilted, treacherous nose, his sunny, lethal eyes. As he began to shave—and the orchestration for Mr. Loesser's threnody was somehow composed of four violins and three electric shavers—he also began to view himself from a variety of admirable angles. Like Michelangelo's "David" or the "Venus de Milo," he looked just as good from all sides. To himself, to us, perhaps even to Machiavelli in heaven. If Horatio Alger's noblest lad had been born a crook, he couldn't have been more charming.

Mr. Morse was also charming—in an alarming sort of way —when he wasn't so sure of himself. His sudden look of deep, seal-like shame when he realized a girl had hooked him for lunch; his habit of using his hands as though he'd skip rope if only he had a rope; his practice of seeming to try to shake water out of his ear whenever a damsel had an undue effect on him—all of these were graphic studies in the nature of man, pre-coordinated man.

We first met this happy spastic as he was being lowered from the flies on a window-cleaner's scaffold, a book in his hand. The book was a young man's guide, circa 1961, to professional advancement, and it wasted no time on such irrelevant matters as thrift, hard work, or personal cleanliness. Its definitions were all more intelligent than that. (Definition of a mailroom: "a place out of which you must get.")

In getting out of the mailroom and becoming all things to all potential victims, Mr. Morse had the opportunity to turn his foam-rubber form into a drooping flower as he bestowed a carnation upon the firm's biggest battle-ax; making the gift, he somehow became the carnation. He was now manic (hopping in and out of chairs that looked like pistachio ice cream cones to speak of territories "where sales have been peakiest"), now depressive (the crash of a cymbal from the orchestra pit warned him he was in love, causing him to go limp as a broken-necked puppet impaled by an arrow to a wall). Whether he was darting around high on a windy pent-house or taking off for the horizon as in a very spiritual movie, whether he was going to pieces or coming to a color (true-blue), Mr. Morse remained an exhilarating zany, a six-teenth-century harlequin with a Dow-Jones soul.

Mr. Vallee was no slouch, either. As a corporation president who steadied his nerves by knitting covers for his golf clubs (popcorn stitch), he was sober, reflective, and preposterous. Despising nepotism because he happened to despise his nephew, a fellow named Frump, he wheezed, "Blood is thicker than water, but Frump is thicker than anything." Dumping his latest cookie into the stenographic pool at the office, and explaining that he couldn't go home nights "because I'm a married man," he ruled his wicked little world with the pince-nez piety of a Woodrow Wilson and the knickerbocker win-someness of a Warren Gamaliel Harding. Mr. Vallee bleated, snorted, and exhaled virtue like a lamb that had absolutely not lost its way.

Yet what most distinguished an impudent evening was—in defiance of all precept—its book. Abe Burrows had done it with acknowledged help from Jack Weinstock and Willie Gil-bert. But what had happened was that, for the first time re-ally, an entire musical comedy had been fashioned along the deadpan, and deadly, lines of Mr. Burrows' celebrated piano parodies ("Good Luck, Boulder Dam"). This was, and I whis-per it, a musical with a mind. A bland and caustic kidding of the American success story, it skipped along all evening with-out ever losing its frosty and lunatic altitude. Gags were subor-dinated to impish running commentary; Mr. Loesser's perky score was subordinated to the merry malice that was afoot; meaningful fantasy was given its head, and the point of view grinned and glowed with its own cocksure effrontery.

La Plume de Ma Tante

If *La Plume de Ma Tante* made hash of everyone's predictions that the musical-revue form was through, it was because the French had discovered an absolutely perfect way of bringing it back to life. They simply left out the words.

Oh, there were a few words spoken here and there as guitars caught fire, chickens hatched bald-headed men, and a tardy member of the orchestra tried desperately to get across the footlights and into the pit, but very little valuable time was wasted on them. A deeply forlorn straggler with a circumflex mouth did poke his head through the curtain while author Robert Dhery was identifying the next unidentifiable number and did try to get a thought in edgewise. He said, "Maybe you will think I am stupid—"; he was met with a very curt "Yes," and he disappeared disconsolately, but immediately, to his dressing room. He was not going to argue.

This same wistful zany (his name was Pierre Olaf; remember it) had some difficulty in hoisting his bicycle over his head smartly enough during an emergency police drill. In a small, shy stammer he explained that he just couldn't do it with all those people out front. Forgiven for the moment, he at last got a second golden opportunity to shine. "They're still there," he murmured, excusing himself.

But silence was the supreme joy of nearly everything else in *La Plume de Ma Tante*. Silence, and a superb sense of the supple, insinuating, and explosive rhythms that underlie the comic spirit at its lowest.

Rhythm alone was what made M. Dhery's after-hours tussle with an insistent customer in a deserted restaurant the miniature treasure it was. Wriggling his fingers after a bit of cork in a wine glass until every ounce of the wine had been exhaustively explored, missing a flapjack with his frying pan in a moment of perfect imprecision, tidily tucking away a flaming scarf in a handy chafing dish, he was the very model of swift, light-fingered, everlastingly resourceful incompetence.

And it was worth it to keep a sharp eye on the four monks who stirred sleepily in their bell tower at the end of the first act. The hour was matins, I suppose, and the good *frères* rose to tend to the stout, inviting ropes that dangled from the belfry above. There was an itch in the spring air, though, and a touch of jazz in one devout heart. Two seconds later the cloister was jumping with surely the most exuberant display of ecclesiastical jitterbug yet seen by mortal eye, and the theater swayed with incontinence.

Having laughed so freely through two-thirds of *La Plume de Ma Tante* that my wife was on the verge of reporting me to the ushers, I did feel a small twinge of apprehension as I watched the beginning of a semiserious dance called "In the Tuileries Gardens." We were deep into the second act now, and here came Pierre Olaf ambling across a stage crowded with straw-hatted schoolgirls in the company of dancer Colette Brosset. Both were dressed in tramp costumes, and the severe streaks of make-up that marked the mouth lines beneath their glowing red noses were turned down. Must the most accomplished comedians, I asked myself, *always* turn ragged and pathetic for five minutes a night? Is there no getting away from the number with the teardrop eyes?

But I wasn't apprehensive for long, although this *was* that same old bit in which buffoons become wistful. In a moment or two I was paying very close attention to M. Olaf's hopeless flirtation with a bright-faced child, to Mlle. Brosset's forlorn shuffle as she turned her back on the sorry spectacle her partner was making of himself, and to the hesitant, almost despairing, reunion of these two strays once the wild-oat impulse had died down. In spite of the obviousness of the bid for

31

pathos, the pathos had quickly come. When it came, it was genuine. The clown's traditional sideslip into sudden sorrow had once more worked its magic.

What is really puzzling is the incredible speed with which any dealer in simple slapstick can turn the tables on an audience. It may take a hard-working tragedian a couple of hours, and enormous amounts of professional writhing, to do the trick; a cartoon in oversize pants and painted eyebrows can do it with the flick of a finger.

The secret, I suppose, lies in the fact that the clown is helpless to begin with. The tragic hero, when you first meet him, is normally a fellow who has it made: he seems to be master of himself, master of all he surveys, and if he does get into trouble—at long last—it is only because he cannot leave his manifestly desirable destiny alone. The fellow in the pancake hat, on the other hand, starts out with the world against him.

How much it is against him—with what implacable venom it scatters booby traps at his feet—had already been made abundantly clear in the earlier stages of *La Plume de Ma Tante*. Interlocutor Dhery had barely been able to get through his introductory speech of welcome what with his obvious fear that everything was going to go wrong all night. The players were ready, he had assured us, though one of them was clearly still shaving at the proscenium. Mlle. Brosset had promised to help us follow the various songs and sketches by appearing regularly with numbered placards, but Mlle. Brosset was to be seen displaying a large "2" before anything recognizable as "1" had taken place.

A baritone forced to do a ballad with a lady in a flowered swing had been utterly unable to establish himself in a position that was reasonably safe. The unpredictable doors of a bathing pavilion, rhythmically clicking open and shut, had refused to accommodate themselves to the heady desires of a frustrated fellow who would have liked to make the most of them. In a leggy line-up of chorus girls, one leg had worked steadily and solemnly against all the others. In another show-girl fantasia on a darkened stage, one showgirl in luminous paint had found it necessary to use a flashlight.

Even now, as the evening skipped to a close, a prince in a ballet found himself nearly unable to go on with his work; he had made the mistake of glancing down at his dancer's tights. Because the exits of a Paris latrine were difficult to find and difficult to manage, two visitors were trapped in it well beyond their endurance. (If this particular inspiration was less funny than some of the others it was only because the rest of us could see an easy way out of the situation, and the hostile universe that the clown inhabits became—in that instant—less real.)

Anyway, as loosened slippers flew wildly into the balcony, as a strip-teaser's pompons stuck to her like burrs, and as a lonely passenger stood atop an airport ladder looking patiently into the sky for a plane that wasn't there, it seemed clear enough why tears should come easily to such monstrously harassed, and undeservedly bedeviled, victims of the outrages that comic flesh is heir to.

The Sound of Music

The sweetness that was best in *The Sound of Music* could be heard, gently and demurely, in an early Oscar Hammerstein lyric. Mary Martin sang the line, with her dimpled mouth spilling upwards and sideways over her dimpled cheeks. She was dressed, at the moment, in the muted garb of a convent novice, but she was determined to list, one by one, all of the things she loved best in the world. One of these, she confided to us with a lift of her chin, was the feel of snowflakes on her eyelashes.

That is a sentimental thought. It is a pretty thought. It may even be, among romantics, a conventional thought. But it soared from the lady's pitch-pipe throat with great joy, and you could only think, "How nice that is!" It was nice because this was a musical, because sentiment is quite proper to this kind of musical, and because it was good to know that so skilled a craftsman as Mr. Hammerstein would be putting the words together for the rest of the evening.

The rest of the evening included certain gifts from the Broadway confectionary. It was hard to imagine, for instance, anyone other than Richard Rodgers finding so much leapfrog gayety for a troubled melody sung by five or six worried nuns. But who was it that decided, after half an hour or so, to abandon the snowflakes and substitute corn flakes? Before *The Sound of Music* was halfway through its promising chores it became not only too sweet for words but almost too sweet for music.

Somehow I couldn't feel that this was the fault of librettists Howard Lindsay and Russel Crouse. When it was time for a moment of melodramatic plotting, the spine of the evening straightened abruptly and we did feel some tension as a principled family found itself surrounded and cut off by boot-clicking Nazis.

Was it director Vincent J. Donehue who made the evening suffer from little children? There were seven tots necessary to the narrative, and I have never been against tots. But need they have bounced into bed in their nightgowns so often, and so armingly? Was it necessary for them to wear so many different picture-book skirts, and fluff them so mightily, and smile so relentlessly, and give such precocious advice to their elders so often?

The cascade of sugar was not confined to the youngsters. Miss Martin, too, was to be seen falling to her knees and folding her hands in prayer while evening breezes blew the kiddies through the window. Always, always she entered as though the dessert were here now.

Always, always the stage pictures—groupings in thunderstorms, groupings at nightfall, groupings singing little concerts with very cute gestures—begged us for an "ooooh" where a decent, simple interest might have been much warmer. The pitch was too strong; the taste of vanilla overwhelmed the solid chocolate; the people on stage had all melted before our hearts did.

The upshot? What might have been a perky and reasonably substantial entertainment aimed itself directly at those who have always found Sir James M. Barrie pretty rough stuff.

West Side Story

The dances in *West Side Story* came up like geysers through the floor of the city.

The curtain rose on a silence, and a pause. It was the last silence, almost the last pause. Against an empty-eyed background of warehouse windows five or six blue-jacketed young delinquents, with the tribal mark "Jets" scrawled across their taut shoulders, were lounging, waiting for the first whisper of violence.

Their impatience came to life in their fingers. A snapping rhythm began to tap out a warning of mayhem to come. Knees began to itch, and move, under the lazy, overcast midsummer sky in Puerto Rican New York.

The Sharks—equally young, equally sick with very old hatreds—appeared from the alleyways in twos and threes. There was a sneer, a hiss, a tempting and tantalizing thrust of an arm, and then—with a screeching downbeat from the orchestra pit—the sorry and meaningless frenzy was on. From this moment the show rode with a catastrophic roar over the spider-web fire escapes, the shadowed trestles, and the plain dirt battlegrounds of a big-city feud.

Choreographer Jerome Robbins did not run out of his original explosive life-force. Though the essential images were al-

35

ways the same—two spitting groups of people advancing with bared teeth and clawed fists upon one another—there was fresh excitement in the next debacle, and the next. When a gang leader advised his cohorts to play it "Cool," the intolerable tension between an effort at control and the instinctive drives of these potential killers worked on the theater with pressure-cooker menace. When the knives came out, and bodies flew wildly through space under buttermilk clouds, the sheer visual release was breath-taking.

Again and again there was striking use of suppressed sound: the rustle of feet being thrust as quietly as possible into toeholds on a wire barrier, the clap of a hand on a leather-clad shoulder as a too-eager Shark was halted in mid-flight. Casual shoulders converged, backs rose in arches alley cats might have envied, stealthy feet slipped sideways into circling pools of hostility until, from a single swift upthrust at the heart of the cauldron, an explosion of venom could roar outward to the wings.

This constant pendulum-swing of pressure and release became the fundamental visual and dramatic pattern of the entertainment. Mr. Robbins' Polish-American Romeo and his Puerto Rican Juliet first met at a gymnasium dance that was going badly: the rival street gangs were already brushing elbows as they warily circled the social floor, waiting for the one grating exchange that would give them the right to act.

As the waiting approached fever pitch, there was a sharp inhalation. Out of opposite corners on a swiftly darkened stage came the spellbound lovers, eyes riveted upon one another. As they met, the silhouetted enemies behind them subtly changed footwork: a mocking, insidiously mincing minuet echoed the lovers' mood without for a moment ceasing to threaten them. The figure of the dance was romantic, but a Satanic rigidity infected its grace. The moment was stretched taut: a longing couple, a coiled crowd. Then restlessness reasserted itself: knees bent with more emphasis, elbows unlocked and jabbed at the air, a picture that had had temporary shape and control broke open toward stomping rebellion. Chaos was coming; the lovers would be lost in it.

The dissolves that carried us—via a rainfall of streamers or a nightmare of spinning fences—from tiny Puerto Rican rooms to garishly lighted alleys were everywhere ingenious, but nowhere more so than in the transition that swept us into the free stage and the extended melodic line of Leonard Bernstein's "Somewhere." Two or three times during the evening Mr. Bernstein asserted a composer's right to be heard on his own ("Maria," "Tonight," "I Have a Love"). The rest of the time, and it was most of the time, he was writing musical phrases in steel, hammering with a stern force at the red, noisy anvil of the narrative, content simply to be part of the furious contraction, expansion, contraction.

I confess that the nonmusical portions of *West Side Story* have always left me unsatisfied. Whenever I have seen the show, I have been aware of some disproportion between the essentially unexplained gutter violence and the vast tragic arena spaces it was expected to fill. Yes, *Romeo and Juliet* could be transposed into contemporary terms with some aptness. The pieces did fit. The girl was both Juliet and a Puerto Rican. But she was not any *one* Puerto Rican for whom we could feel deeply. Her sufferings seemed dictated not so much by this play as by another one: our relationship to her was less than personal.

And the failure to account in some meaningful way for the specific hatreds that tore these lives apart left a question mark stamped on the work. Though librettist Arthur Laurents had given us busy and accurate language of the streets, only once did he seem to hit upon a root for so much pain. A druggist (Friar Laurence, that was) was fussing at his unruly young customers and wearying them with "when I was your age" maxims. One of the grim-lipped amateur gangsters spun on him in unexpected rage. "You were never my age!" he

37

screamed. For one shocked moment we seemed to be intimate with a special time, a special group of mystified, flailing youngsters. But the vein was not opened again. There was violence, and more violence, and no further hint of its exact impulse in the recesses of flesh and brain.

No one in his right mind would ask such values of a musical show that meant simply to be a lighthearted, lyrical *divertissement*. *West Side Story* meant to be, and in several respects was, much more than that. It was an utterly serious musical play that, in its ambition and partial achievement, created fresh new demands of its own—specifically, for an emotional recognition and a character penetration that would match the sober urgency of its orchestration and its dancing. It did not achieve everything it asked of itself. Even so, it was a remarkable piece of work to come from a Broadway tradition that is generally thought of as merely giddy.

ILLEGITIMATES

THERE IS a kind of show business that has nothing to do with plays, bless it.

Flanders and Swann

In this two-man vaudeville, Michael Flanders is the one with the beard, but Donald Swann is the one they are going to take away soon.

Mr. Swann, if I have to be the first to point the finger, is crazy. The authorities are not to be deceived by his guileless manner. It is true that he seems very shy and serious, like an overage altar boy who is losing his hair. It is true that he gives the impression of being absolutely docile. When he leaves the stage because Michael Flanders wants to be alone with us for a moment, he leaves as though he had been sent, dragging his broken spirit behind him. It is also true that he makes a pretense of disliking indelicate jokes (he cannot bear the one about the hi-fi bug whose lonely wife finally decided upon "no fidelity with high frequency"), and that he wears glasses. Those glasses, as Michael Flanders warns us in a rather testy moment, are all "fogged up with passion," and it's no use pretending not to notice.

I didn't know what to make of the man early on in the evening. He started out by lavishing great affection, perfectly straight, on a typically Irish ballad. Well, he's serious, I thought—only the other man is hilariously funny. Let him be.

Then little telltale mannerisms began to crop up. Sometimes his head would fly higher than his hands while he was attacking the piano. In one number ("The Wompom," I think) he began to cackle noticeably. After a while, he stopped everything to do a song entirely in Greek, most enthusiastically. And by the time he was pretending to be a stubborn cannibal child who wouldn't listen to reason and just would not eat people, beating the piano top with his bare fists and then sullenly clasping and unclasping his hands in distraught defiance, the secret was out. This man is dangerous.

Only a dangerous man could remember all of Flanders' waspish monologues word for word. Swann sits there, gripping the piano bench with one hand and steadying the piano with the other, silently mouthing every syllable his companion speaks. Frequently, he nods, reassuring us that Flanders has left nothing out. It must be admitted that this rare ability— probably picked up when he was a school child who could never get a speaking part in the annual play but was resolutely determined to learn all the lines in case of sudden illness—is of some value to the evening. It takes care of the lip-readers in the audience, for one thing. It provides a nice balance, and even counterpoint, for another: sometimes Mr.

Swann gets slightly out of synchronization and has to catch up, so that a rather raffish offbeat is added.

Furthermore, Swann is not jealous of Flanders, and that is a peculiar symptom. Flanders has most of the good lines, and most of the good lines are very good. (Flanders assures us that he has been studying the American political polls and that he and his partner are going to avoid social comment in their little songs for fear of offending the "Don't knows." Then, in a hissed and confiding afterthought, he warns us: "They're going to get in!") But Swann laughs as heartily as anyone at each successful sally. He admires this fellow who can speak so crisply: his own voice hasn't changed yet, and if it has it was a mistake.

Well, perhaps he is right to admire him. Perhaps he is not so much crazy as possessed of an unnatural supply of good manners, humility, and largeness of spirit. Perhaps, after all, it is Swann's way.

If Michael Flanders is readier to take over the stage, it is not because he is egocentric. He is, actually, filled with compassion. He is deeply sorry for wart hogs, especially female wart hogs with whom no one will dance. He has boundless sympathy for a bit of bindweed that was only doing what it was supposed to do, which is climb a wall counterclockwise, when it suddenly felt its tendrils stirred by a slight brush with a honeysuckle that was climbing clockwise, and thereafter found itself in a situation fully as tragic as Romeo and Juliet's. He has a kind word for the hippopotamus, and he has solved, in a single lyric, that problem of identity ("Who am I?") that has been baffling playwrights of all sizes for so long. He has solved it in terms of gnus rather than people, but it is solved now, and I hope we shall hear no more of it.

Of course, during all of this benevolent behavior toward man and beast, Mr. Flanders does keep his sword arm free. He has heard every song he ever wants to hear about Paris, and he is prepared to finish them off by rhyming "safe" with "cafe." Scowling at us now from over his beard, he looks like an evil Peter Ustinov, which is not an easy distinction to arrive at. Distaste wafts from him like a fragrance.

But whatever he finds distasteful in the modern or ancient world he treats genteelly. No vulgar opprobrium. Does someone always park a car in his parking place? He leaves a note pinned to the windshield wipers: "Do not park here. You shall smart for this."

Was 1546 a desperately bad year for the theater, what with *Gorboduc* doing poor business and *Gammer Gurton's Needle* just about played out? He sees no problem: the people who have pawned their doublets and are sitting around in their singlets need only await the arrival of an exciting new script by special Massinger. (No need to wince; Mr. Flanders has a magnificently frosty way with a pun, delighting in it and disowning it at one and the same instant.) Are breakfast-food packages now filled entirely with prizes? No matter. Just mail in the box top and they'll send you the cereal. Courage, says the crisp man with the alert eye. Everything—even Russia, even the British weather, even Mort Sahl—will work out.

Nichols and May

It's a good thing Mike Nichols and Elaine May are partners. How would either of them ever find anyone else they'd distrust so much?

Mr. Nichols has only to look at Miss May for his eyelids to begin fluttering in dire apprehension. Miss May has only to look at Mr. Nichols for her shoulders to give in instant despair. Each seems bound to betray the other in a matter of minutes and in a manner no one can foresee: perhaps by changing the lines, perhaps by leaving the stage, perhaps by saying something unredeemably awful about the world we live in. There is some peril in their very presence on the same stage, some undefined tension, some secret knowledge of where all the bodies are buried. They are the two least innocent comedians I know.

The faint, smirking malice which underlies much of their comedy—initially improvised, later set—may come from the intimation that, as they take a joint look at the insanity that passes for contemporary civilization, they aren't always kidding. They may never be kidding. They may mean it.

Consider, for instance, what appears to be a pleasant bit of nonsense about an atomic scientist talking to his mother on the telephone. That's a good gag situation, to begin with. Mother's worried about her lad during countdowns and wondering why he never does phone her from the launching pad. Our two clowns doodle with this for a while (Mother's been waiting so long for a call that she hasn't eaten in three days, not wanting to have her mouth full when the phone rings).

Then, gradually, it dawns on us that Mother is a real trial, a man-devouring whine who is always ready and eager to be carted off to the hospital on account of her nerves, a tender-hearted leech who wants to be sure that her lad is suffering for her. She asks him if he is suffering for her. How does he feel?

"I feel awful," he says, putting his heart into it.

"Honey, if I could believe that," comes the lyrical response, "I'd be the happiest mother in the world."

There is polite savagery, you see, behind the making-with-the-jokes. There is also genuine, jaundiced, festering observation. Truth snakes in and rears its venomous head, looking sparkling and ugly at the same time and without interrupting the rolling laughter. It's a tricky double play.

But the fact that these inventive entertainers are sociologists and psychologists as well as entrancing lunatics is most thoroughly exploited in what must be their strangest exercise: a dip into Pirandello during which a couple of quarreling children turn without warning into a couple of quarreling

42

adults and then, inexplicably, into a couple of quarreling performers known as Nichols and May. It is a shocking notion—they have been known to bring it off so that your hair stands on end—and it constitutes a perfect commentary on their rich, curious blend of meanness and pure madness.

Beyond the Fringe

If you have any questions, the four solemn counselors who perform *Beyond the Fringe* will always be glad to answer them for you. What attitude should a reasonable man take to all the violence and aberration that have been cropping up in our theater? "I don't want to see lust and rape and incest and sodomy," says a Toby mug of a man named Dudley Moore. "I can get all that at home." Or have you wondered, perhaps, just what sort of customer goes into those bookshops featuring sex manuals and illustrated studies of flagellation in order to purchase, say, a copy of *A History of the Thumbscrew in the Home Counties*? Jonathan Miller, wrinkling his nose like a rabbit with asthma, will take care of that one. "Far and away the largest purchasers of such volumes are your straight warped."

It is hard to tell which of these visitors from England belongs to the straight warped, for there is something irremediably warped-warped about each of them. Jonathan Miller will probably be hardest to straighten out. Mr. Miller has not exactly taken leave of his senses, but the parts of his body have certainly taken leave of each other, and it is going to require all of the Queen's horses and all of the Queen's men simply to collect them, let alone paste them up.

For instance, at the beginning of a line that suggests no emotion at all, Mr. Miller leaps straight up into the air like a comma that has decided to become an apostrophe. Landing again, as even immortals must, Mr. Miller whooshes full speed ahead in the direction of nowhere, making semaphore signals with his arms as he goes. I am surprised that he was not boarded before he was through on opening night.

Boarding him would be tricky, though, for he is always in high seas. The sleeves of his sweater slip down over his hands as he twists himself like a wisteria tendril around a little railing provided for his pleasure. His eyes, when they are closed, fold down over his face like tent flaps, and he does not smoke a cigarette, he makes a small votive offering of it between the crablike crawl of his arched and spidery fingers. Speaking French with distended nostrils, and skipping across the stage with his Punch-and-Judy head lifted nobly to the wind, he is all spirit, blithe spirit, reduced to going it blind. The modern world is in a mess, you see, which is why he wafts himself so far above it, with such blissful and blistering disdain.

Alan Bennett would seem to be milder, but he is a strangler nonetheless. Basically, he strangles words, forcing them up from his thin, piercing larynx only to catch them at lip point and mash them to death. His mouth closes down on a prissy reproof to Bertrand Russell ("As a thinker, he should stick to thinking") so that all that can come out is a trickle of poisoned honey. As a minister delivering a woolgathering sermon, which is about as entertaining as entertaining gets in these sobersided days, he can speak of "that sense of *lack*" in such a way that his tongue seems drained of vitality and then hung out to dry.

Dudley Moore plays the piano when he isn't helping to disembowel Shakespeare ("Now is steel 'twixt gut and bladder interposed") and his repertoire is not only enormous but in one case endless. That is to say, he cannot find a suitable conclusion to follow his mightiest crescendo in a theme-with-variations rendition of that tune from *The Bridge on the River Kwai* and his despair is only exceeded by our helpless happiness. It is exemplary, too, that Mr. Moore never tells you what he is doing, possibly because he doesn't know. He just starts, and cannot stop, and you discover his problem for him, with joy.

Peter Cook has four legs, or so it seems when he crosses them, and no expression at all. In one handsomely sustained monologue he simply sits on a flight of stairs that have obviously been left over from a bad Shakespearean production, keeps his hands in his trench-coat pockets, and, somewhere between a whine and a drone and a nasty nasal whimper, explains why he has never become a judge. If anything ever does happen to his eyes, it's that they seem to cross inward as though searching for the rumor or the remnants of a long-lost brain. They do not find one, at least not during a public address by a certain prime minister.

Beyond the Fringe is a satirical revue which treats calmly and ruthlessly of the hydrogen bomb, the end of the world, religion on television, capital punishment, race relations, and the emerging African nations. It is funny on all subjects. But it is not a conventional revue with conventional sketches with conventional blackouts with funny hats. It has imagined a meaningful impossibility.

It has imagined that all of the tones of voice men use, and all of the gestures they make, could be made free of the men and sent forth to lead independent lives of their own. Inflections walk around. Postures (a man with one foot on a chair and one hand on his hip, pretending ease and good fellowship) are permitted to stand free of the flesh and balance mindlessly in limbo. Notions for scenes do not begin or end; they escape, strolling casually past the guards and then running like crazy. That is the way our words and gestures behave nowadays; and that is the way they are recorded.

GOOD DEEDS IN A NAUGHTY WORLD

WHEN WAS IT that we all became such passionate admirers of perfect plays that we wouldn't think of going to one that had the least trace of a seam showing?

45

That is more or less the position we tend to adopt, or pretend to adopt, at the present time. Told that the second act is a wow but the third is flabby, or that there are interesting scenes leading to a final irresolution, or that there are magnificent performances worked out above and beyond the actual merits of the writing, we nod sorrowfully and stay home. In some curious way we have all become literary critics, or at least connoisseurs of craftsmanship, holding fast to the transplanted phrase "the play's the thing" and refusing to sully our minds with a possible good time that derives its pleasures from something other than an airtight structure.

Now it is perfectly true that the play is the solid planking on which the theater at its finest ultimately rests, that a living library of great plays is what the theater has been aiming at from its dawn in the circle of Dionysus, and that the greatest weakness we must contend with at the moment is curvature of the dramatic spine. But it is really most odd that in a time when drama is patently at sixes and sevens, and when we know quite well that we may have to wait a long while for masterpieces, we should strenuously insist upon precisely the things we can't have and won't get. It is somewhat stubborn of us, as though we wouldn't touch dinner because lunch had been so-so. Our habit may conceal a somewhat horrifying truth: that we don't much like the theater, and are glad of an excuse for giving it the go-by. But our behavior is not entirely natural.

While it is always intelligent to hope for the best, and to do what one can to prod a laggard form along, it is also human and even reasonable to snatch whatever fun is going when Christmas seems so far away. No one waits for the finest day of the summer before he goes swimming—not if he likes swimming.

There are reasons for going to the theater other than bowing down before literary or technical triumphs, and it is surprising that we so rarely latch onto them. The most obvious of these, of course, is the real fascination of watching a good actor act. We surrender to this fascination nowadays, I think, only when the actor is so utterly divorced from his play, or from any play, that we feel free to suspend our penchant for dramatic criticism and observe him in a vacuum. If Marcel Marceau comes along, and there is no play to engage our fault-finding faculties, we are delighted to attend to his accomplishments and to acclaim them. If John Gielgud and Emlyn Williams are wise enough to appear *solus* and to read enough material in the way of sonnets and short stories to qualify the evening as essentially nondramatic, then we are able to say, "What fine actors they are!" and to urge our friends to see them simply because they are fine actors. If a play is generally thought to be unplayable, or perhaps not a play at all, and Charles Boyer and Charles Laughton and Cedric Hardwicke and Agnes Moorehead take two steps forward and affect to read it as though it were an essay, we again give ourselves permission to be utterly enchanted. Acting is a good enough reason for going to a playhouse so long as no play is being acted.

Put the same actors, or any of their peers, into a piece of work that has a perceptible dramatic shape and it is instantly most difficult to see how fine they are: our eyes are on that possibly shaky shape. We tend to be single-minded about our theatrical experiences, and the single thing we have in mind is the thing that comes along least frequently: the play so strong that it could probably survive bad acting.

'Twas not always thus. Apart from four or five first-rate pieces of writing, the entire British theater of the eighteenth century survived—quite handsomely, as a matter of fact—on performing. People did not really go to see the new Colman play; they went to see Garrick act in it. If there were no new Colman play, no one cared, which may in itself have been a sign of good taste; they could always go to see Garrick do *Richard III.* Theater thrived, generally, on the ability of at-

47

tractive players to do something extra with weak new plays and something satisfying with great old ones; with Wilde and Shaw still a century away, it seemed quite enough.

I am not persuaded that William Gillette, in our own century, forged his following out of people whose consciences demanded immaculate playmaking. As it happens, Mr. Gillette wrote a number of his own plays, and, efficient as they were in arriving at dandy scenes for Mr. Gillette to bring off, even the audiences of the day must have noticed that they were jerry-built. If they bothered to notice, that is. Chances are they suppressed whatever they noticed, without necessarily lying to themselves about it, because they so liked the way the man acted.

It can of course be objected that our actors are not Garricks, that they do not even have the flamboyant presence that must have accounted in part for the magnetism of Gillette. The demurrer has some truth in it: after years of playing realism, and playing themselves, and making movies, our actors have neither the command nor the scale we might like. Still, there are astonishingly good men and women among us; and, even below star rank, there are dozens and dozens who are often great fun to watch. But it does not occur to us that watching them may in itself be a sufficient satisfaction for an evening, much less that there is frequently more excitement in watching a good performance in a bad play than there is in watching merely tidy performances in a good one.

Miss Wynyard, Miss Brown

It is my fond belief that one of these days I am going to see a perfect production of George Bernard Shaw's *Heartbreak House,* but until I do I shall rest reasonably content with the last one I saw, principally because of two superbly unreal creatures who call themselves Pamela Brown and Diana Wynyard. The thing about Miss Brown is that she has come out of a lamp: everything about her is smoky, and everything curls. Her nose curls to a point, and may not yet have assumed its final wispy shape. Her mouth is a puckered wreath, perfect for enunciating such flat lies as "I am a rigidly conventional woman." Her whole body drifts into position, as though it had been drawn by a skywriter on a gently windy day, and to watch her whisk downstairs and stop in a shudder, or slip without warning into the trot of a circus pony, is to know how ectoplasm would behave if it wore high heels and were slightly wicked. Difficult as the project might be, Miss Brown should be caught and kept under glass, if only for the sheer improbable glory of that paper-doll profile.

Miss Wynyard is made of more substantial stuff: spun sugar. It was she who moved, in the production I'm remembering, with lavender grace through Shaw's storybook ship, soothing the more unruly of her grown-up children, tucking a feather in here and patting a temperament there, murmuring all the while how lovely it is that "we are able to love liars." Miss Wynyard was Lady Bountiful with sense in her head: tartness and tenderness were the twin children of her smile. Or, wearing pearls to her knees and nipping tea sandwiches for punctuation, was she really Wendy, grown up and glorified? Either way, it was balm for our rattled nerves to contemplate this vision poised patiently on a low Roman couch, one skeptical fist doubled under an elegant chin, for all the world like a healthy Greek goddess who had come in to baby-sit.

Miss Rutherford

Margaret Rutherford has a husband and I have a wife, so nothing much is going to come of this romance. Nothing much came of her appearance in a waterlogged jokebook, *Farewell, Farewell, Eugene,* either, but it at least provided me with an occasion to declare my passion.

49

Miss Rutherford, who weighs in at about twenty-four carats with a few stone to spare, was playing the playwright's mistake more or less on the wing. At least I think that's what she was doing as she hoisted her magnificent bulk onto one dainty toe, flapped both arms wildly like an airplane in a Disney cartoon, and, emitting sounds that would cause gulls to mate with cormorants and cormorants to mate with egrets, soared off to the kitchen to baptize a baby at the sink and then back into the living room to guzzle candies that clearly had been made in heaven.

I am especially fond of Miss Rutherford's ecstasies. They are so noncommittal. When, at the end of the first of the evening's three dawdling acts, the fullback we are speaking of sat down at a table to savor some beer, she didn't smack her lips, or roll her eyes, or anything like that. She might have been paralyzed, for all the animation she put out. But television commercials could well have used Miss Rutherford because she really tasted that beer: she gave it her full, sober, dedicated, critical, uncompromising attention—and every sip was a salute to the inventive gods.

Of course, she showed signs of animation now and then, too, especially when animation seemed least called for. For some reason that I am unable to fathom and unwilling to question, she chose to end certain of her speeches with a little leap to the front, an eccentric ping-pong bounce, and what amounted to a curtsy in her nice pink dress—rather as though she'd now finished her turn on the high trapeze and was coming to a jubilant landing. Sometimes she adopted the stance of a quizzical small boy, sometimes she resembled a shark about to feast on a bather, and always she was modest about the devastation in her wake. Having sprayed the room with a fallout of greeting cards, she quietly scolded herself ("Butterfingers," she said) as though mere accident could have accounted for the havoc. Miss Rutherford, dear Miss Rutherford, is it clear to you that I care?

50

Mr. Levene

Perhaps the only thing to have done with a farce called *Fair Game* was to pick out all of Sam Levene's scenes and play them twice. That would have made a nice show.

Mr. Levene was appearing as a sort of garment-district Mephistopheles, a wolf in men's clothing, a very proud fellow who resented being called an "old lecher" because he was not a day older than forty-eight. To every facet of the role he brought vast spiritual depths. Few men can have been so subject to moral outrage. The horror with which he recoiled from an available girl who didn't want a mink stole, just money, was injured virtue in its utter essence. Mr. Levene could not bear to see good taste violated.

He was a great man for philosophy when things weren't going well. "Penthouses, Cadillacs, a place in Bermuda—what does it all mean?" he cried, wringing his pale hands in anguish and shutting his eyes against the appalling materialism of the contemporary world.

Open-eyed, he was even better. There was a certain predatory sparkle that came into his wrinkled and beaming countenance, shimmering and glowing like a battery of drunken glowworms, whenever he sighted prey. And yet it was as nothing beside the simple, evil appeal of his lamblike suffering when his plans were thwarted, beside the agony that rent him in the presence of virtuous women, his fat wife, and folk dancing.

The powers of this performer extended well beyond the genteel flourish of his worn-down cigar, the arc that his fingers made as they constantly kneaded invisible dough, the upraised arm that called for silence in a manner Cicero might have recognized. They extended, indeed, to the total conquest of some pretty so-so dialogue, raising it to the level of bright comic literature.

51

"That's not Chicago, that's the ladies' room" wasn't exactly Oliver Goldsmith or John Millington Synge. When Mr. Levene said it, it had class. If someone snarled at him, "Can't you tell the difference between a nice girl and a tramp?" and he muttered, "It gets tougher all the time," that was edifying, too. The artist, working with the nervous energy of a ribald otter and the leonine aplomb of a David Belasco, was in such happy, carefree, altogether svelte command that you didn't ask questions, you just grinned—and waited for him to come popping back through another apartment door.

Miss Channing

It wasn't until an inconsequential revue called *Show Girl* came along that I realized how much I'd missed Carol Channing. There she was, a towering cornstalk in a husk of slinky red, bowing and beaming and looking shy and fussed and fearsome, and I knew why it was life had seemed empty lately.

What I like about Miss Channing, apart from her various and voracious talents, is the way she greets you. She is a hearty soul, equipped with great blazing eyes that passing motorists must curse her for. But she doesn't overwhelm you. She gives the impression of being very, very cordial and very, very busy, and won't you come in, and please for heaven's sake help yourself to anything you find, and she'll be right back in a minute after she puts out the fire in the pantry.

Or maybe she hasn't come from the pantry. She's been up into the tower, hanging onto that bell-clapper from *The Heart of Maryland*. She heard you ring, and though her wrists are aching and her fingernails ravaged, she's come down to open the door and turn up the thermostat so you'll be utterly comfy while she goes back to her desperate work of warning the troops.

You see, there's some sort of embarrassed innocence—an air of being caught where she shouldn't be by the high school principal—about the girl, in spite of all her effusive energy. Even as she's starting off with what a composer friend of mine calls a "waker-upper" tune, her two turned-in feet are edging nervously against one another, and abashedly away from the footlights. Whenever she gets a great big laugh, she whips around at you in delighted disbelief, breaking into a surprised smile you could drive a truck right through.

And because she is so quick with a disarming grimace that asks "What did I say?" she can afford to be lethal when it is time to be lethal. She has been such a peach all along that you are not the least bit alarmed when her lip begins to curl for a one-woman rumble called "Switchblade Bess" or when, making a small mess of the feathery thing she is wearing, she decides to haul Marlene Dietrich kicking to the block. Her homespun, Christmas-morning face now deteriorates into a sneer that could be used for sweeping floors, her moist eyes harden into agates you could lag with, and you remain contented and beguiled in the presence of premeditated murder because you don't, no you don't, believe a leer of it.

Mr. Silvers, Miss Walker

A great many people did not like *Do Re Mi* as much as I did. I know, because they have written me letters, grabbed me by the lapels on public sidewalks, accosted me on shipboard when all I was trying to do was take a vacation. Now, I realize that every man is entitled to his own opinion and that vigorous differences are healthy for the theater, if not for vacationists. But what is to come of the conversation if the contenders' premises are irreconcilable? *Their* premise was that every musical comedy should tell a sensible story in sensible sequence, with integrated songs, dances, jokes, and, I guess, orange drinks at intermission. My premise, far more demanding, was that every musical comedy should star Phil Silvers and Nancy Walker.

In *Do Re Mi* Phil Silvers looked like the canary that swal-

53

lowed the cat. I mean, you could still sort of see the cat's outlines bulging here and there beneath Mr. Silvers' bright
checkered vest, its whiskers twitching and its large eyes fixed
in stunned surprise, while above and beyond that checkered
vest rose the proud and triumphant note of our warbler, in-
sanely trilling in his chinaberry tree.

Mr. Silvers has elevation, while Miss Walker expresses the
crushing forces of gravity. He does not so much tiptoe
through the tulips as tiptoe on top of them. She seems always
to be planting her foot on something she has just killed—an
enemy, or perhaps the audience—and announcing, with a
shift of her jaw, "This one's mine."

It is true that Mr. Silvers, forepaw poised as though he
were about to step into a sunken bathtub, does try to get down
to earth now and again. He tries to pose as a realist, or even
as a homemade Torquemada, setting his teeth in the meanest
smirk he can manage as he bitterly says, "I love kids." But the
poor man has the soul of a kindergarten teacher, and a kindergarten teacher who used to sneak his charges into a vaudeville show every Saturday afternoon. To see him make for
the portals like a drum majorette who has lately taken to mari-
huana is to realize that there's a bit of Ed Wynn in him, and a
bit of Harold Lloyd, and a bit of Leon Errol, and a bit of Bugs
Bunny (his cheeks chock full of the most flavorsome nuts),
plus a whole lot of the Mr. Silvers who is the only man left
alive capable of doing these things, for which let our souls
give thanks.

Miss Walker doesn't soar. Mostly she gets her effects by settling one granite hip slightly out of its socket, letting her right
shoulder slump as though someone had planted the office safe
on it and she was just going to let it stay there until someone
had the decency to take it off, and glaring. The glare says
everything: why have you done this to me, when are you going
to cut it out, why were you born?

If the glare seems to be coming more from the set of her
lip than from the force of her look, it is because it is rarely

possible to see much of Miss Walker's eyes: she is the only person I know of who has bags over her eyes instead of under them, and there is a constant sideways sag in the area that makes her appear to be wearing, in lieu of eyebrows, a pair of unbalanced Venetian blinds. On the whole, she looks like a wax image that has half melted in the heat and then hardened into a permanent dribble, and my principal memory of her in *Do Re Mi* is of a moment in bed with Mr. Silvers (they were man and wife, mind you, and meant for each other). He was reading the *Mirror* and she was reading the *News* and after a very long silence she glanced over at his newspaper and asked, "Did a fish bite a woman in Asbury Park in yours?" No, I am against responsible musicals.

Mr. Foy

I grant that Eddie Foy probably should have been jailed for what he was doing in *Donnybrook*. It could not be said that he was behaving well. The nature of the show, and the terms of his employment, clearly required that he settle down, flesh out his busy Irish matchmaker with a pound or so of relative reality, and help his colleagues be decently convincing. For the musical itself, adapted from John Ford's film *The Quiet Man,* meant to be reasonably dimensional and quite above free-for-all clowning.

When Mr. Foy first came on, he did seem subdued, even in those clamoring spats—so subdued, in fact, that he was sometimes inaudible. He was apparently waiting, however, for the house to fill up, as though he were playing a Wednesday matinee in Des Moines thirty years ago. Then, when he obviously felt that we'd settled down and got the sober playlet that had preceded him on the bill out of our systems, he appeared to nod at the conductor, wave to his agent, and remember himself.

Now his hands came out of the pockets of his sagging

jacket and fastened, washerwoman-fashion, to his hips. His feet began to jab, in a stammering rhythm that has no known musical equivalent, at a square foot of the floorboards he had marked off as his own. A mystique grew up between him and this mesmerizing pocket of space. His concentration upon it grew fiercer. Certainly he paid no attention to the partner he was working with while the thrall was upon him. Soon his shoulders began to leave his torso and slip down his back, soon his chest had puffed out as though he were a species of wood dove, and all of a sudden he was getting about on his ankles, his knees, and his elbows.

Once started on this sort of thing, he didn't stop just because the song was over and the plot under way again. On the contrary, he was to be seen ramming a hole in the crown of his hat, responding like an aspen to the force of a thundering speech, fishing for the cuckoo in an unoffending cuckoo clock, and mouthing unheard ad libs to the man on his right. As though he hadn't already spilled far enough out of the frame to be considered avant-garde, he became so impatient to get from one scene to another that he began helping the backdrops to get out of the way. (I don't know why people credit Brecht with the "alienation" theory of drama when a fellow like Foy is still around.)

Anyway, whatever he was up to had very little to do with the rather straightforward characterization and earnestly sung balladry everyone else was pursuing. The funny thing is that, even if we were liking the mood of *Donnybrook* in general, we were liking this, too. If anything, we were liking it more. If Mr. Foy should properly have been jailed, we'd instantly have asked the address of the jail.

What fondness for hooky lurks in the hearts of all theatergoers, even when they are giving assent to something purposively organized? Does the theater itself house an imp in the basement that can never be altogether denied and that makes our eyes light up in welcome every time it escapes its cage and, with a whoosh, comes up through a crack in the planking? Here we were, approving the respectable intentions of a defined entertainment. We knew what the shape of the show should have been. And here came Mr. Foy, who didn't know, taking off on one toe like a ballet dancer put together of old dishrags, and we sat straight up in our seats and craned our necks so as not to miss a single irreverent, irrelevant, irresponsible scissors step. We were terrified of overlooking one small twitch of what everyone who ever went to vaudeville saw forty times over and which hadn't been changed, not by a fraction, since. We pretend to believe in legitimacy, but we can't be serious.

Miss Grimes

The Unsinkable Molly Brown was a most slapdash musical, but in Tammy Grimes it had the kind of musical comedy heroine who might have been imagined by Edgar Allan Poe, and the purloined heart was mine.

I mention Mr. Poe only because there is something unearthly about Miss Grimes. The girl belongs to a new group of clowns who seem to be turning into mystics. In the old days, clowns were just folks who'd dropped in. Bobby Clark used to blink right at us, and if a girl in red satin suddenly stalked across the stage, his puzzled question ("Who ordered lobster?") was addressed to the customers, with whom he shared all his confidences. Ed Wynn used to get so close to the audience that you felt he should pay for a seat, and any outrageous pun he'd managed to work out ("I found the talent for tonight's show on a showboat—I bred my cast upon the waters") was offered as a juicy bit of gossip just between us. Even Joe Cook, the zany who was farthest out before "out" got to be so far, remained on intimate terms with the incompetent and forgetful people who'd come to see him ("Tonight I promise to perform the sensational feat of escaping from a

57

straitjacket in less than ten seconds. Does anyone in the house have a straitjacket?").

But the best new comics are different. As the song says, they hear music and there's no one there. With their eyes fixed upon some impossible eternity where a mysterious comic harmony exists for them and them alone, luring them past the rest of us in a transport of private lunacy, they go about the business of dominating the stage by following a secret and hypnotic star of their own.

I certainly don't know how else to account for the eerie authority of Miss Grimes, who looks neither to the right nor to the left but only onward and upward. One of the difficult things she was asked to do in *Molly Brown*—as the authors struggled to get a curtain down without having thought up a curtain line—was to tuck a pot on her head, wrap a tablecloth about her shoulders, raise a broom like a scepter, and march, march, march, in perfect silence, for what seemed an eternity, across the stage. If I were an actress, I'd have quit right there. But Miss Grimes went marching, spook that she is ("kook," I believe, is the word for it now), and the house held its breath.

The girl has, probably, the strangest shape on the North American continent: square shoulders and foursquare legs, topped by a head of hair that isn't hair at all but tumbleweed. And out of this improbable rag doll, with its faraway stare, comes a falsetto baritone that seems to be a distillation of all the sweet-tempered steampipes that ever played the two-a-day. In fact, I know what it is. Helen Morgan has been crossed with Rosetta Duncan, and here is the gravelly, miraculously liquid result.

As an untidy evening scampered out of her path, Miss Grimes carved her way through a Colorado saloon as though a piece of Mount Rushmore had slipped from its saddle, as though the Rockies themselves had spawned her. One look from her great black-bordered eyes and strong men turned to hitching posts, lashed to the spot. She issued edicts with a clodhopper command ("I ain't settlin' for happiness") and with a bulldozing innocence tossed the sort of social-climbing party that, as the libretto reported, made its way into the newspapers not on the society page but on the sports page. But whatever the libretto was reporting, or demanding, Miss Grimes was *en rapport* with an unseen Svengali hovering just above the balcony. Her basic clown's face glazed with spiritual rapture, she seemed to listen to one clear note striking somewhere, and then to become it, even as she was becoming funny, endearing, oddball, and victorious.

Mr. Ford

There is a kind of comedy that makes you laugh out loud and double up in your seat, alarming those nearest and dearest to you. There is a kind of comedy that lets you settle back, warm and gratified and not worrying about the taxicab you won't get when you leave the theater. And there is a kind of reflective comedy that actually stirs a thought or two, without lambasting you into virtue or precisely driving you to good deeds.

As it happens, it was the happy privilege of *The Thurber Carnival* to possess all three. It also possessed Paul Ford, who finds it difficult to dribble onto the stage without breaking up the very light bulbs. Why is one man shod in fur-bearing slippers so much funnier than any other man similarly clad?

Perhaps it is because Mr. Ford believes. On this occasion he certainly believed in the unicorn he discovered in the garden one morning. As he stealthily tiptoed downstairs to pluck a lily and feed the gold-spired beast, he was the happiest man alive. (No, the second happiest; I was there.) And because he was happy, because he had so much simple faith, laughter was born of his every gentle footfall.

Faith shone from his basset-hound eyes—Mr. Ford has really borrowed his entire face from one of Mr. Thurber's dogs,

59

which is why they all look so sad—as he popped Grandma's lace nightcap onto his head and waited for Little Red Riding Hood to turn him down. It seemed to tremble like a halo over the bright yellow feathers he wore as an island castaway who had spent seven frustrated, but not wholly wasted, years with a mermaid. And the innocent, trusting, earnest appeal he made to wife Peggy Cass to come down into the cellar so that he could murder her ("Aw, c'mon, *please!*" was his tone) was hope—and wistful humor—incarnate.

Mr. Bolger

The last time Ray Bolger was on Broadway—prior to *All American*—he took a charming little song called "Once in Love with Amy" and he danced around it, and he sang around it, and he clowned around it until they had to chase the customers out of the theater in order to get it ready for the next day's matinee. Lord, you thought he'd never stop. And he shouldn't have.

For *All American,* too many years later, was the sort of hodgepodge in which Mr. Bolger was never fascinating until he stood right up and told you he was. The announcement came very late, more than halfway through the noisy, but nevertheless laggard, second act. The number in which it happened was itself called "I'm Fascinating," and its very first bars gave this animated question mark of a performer his first opportunity to lift his lofty eyebrows, tilt his nose in high hauteur, and do a tap dance that was full of disdain.

Now he was on top of things, prim, imperious, and ready to stamp out the plebeian world that barely existed beneath his feet. In great double spins he galloped about the stage, one leg flying to the right while the other wondered whether or not to follow it (and decided no). The floor itself hesitated, and began to go in the opposite direction, just as he touched it in an unexpected descent. His whole improbable frame staggered, threatened to wilt, and then, in the near nick of time, a graceful second leg came up from under—easy as satin and thoroughly proud of itself—to rescue everything. Nothing bothered Mr. Bolger any more. Two telephones rang and he simply placed them in a position to talk to each other while off he went, a stumblebum of a meadowlark kicking the leaves from the trees.

Miss Herlie

Having seen Tyrone Guthrie's revival of *The Makropoulos Secret,* I am in a position to tell you the secret of Eileen Herlie. She isn't Eileen Herlie at all. She is Madame Modjeska, supernaturally returned to us in her absolute prime, and she is using an assumed name so that, whenever she tires of more regal roles, she can work in musical comedies. (The spurious Miss Herlie's first appearance in musical comedy was in *Take Me Along,* where she performed a duet with Jackie Gleason in which you couldn't find Jackie Gleason: with fluttering fingers, a spine you could hear tingle, and the flutelike tones of a ravaged nightingale, she appropriated the number with the skill of a slightly deranged Duse, justifying whatever you had paid for your seat.)

In *The Makropoulos Secret* the fact that the lady, in her elaborately curled hair and her cascade of furs, looked exactly like every Modjeska photograph Mr. Daniel Blum ever collected for an album was beside the point. It was the acting that mattered, acting that seemed to have been spirited right out of the heart of the warm-blooded nineteenth century, given all the flesh and steel and sultry eyeshadow it undoubtedly had when its pulse was beating proudly, and deposited here anew to astonish, amuse, and transfix us.

We were invited to watch, for instance, this Herlie-Modjeska smoke a cigar. The trick seemed to be to get it in your mouth, roll it to one side so that it was firmly gripped in

61

the teeth, and then—head held high—ripple out a waterfall of immaculately articulated, superbly aristocratic syllables. You can try it, but who else could do it?

There were other things that this clear evidence of reincarnation was ready to do for us. Take an astonishing little scene in which a doddering relic of the older European gentry tottered gallantly backstage to an opera star's dressing room. He had brought flowers, wistfully, as he had always brought flowers to the divas of his youth. He was eager to toast this newcomer—Miss Herlie, who rather reminded him of one he had loved long ago—and he had raised his glass. Miss Herlie rested on a chaise longue, turned entirely away from us. The old sport's eyes met hers. In the intake of a breath, and a few seconds' silence, something happened between them—something strong enough to hurl the frail gallant backward, like a wind-blown dandelion, into the lap of the nearest onlooker. It was author Karel Capek's fantastic conceit that the new diva was indeed the octogenarian's ancient love, restored to an eternal youth; but the thought was not here put into words, it was merely let happen. And while actor Eric House had made his own fine contribution to the moment, the look we couldn't see—yet still felt with the force of an electrical discharge—was Miss Herlie's, conveyed through the back of her head.

I don't suppose even this would have convinced me that the actress possessed supernatural powers if nature itself hadn't intervened on that clear fall night. Throughout the evening one of the characters kept insisting that Miss Herlie's voice was "like snow—glittering, marvelously pure—like snow." And when we came out of the theater, it was snowing.

I can see a ghost by moonlight.

REBELLION

THE THIRTY-YEAR ITCH

THE SAME THEATER that bedecks itself in giant musicals and prays that a performer will do something handsome enough to save an otherwise routine show spends a surprising amount of its worrying time and a surprising amount of its money trying to make hasty room for its loners, its innovators, its rebels. It knows that the stage does not live by entertainments alone; it knows that the tricks that work tonight may be seen through by tomorrow morning; it has learned to listen because it knows the hour is late.

In more than thirty years of playgoing I don't think I have ever heard anyone hiss in the theater. I don't remember ever hearing anyone call out a heartfelt "Bravo!" while a performance was going on, though, of course, I have heard audiences applaud from time to time and there are always those slightly suspect cheers that fill the back of the house (why is it always the back of the house?) at curtain-fall on opening nights in New York. Apart from the rhythmic hand-clapping that greeted the finale of *The Music Man*—and from now on we are going to be talking about plays rather than musical comedies—I am not certain that I have ever felt a single, irresistible impulse sweep over an entire audience (for good or ill) and stir it to a response, or a demonstration, that could not possibly have been inhibited.

This is curious. If we are to believe the legends that have drifted down to us from the theater's apparently unruly beginnings in a scooped-out shell directly beneath the Acropolis, and if we are not simply to avert our eyes from the perfectly real evidence of what could happen in a New York playhouse as recently as the century before our own (twenty-two people killed and two hundred injured in a street battle brought on by, and fought during, a single performance), it is somehow or other in the nature of the theater to provoke ardent, if not violent, rejoinder.

Rejoinder is, in fact, the essence of the very first theatrical legend we cherish. The story runs that drama, as we now know it, was born on the day when a headstrong member of a religious dancing and singing group turned away from his fellow celebrants, faced the worshipers who had gathered to watch on the hillside, and, instead of continuing to sing the praises of the god Dionysus, announced that he *was* Dionysus. In daring to speak in the first person, to impersonate the god rather than describe him, a man named Thespis is supposed to have become the first bona fide actor. And a lawmaker named Solon, present at the holiday ritual, is supposed to have risen in his seat immediately and talked back, thundering down to the impertinent performer that he was a damned liar.

Whether or not this appealing—and perhaps highly significant—little scene ever took place, it seems very likely that, not too long after and once the notion of impersonation had expanded into full-scale drama, several of Greece's most popular and distinguished playwrights were, from time to time, forced to take refuge at the central altar from the storm of missiles that came rattling down at them when their customers (most of them in on passes, and having nothing but pleasure to lose) felt bored, cheated, or otherwise neglected.

As late as the eighteenth century in England audiences were inclined to rip the decorations from the walls, break the benches in two, and demand that actors beg forgiveness on their knees if they were seriously dissatisfied with the entertainment being offered them. And while the notorious Astor Place riots in nineteenth-century New York arrived at their twenty-two dead through a complex series of social, economic, and deep-seated psychological aberrations, the hurricane began in a hiss and had as its terrifying center an esthetic debate over the respective merits of two actors: the burly Edwin Forrest and the somewhat effete William Charles Macready.

I don't mean to become involved in a campaign for the re-establishment of hissing, even though Forrest, who was the original hisser in this last imbroglio, maintained to the end that there were two wholly legitimate forms of response in the theater, and that hissing was one of them. Hissing isn't the whole story. A letter I have never been able to forget came to me a few years ago from a long-retired actress who had, as a youngster, been taken to see Edwin Booth play *King Lear*. It seems that toward the end of the play, when the mad Lear was brought face to face with his daughter Cordelia, there was a sharp pause, then—for a second that couldn't quite be caught, or measured—a startled, desperate, longing flicker of near-recognition stirred somewhere behind the old man's eyes, and then—nothing. The entire audience rose, without thinking, to its feet. It didn't cheer. It simply stood up. It was as though a single electrical discharge had passed from one body on the stage, instantaneously, through a thousand bodies in the auditorium. Something had been plugged into a socket; two forces had met.

This meeting is what the theater is all about; it is its greatest power; it is what most distinguishes it from all other arts and makes it the most *personal* of them. A painting rests in its frame, brazen and passive and waiting to be taken. A piece of sculpture thrusts itself into space, perfectly commanding and perfectly detached. A novel lies patient and unprotesting until we are ready to nod to it; it is an intimate, but an intimate born without eyes. Even music, closest to the drama in the immediacy of its restless presence, refuses our handshake; we must turn slightly away in order to know it well.

The stage asks us to look at it so that it may look back, and make something of the eye-to-eye, nerve-to-nerve encounter.

But this is not simply to say, as we have so often and so

feebly said in the competitive twentieth century, that the theater is the last of the "live" arts, the lone citadel of the flesh. (This argument, clearly, has got the theater exactly nowhere; each time it has been advanced the mass audience has struck up yet another love affair with some mechanical, most unfleshly, gadget.) To go to the theater merely to *see* living actors, or to watch flesh passing by, is not all that exciting; we see people, and flesh on the hoof, every day.

To observe "live" actors going dispassionately—or even passionately—about their *own* business is never enough. The rewards of such detached sightseeing are few, and trivial: we may have the satisfaction of looking directly at some well-known personality, of being in the same building with him, of saying later that we saw him "in person"; but it will almost be necessary for the actor to flub a line, or bungle a piece of business, to shock us into an active awareness that something *personal* is really going on (that he is a person, that we are persons, and that some secret is shared between us, if only his idiotic little mistake).

The actor, if he is to do what the great actors of the past seem to have done, must make his business our business, must turn to us and place it in our hands, must ask that we join him in a common activity. The theater gains its natural—and unique—effect not from the mere presence of "live" actors, or the happy accident of an occasional lively audience, but from the existence of a "live" relationship between these two indispensable conspirators, signaling to one another through space. When this exhilarating, intensely demonstrative union takes place the walls of the playhouse can barely contain the spiritual excitement that is bred; actor feeds on audience, audience feeds on actor, a fiery, nourishing pulse races back and forth between them.

It is obvious, I think, that twentieth-century theatergoers have not been getting their share of the theater's most characteristic gift, a thrilling marriage of hearts and minds—with all the lovers' quarrels that properly belong to such a state. We do not hiss; we do not stand in unison on an impulse (what *could* prompt such an involuntary reaction?); we do not even care if we go very often—these are the polite, reserved, thoroughly decent signs of our discontent.

If we do not now behave passionately, one way or the other, toward the theater, it is because the theater itself, somewhere along the line, must have banked its fires and asked that we be more discreet about our own. Where, and how, did the ice age begin? (Perhaps it is only the age of discretion.) The contributing causes are many, of course, and some of them are only mild and minor historical accidents; there is also an inevitable ebb and flow, with frequent cooling-off periods, in the natural rhythm of any prolonged relationship.

Still, two continuing threads leading toward our present placid behavior may be disentangled from the others without too much oversimplification: one of them is physical, the other philosophical.

We are encouraged to behave well in the theater today, and to keep the actors from making unsuitable advances to us, by the very shape of the playhouse in which we sit. We sit chastely outside the experience, as though we were keeping an eye on it from the front porch next door—attentive, but determined not to become involved. The actor, for his part, is safely boxed up in a neat little compartment with an invisible, but psychologically effective, "fourth wall" cutting him off from us at the one point where contact might be made. Each side likes to pretend that it is alone in the auditorium: the actor by scrupulously refusing to notice the audience, except surreptitiously, and the audience by being so quiet that its presence will rarely be betrayed. (When I went to drama school I was taught that it would be wise to abolish curtain calls, since these could only destroy the desired detachment, and hence all illusion.)

Under these circumstances it is difficult to arrange for the sort of violent meeting we have been talking about. The standard theater shape we have come to accept assumed its form gradually over several hundred years; precisely how and why this happened we shall discuss briefly later on, when we are ready to consider the problems facing architects. At the moment, we *do* accept it, virtually without thinking, even though it reduces our players to figures in a landscape rather than friends (or enemies) in a meetinghouse. Because the two parties to the theatrical experience are in effect confined in isolation wards, forbidden to infect one another and to spread contagion, contagion is hard to come by.

The growth of our playhouse in this direction was reinforced, and then temporarily sealed, by an historical event which took place late in the nineteenth century. The mind of the world was moving in a new, and powerful, direction: toward science, toward the glorification of the scientific method and of scientific knowledge as the only method and the only kind of knowledge worth having. Step by step, the theater obediently, and even proudly, marched into the camp of those calm, dispassionate, objective observers who wished the world to stand still while they measured it and who insisted—quite rightly, from their point of view—that impulse and poetic intuition and raging emotion should play no part in the process.

Playwrights caught the hang of recording social fact after social fact, and of presenting the result with a minimum of poetic fancy. In the hands of Ibsen, Hauptmann, Gorki and Galsworthy the new tool was shaped and refined: it continues to do the work of Lillian Hellman and Arthur Miller and to dictate the surface form of such plays as we continue to call realistic or naturalistic. One rarely praises a contemporary playwright by saying that he has struck a nerve so deep it cannot even be named; one praises him most highly by saying that his observation is accurate.

In the fact-finding laboratory of this kind of theater the

roles of the player and the spectator have necessarily changed. The player is not a partner to the experiment; he is the object of it. He goes his little way as "naturally" as possible: that is to say, he tries very hard to duplicate the precise surface conditions of "average" life and "average" language, to be a "fair specimen" held up for examination. If the sample of behavior he offers is in any way extraordinary, if it introduces elements that cannot be measured or promptly verified by comparison with the ordinary life we all know, he ceases to be sufficiently "representative"; as a freak, as an exception to the laws of commonplace experience, his scientific value is nil—you can prove nothing by *him*. The player, as well as the character averaged out for him by the playwright, is meant to be a statistic, and not a particularly variable one. Nor dare he interfere with the work of the man who is studying him; that would be as improper—as inexplicable, really—as the sight of a bacillus turning its head to wink up the barrel of a microscope at its owner.

Nor is the spectator any longer a partner; he is the calm observer who notes phenomena. He is not supposed to express partisanship, to feel passion, to hope for one or another answer. Emotion might blind him, invalidate his findings (have you noticed the tremendous resistance we've built up to being caught out in a show of sentiment?); the notion that he might wish to feel anything other than sober interest in the sampling before him is unsuitable. Intellectual distance, and a rigid indifference to anything that might prove falsely persuasive, is what is wanted. Any sort of communion between the fact being examined and the examining mind might prejudice the outcome, as personal affection or close association might prejudice a member of a jury panel; and there would, in any case, be no point to it.

It is perhaps odd that an attitude of mind should find, at the very moment of its maturity, a perfectly expressive vehicle waiting for it. But that is what happened. The physical theater, steadily detaching the performer from the man out front, had come to look more or less like the glass-slide-under-a-microscope that was needed for controlled experiment. (We were quick to invent the term "slice of life" to indicate how perfectly we understood the scientist's needs.) The shape of the stage met the temper of the age gracefully; and the theater, though it soon lost something of its popularity, could at least congratulate itself on knowing what time it was.

I am in danger of serious overstatement here. If plays did become "accurate" records of observed life, and if the theater building did tend to detach the observer from the sample observed, the wholly dispassionate atmosphere of pure science was not—and could never have been—duplicated in the theater. For one thing, all of the "samples" held up for scrutiny had been invented—and that made them questionable samples. For another, we continued to feel emotion in the playhouse. Certainly we are moved today as we listen to a middle-aged aunt make a fuss over her niece and nephew, crack endless and very noisy jokes, and then suddenly find her hands out of control as she is forced to discuss her sexual failure in such a play as William Inge's *The Dark at the Top of the Stairs*. The squirming figures on stage are not bacilli, they are people; to some degree we "identify" with them, as the theatrical jargon of the day has it; the rhythms of their anguish reach us, and touch us. All is not lost.

But something has been lost. The emotion we feel at *Look Homeward, Angel* or *The Dark at the Top of the Stairs* (let alone *Sunrise at Campobello*) is, at root, a remembered emotion, not a new one. It is an emotion born of recognition in a literal, rather narrow, sense. In a realistic time the playwright must ask us to verify what he offers out of our own experience, to compare what he has done with what we already know (and know that we know); only by gaining our assent ("Yes, that's the way it was, exactly") can he hope to tease us into feeling something for his figures, into a sentimental relationship with them. I am caught almost at once in *The Dark at the Top of the Stairs* because actress Eileen Heckart behaves very much like a half-dozen "aunts" I loved as a boy: she has caught the sound of them. I can now be led toward disclosures that no aunt of mine ever made to *me,* but that are familiar in themselves from hundreds of treatises, scientific and semi-popularized, that have been written on sexual failure and emotional frustrations. Two echoes join, imperceptibly; there is nothing I can question, and I am already committed out of fond memory; I believe what I see and am reluctantly, but effectively, stirred by it. I feel emotion at a contemporary play when I can say, "That's just how she talked" or, "That's how *I* felt" or, "That's what the old place looked like" or, "But this is an actual story!" The playwright seeks out averages; when he finds them, I cannot help but be drawn in. If statistics can be directly related to *my* vital statistics, even a scientific theater can make me respond in a highly unscientific manner. This may be a rather underhanded way for the playwright to seize the best of two worlds —the objective world of the factual theater and the subjective world of my emotional responses—but it does keep the contemporary experience from becoming hopelessly antiseptic.

There is, however, another kind of theatrical experience, the kind we have in coming to know Hamlet or Monsieur Arnolphe or Oedipus even though we have *never* known him, even though we cannot verify him out of our storehouse of perfectly intelligible associations, even though we cannot give him a name and must accept him not with our rational, measuring minds but with our vitals. A friend of mine sat in the control room during a television broadcast of Christopher Plummer's performance of *Oedipus* and came out looking a little shaken, murmuring, "I can't help it, that play is so *visceral!*" An extremely well-known comedian ordered a kinescope of the same performance and played it for himself daily

73

for a week, arriving at a different (rational) interpretation of its meaning each day; but since its meaning was somehow received by the whole body and not simply by the working mind the task was superfluous—and perhaps impossible. (It is said that when the Furies first descended upon Orestes in the ancient Greek theater strong men fainted and women miscarried.)

I am not, let me hasten to say, talking about a theater of outrageously sensual appeal, of simple animal passion. (In all probability no more controlled play than the *Oedipus* was ever written.) The word we are searching for, I think, is the one the late nineteenth century so wished to discredit: intuition —specifically, poetic intuition. Poetic intuition constitutes knowledge of a sort, but knowledge that eludes rational or scientific formulation, that leaps like an electric current from eye to eye, that flares into visceral certainty only in the immediate presence of the person or thing known, and that is of no earthly use once the immaterial thread is broken. It is a great deal like love: sure of itself without being able to explain itself, exhilarated by a conscious sense of increasing well-being, expansive and generous and incredibly excited by the realization that something inexpressible is exactly communicated and exactly shared, gloriously passionate when things are going well and violently disconsolate when they're not. (Those people who broke benches *were* disconsolate; they had come happily prepared to fill themselves with love, and the loss was intolerable.) If we don't rip up theater seats, or hiss, or stand suddenly, it is because we expect so much less, and are therefore far less disappointed.

The climate of the contemporary theater is still largely temperate. But there are signs of a possible heat wave to come, as I shall try to illustrate in some of the following pages. In the meantime, if we can learn anything at all from the legends that have come down to us, it is that the theater is *capable* of provoking a response—a deeply personal and highly

inflammatory one—that is rather unlike the response generated by any other art form. The theater will no doubt become
most perfectly itself when it most perfectly explores and ex-
ploits that peculiar gift.

MAN AND MASK

Do WE HAVE PLAYERS who are capable of sustaining the direct experience we've been talking about? If not, is anybody
doing anything about it?

I suppose these questions were at the back of my mind as I
stood, one summer day, three or four mine-shafts underground (I never did find out just how many layers deep we
were), craning my neck to stare at an impress in the
tunneled-out rock directly over my head. I had come to the
ruins of Herculaneum, which was once the summer resort for
the wealthier people of Pompeii, for the express purpose of
looking at its ancient theater, only to discover that the theater had never been dug out from under its tons of unfriendly
lava and that the only way to see any part of it was to slip and
slide down wet, winding corridors until one came across a
partially uncovered elbow of the auditorium or a hacked-out
corner of the stage floor. The archaeologists had sunk a laby-
rinth of shafts into the buried playhouse without actually un-
covering very much of it, and I was now both damp and disappointed.

When the acrobat who was serving as guide to us motioned
us along still another dripping cavern that seemed to be leading nowhere, I was reluctant to go. Five seconds later, though,
I was glad I had obeyed. Halfway along the gloomy narrow
channel our guide halted abruptly and pointed upward.
Frozen forever in the rough rock roof over our heads was a
face—the sleek, black, shining imprint of an actor's mask

75

that had been caught up in the holocaust, baked in the fire as perfectly as though a skilled ceramist had been at work. The disembodied face was simple in line, severe in execution, and, suspended like a ghostly blessing over the netherworld, quite beautiful. I had a moment's regret that our own theater had long since abandoned the use of the universal face; western dramatists and actors haven't paid much attention to the stylized mask—the face that represents many men rather than simply one man—since the clowns of the *commedia dell'arte* tore off their papier-mâché eyebrows and vast hooked noses in the eighteenth century. We don't care much about the universal image, I thought; we like to see the individual countenances of individual actors—personal, idiosyncratic, unique. In our easily understandable preference, have we lost something? Or did the mask never have much to do with the essential nature of the theater?

A few weeks later I realized that my queries had been wasted. A new season introduced itself with a performance by Marcel Marceau, to whom the idea of the mask is no idle memory. The distinguished French mime, as everyone knows and as *I* ought to have remembered during my musings, paints his face a dead clown-white and gashes it with little more than a morose clamp of a mouth and a pair of exhausted parentheses for eyebrows. That, I think we may take it, is a kind of mask.

But the brilliant M. Marceau was being even more explicit about the nature of his trade in his new entertainment. He began the evening with certain familiar exercises, the sort of exercises that had already made us recognize him, emotionally speaking, as the shortest distance between two points. He appeared as a holiday sport pitching ball after ball at the dolls in a carnival booth. For the fleeting second that each invisible ball spun out of M. Marceau's hand, our hero's face was wreathed in happy, expectant smiles. In the still more fleeting second during which each ball whizzed impotently past its intended object, our hero's face went out like a candle.

Between the hope and the horror, between the trusting confidence and the total eclipse, there was no measurable flick of time. The two basic faces of man, the delighted and the dismayed, simply collided.

The short-circuiting recurred, hilariously, in a wire-walking exhibit. Marceau had strung and tested his nonexistent high-wire. He had clambered up the ladder to a precarious perch. (It is wonderful how forcefully this magician makes ladders diminish beneath him as he prowls rung after rung without ever leaving the ground.) He had made it, teetering, to the center of the wire, and was veering around toward us to take a bow. The bow was foredoomed, of course. At the very moment of glory, one uncertain foot went sawing wildly into empty air. Lightning could scarcely have competed with the transition.

But the special illumination of this particular visit came with the closing portion of the pantomimist's solo performance. In a vignette called "The Mask Maker," he tried on an assortment of grimacing countenances, all of which were accomplished by the barest passing of his modeled hands across the plainness of his own face. As the pace accelerated, we were nearly dizzied by the in-again, out-again sight of a sad little man behind these many borrowed moods.

At last—and I am not certain that the contemporary theater has offered us any surer stroke of visual genius—one of the masks, an especially gay one, became stuck. No amount of pulling and tugging, or even bashing with a chisel, would dislodge it. Now we were treated to mirth and misery as a living, breathing unit. The man shrugged helplessly, but the face laughed. The man clawed the air in panic; the face laughed. The man fell exhausted and sobbing; the face was precisely as merry as before. In this bizarre, ironic fusion of anguish and gayety—and it required an effort of will to remember that there was no mask there, it remained Marceau's

77

own face—the mime seemed to have arrived, paradoxically, at the simplest possible statement of complexity. Misery and mirth in a *single* image summarizes, and virtually exhausts, the content of the theater.

But go back a moment to the earlier business in which mask after mask passed over Marceau's wan countenance. As we were given, with the rapidity of a shutter on an old-fashioned moving picture machine, flashes of every kind of grotesque mood interspersed with flashes of an actual man behind the pyramiding moods, there leapt to mind an explanation of what all honest theater people have been trying to achieve since the wholly rigid mask was formally dropped. In their heart of hearts they want to offer us a vision of both the man *and* the mask in the same, or nearly the same, instant. Here the private, personal soul is made visible; but over it and across it like a light reflected in a windowpane shimmers the universal grimace, the grimace of common terror or common joy that links so many unique and lonely figures into a vast and universal chain. The one and the many are thus on tap in a united, blinding rush of energy, implying one another, reinforcing one another, shaking hands with one another. Two understandings of the human condition meet and pass into one another so that only one hat needs to be tipped.

Clearly, the theater has never succeeded in getting its mask entirely off. Just as clearly, a performer, by becoming more than himself while remaining himself, can fill a large space.

WORD PICTURES

IT HAS NEVER SEEMED to me an accident that the theater should have been at its healthiest whenever it was obliged to evoke, in any old way it could, more than met the eye. A man like Sophocles couldn't, or wouldn't, show you a murder at a crossroads or a suicide in the bath, just as Shakespeare had no lightboard to make the skies over Belmont grow dark: the job of making such things happen so vividly that both the blood and the stars seemed immediately present was a job that either had to be done by words or not get done at all. If words have always been needed to brush in the backgrounds of plays, there have been many times when it was necessary for them to create the very foregrounds; and these times have given us the plays we cling to most tenaciously. The strain of making do with the colors that belong to the spectrum of language has, somehow or other, usually proved an upward strain; it has created more that could not be dismantled when the performance was done.

It was impossible not to think of such matters while watching the players at Circle in the Square paint visual pictures on a physically barren stage during a brilliant revival of Dylan Thomas' *Under Milk Wood.* Here director William Ball had conceived the little Welsh town of Llareggub as a wash of eternal gray. As the actors appeared, to stretch and yawn and begin their histories while the world was "fast and slow asleep," they were clad in gray sweaters, gray skirts and, even where a touch of black was needed, gray scarves to cut across its assertiveness. Somehow even the drowsiness was gray.

Untheatrical? Wait. Something was happening. The visible world was being drained of its usual busy and blinding clamor so that room could be made for the hues of the poet's words. Whatever moved across the open floor of this arena theater refused to claim glory for itself. It had been neutralized in order to reflect the changing shades of language, as though language itself were light.

Thus the nighttime "glasses of teeth and the Thou Shalt Nots on the wall" became more vivid to the mind than the people who were describing them verbally. When a shrew issued her morning warning to the universe—"and before you let the sun in, mind it wipes its shoes"—the sullen sun and the dutiful scraping of feet became outraged realities, naked to the eye.

Was a visual, even sensual, summary of a lost life wanted? And in no more than a sentence? A rueful girl remembered that a young man "kissed her once by the pig-sty when she wasn't looking and never kissed her again although she was looking all the time." (To be shown any of this now would have been vulgar superfluity; everything had been seen in the saying.) Were we after a fierce, funny phrase that would make the shrew leap out at us from the blur of misty faces on an unlimbering Welsh morning? "She'd beeswax the lawn to make the birds slip," someone muttered.

The "fried liver with onion on its breath" was no fried liver condemned to the invisibility of an off-stage kitchen; it crawled through the crack in the half-shuttered window to insinuate itself into the stir of the town. Just as an "all at once wind" whipped into our faces in spite of the fact that the rather dour and overcast theater on Bleecker Street was, to tell the truth, close to airless.

Under Milk Wood is, in a way, the best possible case that can be made for the value of verse in the theater—for the simple reason that it offers almost nothing else in the way of dramatic energy. If it is to survive at all, it must survive on language alone; and in performance it survived to an astonishing degree. There was nothing here of sustained narrative, which is probably the theater's most potent all-round weapon. There was very little of unfolding, and hence binding, characterization; the people were given to us in erratic small snatches and then snatched away. (The evening boasted a remarkable moment during which actress Sada Thompson, doubling wildly as all ten performers were forced to do, spoke a sentence in one character, rose mercurially, and, tugging a shawl tightly as she hustled across Coronation Street, spoke the very next sentence out of another body altogether. Miss Thompson, by the way, had been cannily cast in nearly all the more sensual roles: with her high-fashion voice and her fashion-plate repose there was only a twist at the corner of her mouth to let lust in, lending sly delight to her faintly brazen, faintly bitter "Knock twice at the door of my grave and ask for Rosie.")

It is important to stress the theatrical power of the things that were missing here—story, and the continuing presence of people to whom we might commit ourselves—in order to throw into relief the unbelievable vigor of the tool that had been left to fend for itself.

You could not be nailed, suspensefully, to *Under Milk Wood;* you might even have felt free, now and then, to nod off. (I noticed several members of the opening-night audience doing just this, only to find themselves, once they'd come awake again, instantly wreathed in smiles.) You could not become emotionally linked, in the sense of wanting secretly to offer encouragement or quick warning, to the too-many miniatures that populated Llareggub. The absence of these energies was no virtue. The fact that they were not there made it harder and harder for the evening to acquire cumulative force. If they had been there, the experience might have been tripled in intensity.

But doing without them was, at the very least, a wonderful way of making us hear what we have been missing in our own easy-to-make theater (a theater in which everything is made visible, and language, being unchallenged, goes limp) and of making us realize what breath-taking vitality still bolts from the unaided word. The actors seemed to have filled themselves as at a well and to be advancing upon one another with stored-up reserves that could never be drained, no matter how many lightning-quick and silver-flashing syllables tumbled out. There was no holding a young man's wild and foolish declaration to a girl in a dream:

81

I am a draper mad with love. I love you more than all the flannelette and calico, candlewick, dimity, crash and merino, tussore, cretonne, crépon, muslin, poplin, ticking and twill in the whole Cloth Hall of the world. . . . Throw away your little bedsocks and your Welsh wool knitted jacket, I will warm the sheets like an electric toaster, I will lie by your side like the Sunday roast.

Nor did there seem any saucier animation on the stage that season than in the teasing and inverted narcissism of actress Jenny Egan's sneering flirtation with her own face in a shaving-glass:

> *Oh, there's a face!*
> *Where you get that hair from?*
> *Got it from a old tom cat.*
> *Give it back then, love.*
> *Oh, there's a perm!*
>
> *Where you get that nose from, Lily?*
> *Got it from my father, silly.*
> *You've got it on upside down!*
> *Oh, there's a conk!*
>
> *Where you get that smile, Lil?*
> *Never you mind, girl.*
> *Nobody loves you.*
> *That's what you think.*

Nobody loves verse any more, either. That's what *they* think.

THE PERFORMER ON HIS OWN

THERE IS obviously some special theatrical meaning behind the success, these past few years, of the solo performer. It isn't really likely that an audience accustomed to the clamor of a good many voices, the comfortable distraction of scenery, and the sheer visual pleasure of watching eight or nine restless people busy themselves on a crowded stage should be willing to exchange all this for the limited spectacle of a single man, a prop lectern, and a great gap beyond.

When Emlyn Williams first tried it, with a smattering of Dickens, it seemed an interesting novelty—and something of a stunt. When Marcel Marceau turned up, a white mask in a white spotlight, the possibility that a single figure might conceivably carve out of the unfamiliar void a more suggestive image than a dozen cooperative actors normally succeed in doing became clear. Mr. Williams returned with even fewer patches of window dressing—the Dickensian costume and beard had vanished—to wrestle not with *Under Milk Wood* but with the tumbling poetry of Dylan Thomas' boyhood, and any lingering suspicion that the performer was engaged in highly skilled trickery went up in smoke: this wasn't self-indulgent showmanship but a method of communicating a kind of lyric fire that our regulation plays, and our regulation production methods, have long denied us.

At one lunatic point in Mr. Williams' salute to the ribald, rose-colored, runaway language left us by Mr. Thomas, the performer was to be seen simultaneously impersonating three extremely energetic people. The first of these was gaily rocking in a rocking chair that was perched on a horsehair sofa, the second was regularly ascending toward the ceiling from his base on an innerspring mattress, and the third was wandering wildly through a Lewis Carroll world with a beer bottle stuck on his finger. There was a fourth person present,

83

but she was momentarily out of sight on the floor somewhere.

The three we're talking about were very much in sight. Their boozy flights through space were perfectly charted, drawn with such swift and sweeping strokes by a single player that we could not only tell them apart when they were spouting individual insanities, we could continue to identify them when they were all but crashing into one another. This was the actor in Mr. Williams triumphant.

But there was something more than fantastically fluid "acting" in the solo exercise called *A Boy Growing Up*. Mr. Williams was not wholly concerned with focusing attention on himself, on displaying his virtuosity, on daring us to count the number of concrete physical images he could conjure up out of a boy dreaming he was a bird, a dainty aunt delicately setting a mousetrap, a grim family visitor "smiling like a razor."

He was less intent on "showing" us something than he was in seeing it for himself. Again and again in the course of thirteen excerpts from a Welsh poet's childhood memories, Mr. Williams seemed briefly to dismiss the matter of direct contact with his audience. His eyes flashed slightly upward, slightly over the folk out front. What was taking place was not quite taking place on the stage, but in some actual and continuing world that was visibly, and very vigorously, present to him. And he was not really out to display what he saw: he was out to echo it.

I don't want to turn Mr. Williams into a Buddha. There was nothing the least bit pretentious in the curious images he reflected: of a couple of adolescents quietly drowsing on a hillside, of three idlers comparing not-very-romantic notes under a railway trestle, of a bookish youngster suddenly watching "the future spread out" in a gloriously untidy room. But this adroit and extraordinarily sensitive performer did seem to have stumbled upon a private radar set he hadn't been using when he was having a holiday with Dickens: he was responding to subtle, elusive, almost indeterminate shadows and giving them immediate, glowingly intelligible shape.

And he was, while at it, seeing double. He opened a sequence called "The Fight," for instance, by joining us firmly to the just naturally sadistic mind of a child bent on baiting one of his elders. ("As soon as he loses his temper, I'm going to go away.") Identification with the little monster was complete. Once there had been a roadside scuffle with another such monster, however, the mood changed. Our belligerent hero began to imagine his various revenges, and the reaction of a dozen or so people to his triumph. We were now offered characterizations—very vivid ones—of all these other people, but they were still conceived inside that same small, rambunctious mind. Through one pair of eyes we saw another pair of eyes, and then another, approaching an altogether agreeable infinity.

Equally invigorating, a short time later, was John Gielgud's appearance in an evening of carefully arranged fragments from the plays and sonnets of Shakespeare, *The Ages of Man*.

Mr. Gielgud banished the lectern, with its large and unnecessary promptbook, to an upstage position. He worked at the footlights as though there were no footlights, as though we shared the auditorium, and the resources of a playwright's imagination, with him. Though his use of gesture grew as the evening moved from the youthful fantasy of *A Midsummer Night's Dream* to the harrowing indecision of a Lear who can no longer deal with the bleak and bewildering universe he lives in, the gestures themselves were neither realistic nor important. They were unstudied reflexes, spontaneous and very nearly unformed echoes of a contest that was going on somewhere else: in the spare, tense, unyielding effort of the performer's mind to meet the playwright's, and to report it exactly. Mr. Gielgud was not really offering us snatches of impersonation, or shreds of his forty favorite characters. He was interested in another thing: in the intelligence of Shakespeare, in the infinite response an unbelievably alert human being once made to an infinitely complex universe.

The actor was out to catch the very first gleam that stirred in a playwright's eye as a chance gesture flickered past him. If one of those foolish lovers in *The Merchant of Venice* was settling down to a highly conventional, highly romantic rhapsody in praise of a starry night, there must have been—we sensed—something more than mere lyricism in Shakespeare's head. The actor did not sing the speech, or dismiss it for the pretty thing it was. He looked at it, wondered about it, reached for the precise relationship a very real person once gropingly forged with a very real sky. The image wasn't so much acted as literally fastened to a thought.

As Mr. Gielgud stood alone on his platform, sometimes arching his arms over the auditorium, sometimes beating the knuckles of his clenched fists together in the intensity of his pursuit, he frequently blinked his eyes, as though he were trying to see better. What he saw, we saw reflected in him. The player's insistence on cutting his way through the fog of familiarity to the very heart of what Shakespeare meant to say when he first said it was so successful that we were moved not only by the obvious bid for pity of a sobbing Richard II but—startlingly—by the fourteenth line of a sonnet.

Why are we so moved, just now, by language divorced from all of its customary theatrical companions, and why are we suddenly so willing to submit to the separated experience? I suspect that it is the only way any of us can presently think of to set about putting the whole explosive world of electrifying verbal content and expressive visual comment together again.

It's all very well to say that actors and audiences alike have grown weary of the casual "naturalism" that has dominated our stages for years and years, that the lowered metabolism of indifferent speech, transparent thought, and relax-on-the-sofa behavior is ripe for the junk heap and ready to be replaced by something with more juice in it. The problem of pumping vitamins into every theatrical department at once is a staggering one. Naturalism has had its own kind of consistency, its own interior coherence: the thrown-away line, the cigarette reach, and the conversation tempered to a hotel-room tone have belonged together. It's neither easy to tear them apart nor to expand and enrich them simultaneously.

What we seem to be doing is re-examining the basic tools independently of one another, and independently of the "play" itself. Marcel Marceau plants his feet on the stage, and then begins to discover what they can be made to do, as though the very notion of movement needed fresh investigation—almost as though man's talent for so simple a thing as walking had been forgotten. Mr. Gielgud seems to be asking another question: without feet, how far can thought take us?

Two complementary lines are being extended toward their ultimate boundaries; when their outside dimensions are reached, perhaps they can be fused in the interests of a bigger—and ever better—play. This is guesswork, of course; but our fascination with the powers of the uninhibited solo performer, pursuing his unique bent with single-minded passion, suggests that we are curious about a range to come, and an intensity of vision we may have been missing.

ANGLE OF VISION

No ONE has had the nerve to build an entirely new legitimate theater in New York City since the Ethel Barrymore was sandwiched between a couple of Forty-seventh Street storefronts in 1927. The fact is quite properly dismaying: it means that *all* of our available playhouses are now more than thirty years old and that the normal process of gradually substituting fresh buildings for frowzy ones came to an abrupt halt a whole generation ago. We have torn down some of the more tottering structures during the second quarter of the twentieth century; but we have not replaced a single one of them.

The sudden paralysis that overtook theatrical construction is generally laid to economic causes, and there can be no doubt that the financial hazards attendant upon any permanent investment in so mercurial a business have had a good bit to do with the big freeze. In the late twenties, the movies were a much better risk: the Paramount, not the Plymouth, seemed the profitable theater of the future. At the end of the twenties the depression cut off funds altogether. By the time the depression began to look as though it might go away and leave us to our pleasures for a while, a wartime urgency denied manpower and materials to so frivolous a pursuit. It is hard to see how anyone could have been expected to pour his cash and/or his courage into theatrical real estate from 1929 to, say, 1950.

A suggestive question still begs for an answer. What of the boom years since? Why has no publicity-happy entrepreneur even promised us a playhouse in the past ten years? How does it happen that there were no elaborate plans, wistfully but doggedly drawn up during the impossible years, ready and waiting for that sublime moment when money might become available? When money did become available, where was everybody?

As a matter of fact, money has been spent on the theater in the past ten years. Every cent of it has been spent, however, on sandblasting, whitewashing, and recarpeting old houses. We have stretched new marquees over the sidewalks, several of them equipped with enough radiant heating to give passers-by a sun tan in January. We have installed loveseat divans, at increased prices for the additional plush, and then taken them out again (when these higher-priced snuggle pits, big enough for two, weren't sold on a given evening an appalling gap opened up between the stage and the lower-

priced seats). We have covered dusty old walls with fresh
coats of yellow and powder-blue paint, we have upholstered
dressing rooms so that an actor's family can visit—or even
vacation—in complete comfort, and we have, in the case of
the glossy, candelabra-lit Lunt-Fontanne, torn out the entire
interior and then reconstructed it with such fidelity to the
original plan that no one has yet been willing to describe this
enormous investment of capital and labor as a "new" theater.

Such money as has been earmarked for theatrical renova-
tion has gone precisely where it has gone in the genuinely
new theaters of Germany: into polite accommodations for
formerly nerve-racked people. The German theater has been
building since the war because it has had a paternal source
of funds—the state, dedicated to preserving a theatergoing
habit and a literary tradition very much older than ours. Leaf
any German architectural brochure, though, and you will discover that the state's beneficence has been lavished on exterior arcades that afford "protection from the rain to spectators arriving by bus or train," on cloakrooms and broader
staircases, and, above all, on toilets. Before he enters the
auditorium, the customer is handsomely coddled; when he
enters it, he finds himself in pretty much the same theater,
undergoing pretty much the same experience, that seems to
have paralyzed us in 1927.

I don't wish to suggest that all of these improvements are
not true benefits. There is no reason why a lobby shouldn't be
larger, a canopy warmer, a toilet more accessible, or a dressing room fit for an actor to eat his dinner in. (Some German
actors do sleep overnight on their cozy backstage couches; it
must be comforting for a director to know that his man will
be on time for rehearsal next morning.) Anything that will
soothe player or patron is clearly a gain.

But back to our question. In an American risk economy,
where government is quite above dabbling in the arts, why
has there been such universal agreement among rich-enough

men that an altogether new theater building was not worth the risk? Why has so much money gone into a mere holding operation, and none into high adventure?

I suspect that the economic explanation is not the whole explanation, or even the essential one. Businessmen have their own powers of intuition, rough and rational as they may sometimes seem. It is perfectly possible that a spiritual, as well as financial, censor is operating here, that men of ready cash and unsuspected imagination have sensed—since the Barrymore was built—that we had come to the end of something and that there was no further reason, creatively speaking, for building any more Barrymores. In addition to all the economic difficulties, there has been a drag at the heart: no dream stirred impulsively in the real estate man's soul, no image he could get hold of caught fire in his brain. He has simply waited, a bit bewildered, tidying up here and there.

This instinct—vague enough to keep him protesting that he is in favor of new playhouses and strong enough to keep him from doing anything about it—has been powerfully reinforced in recent years by the peculiar behavior of authors, directors, actors, and off-Broadway entrepreneurs. To look at off-Broadway first, since that is where the oddity first asserted itself, the habit grew of performing plays "in the round."

Instead of fastening like leeches onto old movie theaters, a great many of which were now rapidly becoming available, the young men and women of downtown Greenwich Village or uptown East Eighty-fourth Street tended to prefer abandoned cabarets and hospitable church basements for their expanding operations simply because the shape was different. Here benches sprang up around the actors, or on three sides of them; if a possible auditorium happened to be rectangular in shape, as the Theater de Lys was, a forestage was thrown out at the customers as though to compensate for the defect; facing the fact that there was no proscenium arch to conceal the dozens of spotlights needed to keep the actors visible, producers shrugged and hung their spotlights from the ceiling, plainly exposed; facing the further fact that any sizable piece of scenery would blind the customers who happened to be sitting behind it, these same irreverent fly-by-nighters either ditched the scenery altogether or charitably shot enormous holes through it. Asked why so much activity should suddenly take place in deserted synagogues and bankrupt breweries, a tradition-bound Broadwayite might have given his traditional answer, "It's cheaper." But economy alone did not produce this particular *kind* of theater: a restless, half-understood drive toward another kind of theatrical experience produced it and—in its urgency—drove so many costly things out of its way that it proved, in the doing, to be cheaper. It is possible to paint scenery inexpensively; but it is not possible to see through it, so the scenery went. It is possible to mask spotlights, even though there is no proscenium arch; but masking spotlights might inch us back toward the old naturalistic illusion of the typical picture-box stage, so the spotlights were given their freedom.

Audiences took a surprising interest. As a reviewer, I covered one off-Broadway production in 1951. In 1957 I covered forty-six. If I were a stronger man, and Broadway itself hadn't the effrontery to keep opening plays, I could cover a hundred or more each season in the sixties. Actors took a surprising interest. Before long certain reasonably important "names," and some genuine stars, were giving up substantial portions of their incomes (if no Broadway plays were begging for them at the moment, television might have employed them at handsome fees) to stumble about on improvised platforms, make up in dressing rooms that seemed barely sanitary, and chance the possibility of damaging failure under embryo directors in order to experience for themselves the special atmosphere of a new relationship with the customers "down front" (and now they were really down front). Curiously, some plays seemed better in these circumstances than they had in much richer Broadway mountings, Tennessee Williams' *Summer and Smoke* being the earliest and most celebrated example.

Still, there was—and is—a limitation to the off-Broadway experience, a limitation not upon the size of the audience or the size of the profit to be taken from it but upon the size of the experience itself. The arenas are small. Voices must necessarily be lowered, gestures must necessarily be kept at less than heroic force, sweep and scale are out of the question. Though actors and play are visible in a new dimension —quite round, quite close, not plastered against faraway post cards—both are inevitably drawn into a still more casual naturalism. Fresh contact has been made between audience and performers but made at a suppressed, extraordinarily discreet level. It is possible to sit through whole productions in which no voice is ever on tone, in which players use a lower and less theatrical pitch than they would in their own living rooms, speaking normally to their wives. The small arena breaks down every formula but one: the formula of subdued, tape-recorded behavior. It achieves the shape of a circus in the size of a bandbox.

Franchot Tone has acted off-Broadway but Elia Kazan has not directed off-Broadway. Our most vigorous directors have not been tempted to dalliance, I think, because of this unappetizing reduction in scale, volume, and velocity. They have, however, been going through wrestling matches of their own.

They have been wrestling with the only theaters that are big enough for the noise they want to make—the standard theaters of Broadway—but that were built a generation ago by men they never met and with whom, if they had met them, they would have had nothing in common.

The impulse that has dictated the shape of the off-Broadway stage burns just as feverishly, if much less freely, in the imaginations of the established professionals who do most of the work uptown. Is Elia Kazan satisfied with the picture-

frame stage, the defined curtain line, the sharp division between platform and auditorium that waits for him as he
crawls out of a taxicab to rehearse a company of actors on
Forty-fifth Street? Apparently not. For *Cat on a Hot Tin Roof*
he had designer Jo Mielziner throw a pie-shaped apron across
the orchestra pit so that Barbara Bel Geddes could tiptoe out
on it and soliloquize into our faces. For *J. B.* he expanded this
platform and dropped steps from it to the orchestra floor so
that Christopher Plummer could dance back and forth between the action and the rest of us; he also abandoned the
curtain that normally protects us from the stagehands until
the play has begun, invited designer Boris Aronson to construct a setting of interlocking platforms that tilted toward
us so that we could see the stage floor, and then carefully
called our attention to all of these formalized features by
taking three or four minutes at the opening of the evening
to have men in overalls stroll out, test them, and complete the
job of rigging.

Mr. Kazan is, of course, not the first to engage in this thrashing effort to escape from a straitjacket, nor is he alone in trying to drive a psychological wedge into the center of the house.
The matter of that tilted stage floor, for instance, is interesting. At the opening of José Ferrer's *Edwin Booth,* a friend of
mine came out at intermission time wondering where the odd
rake, causing the actors to act on an incline, had come from.
It was easy to explain where it had come from in this instance:
Edwin Booth had been conceived as a pastiche of American
nineteenth-century drama, and all American theaters in the
mid-nineteenth century had sloped their stages (some of
these can still be seen in the "ghost" theaters of the West). It
was less easy to explain where the same slope had come from
in, say, Eugene O'Neill's *A Touch of the Poet* (here my friend
hadn't even realized he was looking at a slightly lopsided
world because Ben Edwards had so cannily forced his perspective in creating his stunningly "primitive" image of a New

93

England tavern). The truth of the matter was that we had run into five raked stages on Broadway in as many weeks that season, so determined had our directors been to dump the players—and the play—into our laps.

What we appear to be watching on Broadway is the struggle to burst from a cocoon. The off-Broadway experience of being close enough to an actor to hear him breathe has suggested something to us; a nerve has been touched that had been subconsciously twitching for some time past, fervently waiting for the moment when it could infect the whole sensory system of the theater; a scent has been taken up that is being hotly pursued. Somewhere, just beyond our immediate reach, hovers a tantalizing image of what theater *is*— what it is that is *not* like the experience we have become familiar with, and wearied of, during the last hundred years.

But the full image continues to elude us. For all that our youngest playwrights have virtually stopped writing the photographic realism that made so much of the practical doors and the perpetual laying of dinner tables which David Belasco's box set and minutely detailed property list bequeathed us, headlong pursuit of a new and exhilarating freedom is impossible. The theaters were built for Belasco. The cocoon is snarled, and binding; some of the threads simply cannot be broken.

The actors can be pushed toward us, but only a little way —only so far as the orchestra pit and the rectangular shape of the auditorium allow. To force even a sliver of an apron beyond this point would destroy all of the sight lines around it; it would also wipe out a number of those high-priced seats needed to keep any production solvent and there is no room anywhere, in this narrow channel of a house, to compensate by piling up further banks of customers. More than that. In an auditorium built like an alley looking toward a view at the distant end, the surge over the orchestra pit does not alter the essential nature of the view: we are still looking at the actors *against* the scenery, we are looking at them flat. They live in their house, we live in ours, and all communication is through windows.

Given the fact of a new impulse that will not be denied, the fact of an old theater building that effectively denies it, and the fact that we cannot even be sure what the impulse means until we have got it into the open and looked at it, what are we to do? The first clue has come from an old friend, whose plays were good enough to demand continuing production. We knew two things about William Shakespeare: that his plays seemed slow, overburdened, and disconcertingly ghostly against the massive trappings of the picture-book stage; and that they had been written for, and first performed on, another kind of stage altogether.

Scholars began, in the quiet poverty of their university or otherwise out-of-the-way theaters, to rebuild the jutting platform (originally it had plunged halfway through the auditorium), the single side wall that was very little more than an escape hatch for the actors, the limited stage balcony for such scenes as required elevation, and the tiers of seats that rose in stadium fashion around three sides of the acting area. However academic an activity this may have been, it proved something: the plays changed their character, became busy, bustling, personal, dimensional; the author seemed a new man, and a better one.

The experimentation opened a good many eyes: stage architects began to wonder if what was really an anachronism mightn't be reduced to its principles and then adapted to contemporary, or perhaps universal, use; audiences looking at old-fashioned and overdressed productions now saw them more clearly for what they were and came to be intelligently, rather than vaguely, dissatisfied with them. Indeed, it was the stubborn clinging—in some quarters—to picture-frame methods that paved the way for the apron's victory. The Memorial Theater at Stratford-on-Avon, England, was built in 1932 on conventional proscenium-arch lines. It was no sooner open than an uncomfortable sense of its wrongness—not only in its "jam-factory" outlines but in its interior conventionality —swept intuitively over the British theater world; belated, hopelessly hampered efforts to pretend that the curtain line isn't really there have been made ever since. When, thirty years later, the good Americans who built the Festival Playhouse at Stratford, Connecticut, permitted themselves to make precisely the same error of dividing the familiar stage from the familiar auditorium they found themselves instantly engaged in the same frantic pretense: to this day more and more lumber is being laid down over the footlight trough as harassed directors try to catch up with an awareness that has already galloped away from them. For Shakespeare, at least, the day of canvas and paint is done with.

The real breakthrough came in a tiny Canadian town, also called Stratford, when director Tyrone Guthrie, designer Tanya Moiseiwitsch, and promoter Tom Patterson set up shop under a circus tent. The auditorium itself was solidly built and brazenly original: one entered it, in 1953, to look down steeply-banked aisles toward a three-sided arena (the bleacher-style banking has the simple virtue of enabling everyone to see) which fed its actors onto an open platform from passageways directly beneath the audience (the passages are technically called vomitoriums) and from a rear wall composed of intricate stairways and pillars supporting a small, but wonderfully useful, stage balcony. Seated, one looked at the fluid, swift, uncluttered performance with some astonishment. Though the actors were below us rather than above us, they seemed larger. Though they had no scenery to provide them with a literal environment they seemed to be their own environment, to carry a world with them, and to be the fatter for it. Though our eyes never quite met, they were speaking to us, or at least to the man seated directly behind us. Though we were perfectly aware of a vast blur of faces across the platform from us, the presence of our fellow men was not so much distracting as enlivening. We were, all of us, players and playgoers alike, at last in the same building. The actors were doing most of the work, as usual, but we were engaged in a communal and reciprocal experience, candidly acknowledging each other's presence, sharing the field on which battle was to be done, engaged and involved in a meeting that could not help but straighten our spines, alert our ears, and heighten every capacity for response. Being thoroughly present, and not merely eavesdropping, we longed to participate, and savored the sense of being permitted to. The circus shape had now expanded to full size, and the big, booming plays seemed bigger and richer for being allowed to exhale.

Audiences found this inaccessible town and this impertinent theater in such numbers that by 1957 risk money was available to erect a permanent superstructure. Without altering the three-sided stage and the three-sided auditorium in any essential way the circus tent was turned into steel and glass, preserving the exterior contours of an interior revolt. It made no sense to call this adventurous, self-determined house the best new theater on the American continent; it was the only new theater on the American continent. It remains exciting simply to approach it across a dusty path from a parking lot: it stands up for itself, proudly, set apart, built for the things men mean to do in it.

Still, only Shakespeare has been taken care of, unless you want to make special note of the fact that Sophocles' *Oedipus* has been performed, not incongruously, on the same platform. Some instinct tells us that we must not rest on the effective restoration of another man's natural stamping ground: we must arrive at a home of our own.

What this streamlined, wholly successful adaptation of the Elizabethan stage *has* done for us is prod us into asking a series of fundamental theatrical questions. Is it possible, for

97

instance, that however closely Shakespeare's playhouse was related to the particular spirit of a particular time it also embraced principles that were in some way universal, that it belonged—as our theater buildings do not quite belong—to some sort of mainstream? Ought we to look back over the whole range of theatrical architecture to see if we can discover what features recur most often, most spontaneously, and most profitably? Dare we believe that one shape is literally better than another, that it not only produces better relations between actors and audiences but also better plays?

Looking back, we discover the first great body of western drama, and the first period of great excitement over drama in the body politic, in Greece. The Greek experience took place in an amphitheater: the performing area was circular; the stone seats for the spectators rose steeply on three sides of it, leaving a fourth side open for entrances and perhaps for a shallow building in which the actors might change costumes.

The conquering Romans were the first to slice off any sizable portion of the circle. The Greeks themselves had quite naturally learned to use the makeshift building, or scene wall, at the fourth side of the circle as a point of environmental reference: if the lines spoke of a palace, temple, or any other kind of dwelling, the actors might well indicate the handy façade, especially since they must come and go by it in any case.

The Romans moved the façade forward, sometimes halfway into the circle, and began to overload it with decor. The movement—and a destructive one it is—can be seen in what is left of the most important of all Greek theaters, the Dionysus that slopes so gently and so warmly up the base of the Acropolis. Here the playing space has not been severely reduced, but the ground on which Thespis and Aeschylus and Aristophanes worked has been cut into by an assertive lump of carved stone.

At home, the Romans grew fonder of the carved wall than of the plays that were meant to be played before it. Tiers of pillars, flanking more and more statuary, rose high in the air over what must have seemed miniature players; the players were confined to a narrow pathway at the foot of the wall, moving from right to left against mountains of masonry. To see the best-preserved of Roman theaters today—at Orange, in France—is to understand why Napoleon proudly proclaimed that he owned the best wall in Europe. He did not say theater; he said *wall.*

Drama, during the Roman experience, was neither very good nor very popular. The connection between the monstrousness of the façade and the feebleness of the drama need not be overstressed, but it is possible that some connection existed.

The medieval theater, inventing drama all over again for itself, moved quickly from the vaulting cathedral interior to the open churchyard, the town square, and the pageant wagon, a primitive explosion that did its best work with little more than "two planks and a passion." Literary merit was some time coming; but the carnival circumstances made the form immediately popular.

Shakespeare's playhouse seems to have been crossbred from the pageant wagon and the innyard, two holiday meeting places. Once more a sea of faces sweeps around a three-sided platform, with a scene wall at the fourth side so that actors may get on and off and may make what reference is necessary to orchards and tombs. Once again drama is at its most vital. As France, a little later, finds its own way to mature and sophisticated theater, some interest in the old Roman façade, dug from the past by the Renaissance, is in evidence; but Molière's players can perform anywhere, on the almost empty, bare-bones stages of the provinces or in the "round" of a ballroom at court.

Are we at last forced to believe that drama thrives best

when it is smack in the middle of things? No answer is possible until we have re-examined the alternative, the picture-box stage at the end of a gallery that has led us, over three hundred years, to the Barrymore. Where did it come from?

Its remote sources lie, of course, in the Roman façade, in the image of an independently interesting background—with a defined shape of its own—*against* which the actor plies his trade. Dredged up by the Renaissance, and given fresh interest by the discovery of perspective painting, it made its first conquest in Italy and found its way to post-Shakespearean England by courtesy of the court masque, the love of tableau, and Inigo Jones' passion for chiaroscuro. Court circles became interested in *pictures;* if actors do not need a frame, pictures do—and our proscenium arch was born. The arch is not a product of drama, be it noted; it simply sets boundaries to a flat landscape against which drama may or may not be played.

In England, all of the public platform theaters were forcibly closed during the Puritan experiment; since the experiment went on for eighteen years, none of these buildings survived. When theater was revived at the Restoration, only the "court" theater was tolerated, the theater that had grown fond of fashionable tableaux. But at least the revival began in a compromise: the painter was given the frame he needed while the actors were given a decent measure of freedom. The frame contented itself with enclosing the scene panels; the action took place on a deep apron in front of it; doors in the frame permitted the actors to escape. For a time it must have seemed as though the theater had possessed itself of the best of two possible worlds.

Something had changed, though. The eye of the spectator had altered its angle of vision. It had formed a new habit of looking not at an actor loose in space but at a total image, rectangular in shape and given its character by paint, in which the actor might be found. Actor and scenery were, at a glance, one. So long as this habit of vision persisted, so long as we continued to look for the actor as a two-dimensional inhabitant of a craftily designed but essentially two-dimensional world, an increasing fusion of the two elements was inevitable. The frame was visible, dominant, and potentially all-encompassing; it was bound to swallow the actor, too.

In the eighteenth century the apron was foreshortened so that less effort should be required to imagine the character as really moving about in the elaborate environment behind him. In the nineteenth century the environment won. The actor moved indoors, put up his curtain, and forgot all about the veranda-like wedge that lay, a reminder of his youth, at his feet. The apron, no longer meaningful, was at last chopped off. The theater was now not one house, but two: the players', and the patrons', each perfectly private and perfectly defined, save when a permissive drape was temporarily raised to expose the two parts—at a discreet distance—to one another.

This two-party playhouse which we have inherited has, then, come about through an interior logic of its own— granted the picture frame that dictates its growth. It is an intelligible form designed to produce one kind of experience: the experience of viewing an isolated world in a spirit of detachment. What we must now ask ourselves is whether or not we like the particular experience it has carefully arrived at, and whether or not it has produced as good plays as any other kind of audience-actor relationship.

The last question will be answered differently by men of different tastes: the man who is satisfied that the middle (or realistic) period of Ibsen achieves a level of theatrical power roughly equal to that of Sophocles or Shakespeare will rest content with the equipment at hand; the man who feels, as I confess I do, that three hundred years of progressive experiment inside the tennis-court shape has mysteriously but consistently fallen just short of greatness may conclude that it is time to try something else. During those three hundred years there has been no want of energy, of dedicated theatrical effort. Nor has there been any serious lack of creative power in society as a whole. The novel, for instance, arrived at what we are willing to call "greatness" at the same time that the stage was producing flimsy, heavily scenic, melo-drama. Out of the full three hundred years in the English-speaking theater, what are we eager to keep, what plays be-long in the continuing repertory? Restoration comedy, some of which is viable, was written at the beginning of the experi-ment, to be played on a platform. Sheridan and Goldsmith came along when the process was only half completed and a degree of nonrealistic formality was still quite possible. Out of the center of the nineteenth century, when the telescopic theater was being pulled into its ultimate shape, nothing survives to stir us. The turn into the twentieth century is saved for us by Shaw, Wilde, and Synge: curiously enough, all three are stylistic and verbal, virtually independent of the scenery in which they were first acted, and just as effective —as we have discovered with such a production as *Don Juan in Hell*—played on a naked platform or in the unadorned "round."

Whatever resistance continues to assert itself against the new leap into space is pretty much confined to a single fear: the fear that in abandoning our proscenium arch and wholly enclosed stage we may be forced to abandon certain valuable plays that were explicitly written for them. I find myself un-able to name these plays. Chekhov, theoretically the natural-ist's naturalist, has already survived transference to the small undecorated arena, and the best of Ibsen has had some suc-cess there, too. Apparently one need not worry about losing these men altogether in the shift of perspective that is taking place. The most respected of contemporary playwrights, Ten-nessee Williams and Arthur Miller, have already given lavish evidence—in their use of such devices as simultaneously vis-ible multiple settings, bold soliloquy, and conveniently trans-parent walls—that the enclosed stage and the detached experience have ceased to have meaning for them.

At the same time that we have begun to recognize a certain limitation upon quality in the divided playhouse, certain historical and social circumstances have appeared to hurry our thinking along. By the beginning of the twentieth century we had perfected the box image. At the same time a succession of scientifically-devised box images—the motion picture and, later, television—came along to duplicate the pictorial and essentially two-dimensional experience with far greater flexibility. The theater had spent a great deal of time tidying up a style that could now be handled better by rival media: its claim to uniqueness had in large part been lost.

The loss in uniqueness meant a loss in patronage and a constantly tightening economy: higher-priced seats, and more of them, were needed to keep the institution afloat. The long narrow channel that the contemporary playhouse had become was not well designed to meet the problem. Too many seats at too great a distance from the stage proved a liability. They were neither desirable in themselves nor subject to any increase in prices. What was needed, quite simply, was a larger supply of "good" locations, closely bound to the performing area—a need that once more suggested a banked semicircle with a platform equidistant from all sections of the auditorium. As designer Jo Mielziner has pointed out, the typical New York theater of today, with a floor capacity of approximately 1,130, carries its seats as far as 96 feet from the stage; anything beyond 65 feet may be justly described as an inferior location. A three-sided arena with the same floor capacity would bring *all* seats within 65 feet of the stage. The advantages to the viewer, and the economic advantages to producers that follow from them, are obvious.

The pressures toward a new shape, then, come insistently from all sides: from writers demanding the freedom to tell a new kind of story; from directors reaching desperately for fresh contact with their audiences; from audiences that must be wooed by the promise of an experience unlike that offered by rival and more accessible forms; from real estate men who are realistic about what it takes to keep a playhouse solvent. All of our urges, whether generously creative or crassly economic, seem headed in a single direction.

The universal impulse is evident even in those conventional playhouses that have been built—in Germany, say— since the war and that have concentrated mainly on creature comforts. The new theater at Bochum remains a two-part structure: but the struggle to annihilate the old sense of duality, to embrace both halves of the house in a single rounded line, is clear enough. The building at Mannheim goes a step further: here it is possible to extend the apron slightly and to move some of the customers up onto the stage, should anyone wish to. The principle of the arena creeps in, as it were, through the side door.

In England and America new houses are turning up, here often on college campuses, in which everything can be taken apart and rebuilt quickly, more or less in the manner of a Tinkertoy set. Proscenium productions, apron productions, productions wholly in the "round" become possible.

There is, as most theatrical architects realize, a built-in hazard clinging to these transitional houses: the possibility, even the probability, that an all-purpose theater will become a no-purpose theater, that it will lack the courage of any one conviction, that it will tend to revert—by force of habit—to the practices of its most familiar and least flexible variable, the enclosed stage. The very equipment for enclosure—the dominating arch, the deep space inside it, the groove for the curtain that is every bit as psychological as it is actual—may keep us from clearing our heads and beginning to imagine what a genuine alternative might really be like. It is easier to take refuge than to take off. In *The Dramatic Imagination* Robert Edmond Jones enunciated what is surely the simple truth: "The best thing that could happen to our theater at this moment would be for playwrights and actors and directors to be handed a bare stage on which no scenery could be placed, and then told that they must write and act and direct for this stage. In no time we should have the most exciting theater in the world."

How soon we are to have it may depend—at *this* moment in time—on the men and women who are engaged in shaping the structure of the repertory theater that is to be incorporated in the Lincoln Center for the Performing Arts. This, the first new playhouse to be erected in New York since the Barrymore, is the work of architect Eero Saarinen and designer Jo Mielziner. The promise is that it will be *new*.

George D. Stoddard, temporary chairman of the project's Advisory Council, has emphasized that the building is "not to be the last of one kind, but the first of another." Though completed plans have not yet been made available, the expectation is that a fan-shaped auditorium will surround a stage with a thrust to it.

The precise design, whatever it may prove to be, must provoke questions. Will the thrust of the stage be sufficient to impel the actors forward on it and away from their familiar sanctuary? Will the shape of that thrust seem an independent, assertive, self-contained shape rather than an enlarged lip at the base of a wall? The difficulties of shattering an ingrained habit of vision, of standing at a new point in the playhouse and looking at the action from an undreamed-of perspective, are enormous.

But the promise has been given, and that at least is exciting.

BREAKTHROUGH?

WHEN John van Druten paused to jot down his reflections on life, death, and the theater, he spoke of a hint of glory that had often nagged him while he was attending conventional performances of conventional plays. Mr. van Druten was a conventional playwright himself, one of our ablest; he worked in the light realistic tradition of our time, and found it profitable; but, like a good many other people who are willing to settle philosophically for the best that can be had at any given moment, he still had an itch.

Here is Mr. van Druten's report on what tantalized him:

In work that I truly understand, with which I have some professional acquaintance, I am longing always to see form broken, as I have seen it broken occasionally in the theater. I am tired of the traditional play, and I long for a new and other kind. I am waiting always for some one to show me where it is to be found, feeling that just behind that closed door, if one knew how to open it, just around that corner, if one could find the right way to turn it, there is another kind of play, a new and exciting play of fresher vision, wider understanding and portrayal. I have seen what have seemed like hints in other writers . . . that suggested where the path might be found, but it still shades off into darkness when I try and approach it. I know that this is true in all the arts, and that the theater is perhaps the slowest of them all to break traditions, but I have seen those broken. I want to see them broken wider apart.

The yearning strikes a familiar chord. Most of us, I think, have sat in the playhouse at one or another time in the last ten years and, in a sudden and fragmentary glimpse of something unexpected, *almost* detected the whisper of an opening door. "There it is," you say to yourself, "that's the way the next dozen important writers are going to do it"; but even as you are half leaning forward, straining to hear the fleeting inflection as a fully formed phrase, the intuition vanishes, the evening comes down to earth, the future is once more somebody else's property, and you cannot even quite say what it was you thought you noticed.

This is, by and large, a fairly recent phenomenon. The twenties were generally comfortable with tea cups, dinner tables, and "Won't you sit down?" prose. The thirties were violently absorbed in making these same things socially significant. The forties marked time, with a slightly collapsed look about the gills. But the fifties began to grow restless, and the sixties are urgent. It's *time*, some secret nerve seems to be saying—time for the next exciting thing in the theater to happen.

What's holding us back? Well, there is always the possibility that our culture itself is sedentary, sitting on its complacent, magnificently cushioned backside: the playwright is in a measure chained to his culture and he may have to wait for it to wake up. There is the further bother that most experimentation, when it is tried, tries too hard. It shoots for the moon, and skips over man. When this happens the cause of experimentation is not advanced: we simply learn to doubt its advisability. It's often hard to remember that the most successful experimental play of our time, *Our Town*, had the grassiest roots.

I can think of another inhibiting nuisance, a real mental block. The most frequently written theater essay in the twentieth century is the one in which it is solemnly explained that we cannot hope to produce great tragedy. The explanations are various: we are a mechanical society, we are a nonheroic society, we are an irresponsible society, we have run out of quill pens. In short, we are constantly warned that we had just better not try for greatness. Other societies may have managed it; we'd be darn fools to think we could bring it off.

In this connection I'd like to quote a letter I've received from a young doctor in Cairo, Egypt. The doctor is fed up with the "poor us" attitude. He writes:

Because Chekhov and Shaw were masters, and Shakespeare was their master, is that a good reason why we shouldn't do other things and do them even in a wrong way? What are we afraid of? Why are we still gazing speechlessly and motionlessly at things done hundreds of years ago as if those who did them were the only human beings in the whole human race capable of making people cry with joy and gasp in pain? Things can always be done. First we must be convinced that we are capable of doing them.

Good. Reverence for past masters is fine and dandy; when we permit it to turn into a paralyzing awe, we are simply being unrealistic, forgetting altogether that Shakespeare and Sophocles were middle-aged men with backaches and sore feet who were dead certain their next plays were going to be humiliating failures. In any case, and whatever they were, they didn't spend their working hours writing learned treatises on why the Periclean Age was too postwar for tragedy or why the Elizabethan Age was too violent for the proper sort of creative composure.

The next greatness will come, all right; the only question is when. And the *when* might be speeded up a trifle if we could tell ourselves, and half believe, that it might be tomorrow.

In the meantime, playwrights are not really waiting to see what actors, directors, and architects can do for them. They are plainly thrashing about; some are even thumbing their noses.

The Hostage

During the first moments of *The Hostage* it was difficult to know whether author Brendan Behan was simply committing a nuisance or renewing the life of the stage. One character was heard to remark of another that he had "a face like a plateful of mortal sins," which is just how the play looked.

The curtain rose on a grinning and feverish jig which was no part of the narrative but intended solely for the audience's macabre, and slightly startled, delectation. The jiggers included an old crone in black with her front teeth missing, an amiable ex-revolutionary with his one leg useless, a redheaded tart, a couple of homosexuals and a hymn-singer hiding behind spectacles.

When this broth settled down—though it never did settle down since all were back on their toes the minute a tinny piano chose to tinkle—we learned that we were housed in a brothel and that while a dozen raffish idlers, guzzlers, lechers, and perverts pursued their nightly devotions the seedy place was fated to become the temporary prison of a captured British soldier.

What sort of a play was this to be? We were not kept in the dark, only dizzy. When the browbeaten but ebullient inmates were not leering over the footlights to sing us a song (Mr. Behan had written outrageous lyrics for every standard sentimental song that ever dampened a pub), they were telling us jokes, right in the middle of the plot. Glancing at the unhappy prisoner, the housekeeper inquired of the officer who had brought him there:

"Have you got the place well covered, sir?"

"Yes, why?" snapped the officer.

"It might rain."

Shocked laughter from the audience. At which the officer wheeled on the customers, threatening them with a gesture. "Silence!" was his command to Broadway. "This is a serious play."

This was a serious play which had to do with the howling foolishness of bothering our heads over all our minor skirmishes and empty civil squabbles while the hydrogen bomb is waiting in the wings. The seriousness was obvious, and did not have to be stated often. ("The I.R.A. is out of date—and so is everything else.") The howling foolishness of it was given much more footage. Bouncing guards that seemed to have been borrowed from the line of ducks in a shooting gallery wheeled in and out and roundabout; for a while nobody entered except in the act of zipping his trousers, or even his kilt; tea was served, and the teabags haughtily rejected, between ballads. As the evening skipped and tugged until its seams were nearly burst, Mr. Behan seemed to be suggesting that we might just as well kick our heels, grinning, on the edge of the grave—if that's all we can think of doing.

And there was another way of looking at it. One of the things the irrepressible author may possibly have had in mind was the creation of a scatological version of *Everyman*. The soldier who was plucked from nowhere, for no reason, and promptly earmarked for Death was an ordinary young innocent, Cockney to his teeth and bewildered to his toes. Around him scampered all of the Vices contemporary man has succeeded in bringing to a pitch of refinement, each of which was prepared to make the jolliest possible case for itself. Only the Virtues were missing, which may have been Mr. Behan's method of suggesting that we are short on them. The rambunctiousness, and the savage-sweet ending (the innocent was shot, the mood sobered abruptly, then the dead man rose and joined the jig) united death and dance in an almost classic Dance of Death.

In dashing all of this off at breakneck speed, Mr. Behan was three or four persons at once. He was a kind of infant exhibitionist, proud of his never having been trained (the number of calculated shockers was enormous, and this may well have been the play with something to offend everybody). He was a random humorist, ready to borrow from absolutely anyone. ("I'm as pure as the driven snow." "You weren't driven far enough.") He was, again, a better humorist than that, an original piece of salt who might have reminded you of Mort Sahl, or the more extravagant Mark Twain, or simply of your drunken uncle who happened to be a true wit.

And he was an astonishing man of the theater. Whatever the willful excesses or woolly inspirations that overtook him,

Mr. Behan could make the actors on stage blur into the folk out front with an intimacy and a dour communion that was infectious. The ribald evening was blatantly, boastfully, un-self-consciously alive.

Why? The energy that stirred so mysteriously at the center of the stage, tumbling over all the usual conventions of the theater as though they were so many unimportant ninepins, came, I think, from two definable sources. One of them was the plain certainty that Mr. Behan, for all his celebrated toss-pot habits, does possess the single-minded, self-generating, intuitive power of the natural-born artist. He may have nei-ther discipline nor taste; but he has a gift that speaks, in how-ever irresponsible and unmodulated a voice, for itself.

Nothing here should have been cohesive, and everything was. Simply, it seems never to have entered the author's head that his lapses of invention or his headlong determination to make hash of the proprieties should in any way compromise the truly lyrical or observant or just plain funny things that represented him at his individualistic best. And, somehow, they did not get in the way of our hearing "He couldn't knock the skin off a rice pudding" or of our exploding into laughter as a Negro boxer marched into a melee carrying an enormous placard, "Keep Ireland black!" The borrowed, the blue, and the Behan seemed all the same man: a gregarious and all-devouring personality shouting its own name from the Dublin chimney pots. Everything on the menu was malicious.

The second interior strength of the evening lay in director Joan Littlewood's high-powered hearing aid. Miss Littlewood's radar was able to detect, at all times, just where her author's uniqueness lived; she could hear the cockeyed private inflec-tion that bound so much malarkey and so much inspiration together. Another director might have been frightened by the pantomime fantasy—stomping soldiers, crawling bodies, wan-dering shadows—that opened the second act, and so botched it. Anyone might have wondered what to do with a madman in a kilt, a spinster given to outbursts of plain chant, a frustrated lecherer who went over to the other camp, where he camped.

Miss Littlewood's assurance never faltered. She played the outrages as though they were casual commonplaces, and the casual commonplaces as though they were vaudeville routines. You were not permitted to catch your breath and consider what you had last heard: the lines and songs kept tumbling out, they came from the throat of a willful man and a witty man, one who loves to pretend to be wicked; and you wouldn't want to miss the rest of the nightmare party, would you?

Excesses of every kind? Yes, indeed. But a wild night and a welcome one.

Rhinoceros

Rhinoceros was an entertainment in which an extremely talented rhinoceros played Zero Mostel. At first sight you thought it *was* Mr. Mostel, sitting there at a sidewalk café, pronouncing "as usual" as though it were spelled "ash zhushuyewel" and occasionally patting those few fine strands of hair that swirled across his glistening pate as though they'd been painted there by Aubrey Beardsley.

When this weighty, though delicately balanced, object got to its feet in anger, when it became quite apoplectic enough to create its own steam bath, you were still not ready to swear that it wasn't the actor you'd seen before, with his Equity dues paid up. Then came a moment—a moment of truth—in the second act when the whole of playwright Eugene Ionesco's world was rapidly abandoning whatever was human about it and violently returning to the jungle.

Now the rhinoceros beneath the skin began to bulge a little at the eyes. The Kaiser Wilhelm mustache that had earlier adorned the supposed Mr. Mostel lost its spiky endpoints, drooped, disintegrated into a tangle that made it second cousin to a walrus. The voice began to change. "I hate people —and I'll r-r-run them down!" came out of a larynx that had stiffened, gone hollow as a 1915 gramophone record, and was ready to produce a trumpet sound that might have emptied all of Africa. The shoulders lifted, the head jutted forward, one foot scraped the earth with such native majesty that dust—real dust—began to rise like the after-veil that accompanies a safari. The transformation was on, the secret was out, evolution had reversed itself before your horrified, but nevertheless delighted, eyes.

It should be stressed here that Mr. Mostel—for it was he, and he *is* an actor—accomplished this Hyde-Jekyll switch (or have I got that right?) while dressed in a beret and bathrobe. Director Joseph Anthony had not elected to give him, or the rest of us, any visual aids as society decided to head back to the swamps—no greenish plate-armor, no swollen ankles, not even so much as a burgeoning bump on the forehead. If the decision to let us imagine the decline of the species with our own inward eyes needed any justification, it was here in what may forever after be known as the Mostel syndrome. Being a rhinoceros is a spiritual, not a physical, matter.

This point was made, by the way, in the play. Hero Eli Wallach's brow wrinkled in worry as he watched the earlier stages of Mr. Mostel's metamorphosis. By the time the ever-swelling Mostel had ballooned three feet off the floor and then dived to a predatory crouch behind the cagelike bars of his own brass bedstead, Mr. Wallach was at last moved to speak out. "John," he said, "you seem to be going through some moral crisis."

The line was funny; it was also meant, of course, to be taken literally. *Rhinoceros* was a moral exercise, apparently in defense of the intellect. Why were all of the "people" in an unnamed small town so quickly surrendering to an impulse to snort, bay, and roar through the streets? It had become "the thing to do." When Mr. Wallach, increasingly lonely in his humanness, wistfully begged a friend not to join the herd but to hang onto his mind, the friend quickly countered with a question: "Are you sure your standards are superior?" Every sort of rationalization was put forth to justify quitting: "We must move with the times," "There's no real evil in doing what comes naturally," "If you're going to criticize, it's better to do it from within." M. Ionesco's point was a provocative one, and large portions of the evening were most accomplished.

Director Joseph Anthony had conceived a fine mood of defeat in a publisher's office as three or four surviving humans faced the fact that they would not survive long. And the author managed a short but sizable triumph in a scene in which Mr. Wallach and Anne Jackson hurried through "twenty-five years of married life in the space of a few minutes." The leap from lyric love to crosspatch debate to open anger and to a horrendous parting of the ways was subtly and scathingly outlined.

Still, I had reservations about *Rhinoceros*. To begin with, the number of *deliberately* unrelated elements bothered me. At a rough guess, about half of *Rhinoceros* was very careful, and carefully arbitrary, nonsense: not the exuberant nonsense that romps through the irrational according to rational laws of its own, but that much colder nonsense that means to be irrationally irrational. Office workers marched in lockstep, then threw paper wads at one another; conversations were arranged like logarithms, the next speaker being determined by the permutation of numbers; if two people were going to become entangled in the same coat, it was not for due cause (Chaplin, say, performed this business when drunk) but because tangle itself was the only essential requirement of this universe and had to be soberly, even morbidly, respected.

Some of this was charming and some was openly funny; there remained a good bit that was merely determined, antiseptic, forced. But the question was not really whether the side shows worked by themselves. What we most needed to know was why they were there.

Offhand, there were several possible answers. They may have been padding—antic distractions meant to keep us from realizing how slender Ionesco's thread of content actually was. Or, to take a more respectful view of the matter, they may have been there to illustrate and to stress the witlessness that dominates contemporary life and that makes contemporary man ripe for the rhinoceros heap. The arguments we take part in are meaningless: "The fact that I despise religion doesn't mean that I don't esteem it highly." The very logic we use is corrupt: if a cat is an animal with four paws, and a dog has four paws, is a dog a cat? Each mocking inversion of the values we live by may have been inserted in order to call our attention to the peril we are in—and may in that case have belonged, quite properly, to the play.

But if this was the fact, and if the author was to succeed in showing us one man with a real mind bravely refusing to surrender to the madness of the mass, M. Ionesco was faced with a clear theatrical duty: he was obliged to show us the real man with the real mind. This he had not done, with the result that we came to feel, uneasily, that pitted against the vacuum was only another near-vacuum.

It could not be supposed that Eli Wallach, as the clerk who defied his fellows and clung to his humanness, was at fault. Laurence Olivier, whose credentials need not be offered here, had played the role in London; I am given to understand that the results, until the final few moments of the play, were not honestly any better. The role itself was shadowy, underwritten—a pale echo among louder ones, without the color to conquer or even the distinction to point a contrast. With this balance gone, Ionesco's thesis was thrown out of kilter: the mindlessness became heavier, the possibility of even a single survival less likely. An intriguing piece of work, bolstered by one unforgettable performance, became lopsided and ultimately thin.

The Caretaker

I was instantly fearful that *The Caretaker* would become popular for the wrong reasons. There was the chance, for instance, that it would be regarded as zany comedy, and forcibly laughed at. One response that is regularly made to contemporary plays of the profoundest despair is the tittering pretense that the author has carved his vast zero as a joke. This is not emptiness, the nervous laughter says, but an irresponsible playfulness. People are always mentioning the Marx brothers in connection with the "comedy" of carefully illustrated nothingness, as though we had once laughed at the Marx brothers because they struck us as irrational in the clinical sense.

Thus laughter was felt to be obligatory as three remarkable actors played out the following sequence in Harold Pinter's remarkable play. A filthy old ingrate who had been given shelter in a refuse-littered attic was offered a satchel by the vacant-eyed brother who had admitted him. Another brother, hostile for no known reason, intercepted the satchel each time it was presented. The satchel was thrust forward, snatched away, thrust forward, snatched away, thrust forward, snatched away, finally hurled to the floor in a burst of dust. The repeated gestures did have an echo of a vaudeville routine in which a chair was invariably whisked out from under the comedian as he was about to sit on it. But the routine we once laughed at had had a rationale: we understood the sequence of events, however unlikely or unlucky, that led to each experience of frustration. Here, deliberately, no causes were indicated. The bag was offered without charity and retrieved without reason. The old man's frustration was absolute; it was also—to him, as to us—incomprehensible.

To laugh at it almost suggested malice. Or, at the least, the defensive sound of the giggle that is meant to ward off a threatened dissolution of the mind.

There was, further, a strong likelihood that *The Caretaker* would become necessary theatergoing merely because it was, as dramaturgy, novel, eccentric, hence a conversation piece for tired dinner tables. Three characters moved in and out of a domestic graveyard, most often with a sense of stealth, to sit and stare at one another, to recite unseeing monologues (on several occasions the listener on stage simply went to sleep, or otherwise abstracted himself), sometimes to engage in eye-to-eye conversation in which each participant pursued his own thoughts and failed to grasp the other's. All three were kept at arm's length from us, almost at species' length. The homeless old man was indecent at every turn of mind: he hesitated to use the toilet for fear the "blacks" next door might have used it; he treated the benefits doled out to him with fastidious contempt ("Them bastards at the monastery let me down"); he threatened to usurp, with a snivel and a whine, the refuge he did not deserve. The brother who was his benefactor was mindless; doctors had done something to his brain. The brother who visited came to challenge, to sneer, to torment; he was the brazen, mesmerizing pseudo delinquent none of us understands. Such sympathy as stirred in us went, by inversion, to the disreputable vagrant; horror that he was, he was recognizably human and not a robot or a Martian. But in general we were in the company of the loathsome, the lamed, and the spiteful. It was lamentably easy for so defiant a play to become, through its very violation of our ordinary tastes and our ordinary expectations, simply fashionable.

The Caretaker merited, and I think required, another kind of attention. There were two levels on which it might have been attended to, one with deep communion and hence satisfaction, one with detached but genuine curiosity.

To have been deeply satisfied, perhaps even moved as one is moved by an instant recognition of a kindred soul, it would have been necessary to share Mr. Pinter's vision of the present state of man. This vision was not reduced to a series of editorial statements; it stood as a vision, as a fluid image, as an atmosphere. But what it saw and showed us was a world wholly opaque, wholly impermeable, and, beyond the fact that we could neither see into it nor probe it with our fingers, wholly hollow. Mr. Pinter had attempted to construct, and had succeeded in constructing, a poetry of the blind: the sensed experience of a man who has suddenly lost his sight and is now in an unfamiliar room. This man gropes his way, hesitantly, talking to himself to keep himself company. There are objects about, and they can be touched when they are stumbled over; though they can be vaguely identified by cautious exploration, they remain unfriendly. There are people about, and they can be called to: but what they say is misleading because the tone of voice is not supported by the expressiveness of a face. One can guess, and do the wrong thing. One can plead, and not know when the others present are exchanging cold glances. Man—and the grimy caretaker was most nearly man in the play—is lost, rejected by what he had thought were his own kind, ousted from what he had thought was his home. Appeal is at last impossible: there are no hearts or heads to be reached.

To say that this tense, concentrated, sustained position was superbly illustrated in performance is to say too little. The play itself, given its particular insight and its precisely appropriate method of articulating that insight, must be regarded as perfect. For it to have been perfectly satisfying in the theater, however, one would have had to be ready not only to attend closely but to nod firmly and say, "Yes, beyond doubt this is the life we live."

Short of such utter identification, there was a second level at which the play's fascination might have been honestly felt.

A playgoer might have gone to the play without having yet surrendered all hope of speaking to his fellow men, without having concluded that all dialogue is a dialogue with the figures on Easter Island, without having agreed to regard the world about him as a disarray of ripped umbrellas, broken Buddhas, and empty picture frames. It is nonetheless true that a considerable segment of twentieth-century society has so come to see the neighborhood it inhabits. The antiworld is with us, late and soon; it faces us from the paintings on our walls no less than from the increasingly impotent people within our prosceniums. What exists—in the public reality or the private mind—had better be known, whether in detachment or in surrender, whether in cool appraisal or in assent. There may have been no better way of knowing it in the early sixties than through the already cool, ruthlessly framed, astringently orchestrated survey of the wreckage called *The Caretaker*.

The Blacks

There are plausible justifications that can be made for dramatist Jean Genet's return, in *The Blacks*, to the most barbaric form of predramatic ritual—to the mimed immolation of a victim who is both real and unreal, accompanied by the fierce incantations of a bloodthirsty chorus and the orgiastic release that comes of a physical and psychological stomping among the entrails of the dead.

The clue to the first of these may be heard in a line meant to mock one of the commoner and more vacuous claims to white superiority. A member of the cast whose character name is given as Stephanie Virtue Diop begins to weave her fluid hips down a spiraling ramp, swinging a rose in the rhythm of her narcissistically displayed body. As the streamers and beads that bedeck her sway in an increasingly graceful arrogance, she announces that she has decided hereafter to be white (color is a value that exists only in the mind, and hence is subject to such capricious election), that at least one of her given names is going to be changed to Lily, and that "only centuries of breeding could produce such a miracle" as her lissome, glistening self.

Genet's point here, impudently inverted, is that centuries of white cultivation have produced no noticeable miracle, that the "pale and odorless wraiths" who take such pride in their intellectual grooming now possess little more than a paper-thin façade: a drained and weary mask of whiteness that barely conceals the unregenerated primitive behind it. (The point is reinforced everywhere: in the detachable masks worn by the "whites" in the play, in the animal ferocity of the "whites" when they become directly engaged with the rather more candid "blacks," in a grotesque ceremony which transforms a Negro male into a chalky, insipid, and truly terrifying Little Eva.)

The line, and its implications, can also be translated into theatrical terms. Only centuries of dramatic breeding could produce the routine drama we now know—and what a pale, tired, odorless, artificial, exhausted thing it is! How are we ever again going to uncover a brutal, or at least an honestly faced, truth about human nature unless we can rip from drama its veneer of accomplishment and its empty habits of conventional gesture, unless we hurl ourselves back into the stained arena and the frenzied openness of tribal dance in which our present forms began and from which our "progress" progressed? To see the human situation naked, we had best go back to the initial sacrifice.

Thus the evening begins with the placing of flowers upon an altar beneath which the victim (a human victim, to be eaten later) rests. A white member of the audience is invited to place his own flower upon the significantly white bier (this is a ceremony, and we must all take part). Five or six well-dressed acolytes stoop to the unseen body to incense it with billowing clouds of cigarette smoke. Litanies are chanted, jungle drums sounded, shod feet pounded against the shivering floorboards. Obscenities erupt, but never to titillate; they are meant to exorcise, mock, expiate. The circling figures join —for more than an hour—in a now spoken, now sung dithyramb that throbs not only with voodoo cries but with jazz and Strauss and stockmarket quotations. As the first half of the murky, sardonic, and abrasive revel rises to white heat, the effect is dynamic.

The second sense in which the plunge into primitivism is justified is this: a theatrical form which has not yet developed beyond the excited pulse of an abandoned exhibitionism is precisely appropriate for M. Genet's vision of the contemporary world about him, a world that has itself developed no further than that. In the dramatist's view we are one and all still barbarous—the whites behind their pretentious faces, the blacks because they must behave as we expect them to behave. A white queen sits on her throne ticking off an empty, insane catalogue of white achievement: Chartres, Aristotelian principles, Tyrolean songs, and so on in a juxtaposition that makes each term meaningless. One Negro cries out bitterly that "God has been white for two thousand years" while another gets to his knees in an excess of Uncle Tommery and smiles slyly as he asks, "May we whimper?" Between two latent savageries there is really no choice. All we can do just now is know that they are savageries. A savage theatrical form helps us to know it.

But an inherent difficulty survives to make us restive once the ceremony's fever pitch is past and its hangover close upon us. (The second act is literally an act of exhaustion and, let it be said, disenchantment.) The seed of ancient drama lay in just such maddened celebrations. But the celebrations were not themselves drama, merely a boiling kettle from which the future was plucked. These were not only predramatic in nature, they were also in some degree precoherent in nature. Such values as they possessed were almost exclusively intestinal: shape and significance and intellectual satisfaction came later.

Indeed the very advance from barbarism to clarity that M. Genet would surely like us to undertake all over again depended not upon the continued existence of an inflamed primitive ritual but upon the suppression of its inchoate frenzy in favor of a dawning form. The emergence of architectural clarity, of structure, even of sustained narrative was, in fact, an actual progress—whether we have become deadened to its implications or no.

The promise that the evening is going to be "unreasonable and hostile" is exciting. The act of bathing, briefly, in an "architecture of emptiness and words" constitutes—for us—a new experience and, in its reminder of our roots, a stimulating one. But as the evening takes one more step, in its second act, it does not mean to take the step that ancient man and the ancient theater actually took—the step into defined meaning, into controlled illumination. It simply sinks back, slavering rather, breathing hard and refusing the effort at conscious shaping, the struggle toward intelligibility. In the circumstances, and in spite of all there is to be grateful for, we find ourselves dissatisfied. How should we not? Barbarous as modern man is, white or black or polka-dotted, he has by now at least *seen* more than the exhausted tribal dancer did, has long possessed an intuition of something more complex and gratifying which he may not have lived up to but which none of us can wholly disown. And as we watch the falling action in the theater—it is really a helpless inaction—we become aware that we do not now want to see less.

Who's Afraid of Virginia Woolf?

Edward Albee's *Who's Afraid of Virginia Woolf?* is a great many things. It is a horror play written by a humorist. It is a western, a decline-of-the-western. It is an evening in the parlor with people who play nothing but games, war games. It is an admirable piece of writing, with a sizable hole in its head. It is a fantastic jest, but only as Swift is a fantastic jest; face man at his worst and he will not seem sad, he will seem preposterous; face everything all at once and everything becomes much too intolerable for tears, it breaks up into laughter or insanity or both at once.

The horror, with guffaws, first. On the play's memorable opening night, George Grizzard, a freshly hired biology teacher in a New England college, came with Melinda Dillon, his spectral infant of a wife, to ring the chiming doorbell of historian Arthur Hill. It was two in the morning, there had been a faculty party, the historian's wife had suggested they drop by for a nightcap. Mr. Hill opened the door, but it was a five-letter expletive, spat across the room into everyone's face by a grossly tipsy Uta Hagen, that constituted their welcome.

Mr. Grizzard, a pragmatic square who had acquired all of the fashionable words, was as quickly uneasy as his spouse was airily obtuse. Hell lived here, but all the devils were great jokers. They crept along sofas, spouting calculated obscenities. They reached for more drinks, until their brains seemed thick with baby fat. Miss Hagen lifted her upper lip as though any stranger were free to kiss it, while reserving her lower lip and teeth for a hiss at husband Arthur Hill. Mr. Hill walked lightly at first, holding his elbows close together, suggesting that the fires had gone out and eternity was cold. But his quick, callous, fiercely fanciful tongue was busy, without rest, stripping the skin from Miss Hagen's middle-aged back in much the same way that a brandy bottle was later to be gouged of its label.

By the time Mr. Hill bolted into the room, under an archway dripping with books that had consoled no one, to sling a shotgun to his shoulder and aim it point-blank at his wife, we were ready for two things. We were ready for the spontaneous scream of belief that came from the visiting Miss Dillon; we, too, believed that the cankers of love had come to this. And we were just as ready for something else. Author Albee had walked such a tightrope of nerve-racking abrasiveness and overeducated wit (the wit leaving scars, the wounds opening into laughter simply to ease themselves) that we were perfectly prepared to see the shotgun blossom into a red-and-yellow umbrella.

Mr. Albee, in his earlier and shorter pieces, had never been precisely a playwright of the Absurd, but he had here brought something of the Absurd's shrill surrender to unreason into the environment of the perfectly reasonable: the world in which clocks do tell time and girls who have taken too many drinks do get sick and academic promotions do march along in orderly, self-seeking sequence. In the contrast between a plausible, even homey, surface and the uninhibited spewing forth of its baldest, ugliest underpinnings, the crack of comedy was heard: people said not so much what they were thinking as what they dared not think they were thinking, and the uprush became outrageous, mind-curdling, explosive. Mr. Albee's ear did not seem to be listening for speech; it listened instead for a twist of the intestines and then phrased the spasm as though it were possible conversation. Wit was not only in the phrasing, but in the method, in the shock of precognition. The author was functioning as a mocking clown and as a clergyman reading the obsequies in each fetid, funny breath.

The play at its best communicates as a blister does; you don't have to ask what's the matter, you feel it. Authority attends its finger-down-the-throat impulse ("Disgorge!" is both the command and the activity of the play). The thoughts and experiences that are vomited forth are near-hallucinatory: memories of hysterical pregnancies ("She blew up and then she went down," the biologist says of his thumb-sucking wife, explaining that he married her while she was up) and memories of mothers molesting their sons in the bath are explored in detail. Yet the weaving, bleary, bankrupt vision set before us has—for two-thirds of its length, at least—a wild stability of its own. Staggering under the blows it is raining upon its own head, it exists. Only when Mr. Albee is trying to pin himself down, cerebrally and then verbally, does he falter.

There is talk—much talk, though some of it is veiled—about the abyss we inhabit just now, an abyss which sets some men to looking backward (history) and some to looking forward (biology, with a promise of a change in "the genetic make-up of the sperm cell") but which keeps most men from looking squarely into the mirror of what is. The games we are playing, whether they are sex games or career games or any other kind of games, are all one, really: the game of "truth or illusion." We're kidding ourselves, you see, marking time, making up our life preservers. And we have at last come to the time of our lives when only our despairs are true and when everything we have always used to ward off those despairs must be recognized as "illusion" and declared dead.

The thought, honored in one way or another from Pirandello to O'Neill, is by no means a new one. Further, Mr. Albee's central demonstration of it—the secret lie which the historian and his wife have been telling each other for years—calls for some nervous playmaking. The couple hint at the secret as though they were serving up machine-made exposition for a mystery thriller, interrupting the author's grim, gay, knowing personal tone. References to "our son," and elaborated reminiscences of a child no one has ever seen, take on an alien, oddly mawkish air. The same people do not seem to be talking. And when the secret is out, it is both thin and familiar, neither vigorous enough nor inventive enough to account for the size of the scab we have so painfully been picking off. In the third act, the play gasps; the author, too, seems to be sucking his thumb; we become conscious that the surgery was not as major as we had thought it, and that the operation has gone on too long.

But, looking at the play, for two exacerbating acts we do

not think about length, or even particularly about the theater. These damned, dancing souls possess a naked vitality that may be in excess of any rationale the author can conjure up for them but that cannot in itself be challenged.

A Taste of Honey

Quite apart from the fact that A Taste of Honey encouraged a strange affection for some people who seemed not to ask for affection at all, the importation from London raised a series of further questions about what may be happening to the blood pressure of our stage.

The pulse of the funny, distressing, and finally touching evening was not controlled by the shape or length or beat of the scenes the actors played out. It was controlled by a small jazz combo that sat forever at the side of the stage, always in view, restlessly ready to interrupt and alter the rhythm of what was going on, plainly sympathetic to the frustrated outcasts who were raging about an attic room but just as plainly in charge of them.

This itching group of musicians has been turning up more and more often of late at the edges of our theatergoing, not only in an essentially verbal revue like The Thurber Carnival or in an essentially nihilistic experiment of the sort that is favored by the producers of The Living Theater, but in plays that seem otherwise thoroughly realistic—fact-of-life reports on matter-of-fact people. Indeed, it is now thrusting its way into the generally plausible action in a manner that is downright aggressive, which may make it at first sight irritating. I know that when the curtain went up on A Taste of Honey and instead of our being immediately introduced to some interesting characters we were required to listen for a minute or two to some apparently unnecessary musicians, I made a tiny note to myself that I liked this sort of thing better when it was kept offstage—as in The Glass Menagerie, say.

But the device, I soon discovered, was no longer meant as atmospheric counterpoint drifting in from the nearest alley. It had become a metronome, a beat handed down from the guiding heavens to dictate the rate of breathing for the entire dramatic population. It came first, they came in on cue. When Joan Plowright and Angela Lansbury and an assortment of one-eyed drunks and one-night lovers did come in, the dominating downbeat did not leave them. It lay in wait, listening, and when Miss Lansbury casually remembered a music-hall ditty she had once given her all to, it was instantly with her, urging her on. In fact, it listened for every footfall. If some new Lancashire sport was about to roll in from the hallway, the musical thread anticipated him, announcing his near-presence and then pulling him into view. If it was time for someone to bolt angrily for the streets, or time to chop the scene off without anyone's going, the movement was begun and terminated by piano, bass, and drums. (It's been more than fifty years since the theater last employed this particular kind of underscoring; not since villains wore mustaches and heroines curls have we heard obvious "exit" and "entrance" music.)

When one of the figures made his final forlorn exit, the scoring did not simply wave him farewell; a saxophonist actually accompanied him on his deflated journey, weaving down a stairway and into the wings. And at all times the pace of the dialogue took off from the stand-by syncopation: Angela Lansbury rasped and clattered at a rate that had been determined by the introductory jive, Joan Plowright lazed about at midnight in a blues mood arranged for her by the omnipresent accent composer Bobby Scott had laid down.

What was going on here? *A Taste of Honey* was neither a musical nor, precisely, a mood play. The text itself offers us an ugly and unhopeful account of the lonely, meaningless life led by a girl who "works all day in a shoe-shop and all night in a bar" to pay her room rent. She loathes, and still

wants to live with, her mother—who is worthless. ("Have I
ever laid claim to being a proper mother?" screams this sensual virago, as though her candor squared everything away.)
The girl permits herself to be seduced by a passing Negro
sailor and then to be cared for, during her pregnancy, by a
motherly homosexual. The homosexual, looking at some draw-
ings she has done, remarks that they have "no design, no
rhythm, no purpose." Neither does her life. She can say no
more for this life than that it is the one she has somehow
been dumped into just now. ("I'm contemporary, I live at the
same time as myself," she says.) No one present has any
illusions about the chaos into which he has fallen. Mother has
even stopped going to the movies. "I don't care for the cinema
any more," she shrugs; "it's getting more and more like the
theater." Both the people and the play know where they are
at: disillusioned slice-of-life, with no butter.

Whence the music, then? Though the Broadway production had been directed by Tony Richardson and George De-
vine, the original London production was the work of Joan
Littlewood, who had already made use of music as a unifying
force in *The Hostage*. Miss Littlewood and such other new
directors as have embraced the combo are, I think, in search
of something more than a merely convenient device for making untidy exhibits hang together.

I suspect that we have come to a time when the rhythm
that formerly propelled our regulation, prosaic, down-to-earth
life-studies across the space of an evening has lost its power to
drive an audience with it. That earlier rhythm was, quite simply, the minute-to-minute rhythm of ordinary life. It was established by the actors, speaking quietly and casually, as the
curtain rose; it followed the "natural" curve of plausible life,
and it was not only plausible but utterly complete: between
curtain-rise and curtain-fall every moment of time, every
inch of movement, was properly accounted for. Let's call it
the rhythm of the believable clock. This steady tick, which

served us so long, has apparently grown monotonous and grating and left most of us restive. We don't necessarily want to part with all realism of vision, but we might like it offered to us at different beat, under a kind of auctioneer's hammer that says "gone" when the scene is done and gets us on—with some acceleration and a canny selectivity—to the next bargain at hand.

Miss Littlewood and friends appear to be using the hammer of the piano, the percussion of drums, to strike time on the stage, to sound the note that determines when a character may enter, may leave, may quarrel or cry. We are thus whipped into the heart of things—the heart may be hard or soft at a given moment—by a compulsive force that stands outside the action and outside the people, ringing an alarm bell when there is work to be done.

Look Back in Anger

The blank look that my own generation has been giving the younger, bitter, so-called "beat" generation was not wholly dissipated by the writhing excitements of John Osborne's *Look Back in Anger*. But some degree of focus was achieved, some sort of contact made. The disenchanted striplings who are now snarling at the world's heels may be unattractive in the incoherence, the fuming aimlessness of their outrage: but the outrage itself, as Mr. Osborne's electrifying play made clear, is painfully and powerfully actual. With such an evocation as this, the howls of the banshees in sweatshirts can no longer be dismissed as a pose; they sound like something closer to demonic possession.

The perfectly real hero of *Look Back in Anger* is a man furiously intent upon defining himself and just as furiously unable to. The father he admired and loved is—no doubt symbolically—dead. The work he does—running a candy shop—interests him not at all. The wife he has snatched from a contented home is, largely as a result of his lacerating cynicism, an almost faceless wraith. What seems to exist, he destroys. What does not seem to exist (he is aware of "some promise that has not been kept"), he slashes at, as though the very slashing might give it shape.

There is a purpose in this firebrand's random savagery, and it is the sense of purpose that gives Mr. Osborne's play its special distinction in a period of self-pitying literature. Gadfly Jimmy Porter may taunt his wife until nothing but a scream will clear the air. He may turn on his best friend with a merry and merciless sneer, and succeed in driving him for good out of the attic flat they share. He may bully, cheat, mock and spit at the whole world that is available to him until his victims can only draw away whining, "Why do you try so hard to be unpleasant?"

The "why" has an answer, or at least part of an answer. When Jimmy gaily and contemptuously invites his wife to go insane, and announces with a colossal shrug of his shoulders that "that would be something, anyway," the whisper of an explanation is heard. Jimmy wants a response—*any* response, any living and breathing and even flaming reaction that will show him back his own image, that will give him a clue as to who and what he is.

He prods the flesh about him in the vain hope of drawing a cry that will define him: he strips the paint off the universe in long, cruel shreds because he thinks he may at last find a mirror—and in it a meaning. Caught going through his wife's purse, in her absence, he murmurs with a leer that "I was looking to see if there's anything of me in there." Confronted with a conventional letter from the wife who can no longer live with him, he says simply and directly, "I'd rather she'd hit me."

He is not, in the vision Mr. Osborne gives us of him, a weakling. His despair is not the untidy collapse of the feeble, self-anointed patsy; it is an agitated, feverish, determined despair that stems essentially from strength, from a strength that is not being used and does not see how it *can* be used.

The author's own inflammatory writing style is so quick and so stinging that he is able to give his man genuine sources of strength: a tart intelligence, a lively resilience, a fund of caustic humor. The people who inhabit this British hovel are all there: minds, talents, unfulfilled emotions. Because they are all there we see that we must respect them even when we are unable to understand them.

The play is neither conventional in form nor sparing in its insistence on rasping, painful failure. Apart from one or two minor theatrical extravagances, it takes its shape directly from the lunging, erratic movement of the characters themselves and its power from its unwillingness to soften the sound of an infuriated time.

TENSION

TUG OF WAR

As we move with some excitement and considerable bewilderment through the theater of the 1960s, we begin to feel as though we had hold of both ends of one of those firecracker favors that are popular at children's parties. By tugging firmly and simultaneously at the two little tabs—and in opposite directions—you can pull the whole tissue-paper structure apart with a most satisfying *pop!*, after which you can rummage in the fragments for a clue to your future.

What tabs—or bears' tails—have we really got hold of just now? We are wrenching vigorously, with one clenched fist, to rip the ancient concepts of style and form from the face of our pleasures. Just as vigorously, with the other fist, we are trying to stretch the delights of style and form as far as they can be made to go. Form and antiform are the opponents of the hour, and the crackle they make as they scratch in passing is apt to become deafening before the party is over.

This tug of war, by the way, does mean to shatter the shape of the theater as we know it, just as the favor disintegrates in a delighted child's hands. It is also a duel to the death: one side means to come out with a longer straw than the other, and never the twain shall be twined again. And it is a contest that is in no sense confined to the theater. In point of fact, my own sharpest awareness of it came not while I was sitting in the playhouse but while I was making my way, fascinated, through a very long short story that was determined *not* to be a short story in *The New Yorker*.

"I don't dare go anywhere near the short-story form," confided J. D. Salinger quite early in his "Seymour, an Introduction." As though he were painfully concerned to tell the truth, the whole truth, and nothing but the truth about a brother he'd loved, the author was careful to erase, systematically, every trace of artificial coloring that might have come into being as part of the process of producing literature rather than reality.

Were we in danger of being intrigued by Salinger's own highly personal style? "Woe is me, there's a prose writer in our midst," exclaimed a parenthesis meant to shatter our beginning comfort in the writer's rhythms. Were we being seduced away from the subject and into a love affair with someone's words? "I apologize for that verbiage," intruded another aside, adding that "unfortunately, there's probably more."

Were we in danger of becoming charmed by the progressive dance steps of a sustained narrative? "A Day has passed since this last sentence," interrupted the author's voice, calling deliberately disillusioning attention to the presence of the author's hand. "Between the last paragraph and this, just over two months have gone by," warned a further and still more alienating whisper. Not for us the idle amenities of cantering easily along a style-smoothed roadbed beneath a fiction-enriched pattern of sheltering leaves. We must be reminded that a writer is present, and *working*. We must be told that syntax is inadequate to the purposes of truth. We must not be lulled into an illusion of continuity, into mistaking the graces of artful management for the essentially unmanageable presence of life.

Reading the piece with that drugged, slow-paced, cocoon-warmed avidity all Salingerers share, I was endlessly haunted by echoes of my theatergoing. For all their buzzing, these were somewhat ambiguous at first. It wasn't until I came to the last column of type that they leaped into formation and began to march forward.

"I'm finished with this," Salinger announced. "Or, rather, it's finished with me. Fundamentally, my mind has always balked at any kind of ending. How many stories have I torn up since I was a boy because they had what that old Chekhov-baiting noise Somerset Maugham calls a Beginning, a Middle, and an End? Thirty-five? Fifty? One of the thousand reasons I quit going to the theater when I was about twenty was that I resented like hell filing out of the theater just because some playwright was forever slamming down his silly curtain. (What ever became of that stalwart bore Fortinbras? Who eventually fixed *his* wagon?) Nonetheless, I'm done here."

What echoes were firmly on the march now? Several thousand, no doubt, if one were to include all one's memories of the plays Chekhov had influenced, the plays Maugham had influenced, and the plays that had begun to take note of a certain restlessness and resentment in the audience that had already had Chekhov and had already had Maugham. But essentially three.

The first and most easily dismissed of these, of course, is the plainly carpentered, safety-inspected formula play of the twentieth century. It doesn't much matter whether one is thinking of the drawing-room neatness of the second decade (*Our Betters*), the tougher tidiness of the third decade (*The Front Page*), or the sociological orderliness of the post-depression years (*Deep Are the Roots*). All of these specimens are really constructed in the same way, upon the same basic assumptions as to what a play—whatever its content—should look and sound like. The beginning? A tucking-in of unobtrusive but slyly adequate exposition presented as though people were really talking to one another; a casual and plausible laying-in of the plot points. The middle? Our just-folks exposition leads logically, and with no lapses, to something louder though no less natural in the way of a crisis. The end? The crisis scatters a fairish debris about the stage, which debris will be gathered up in a handy dramatic dustpan called The Big Scene or The Big Speech so that the curtain may come down upon an action that has been completed architecturally, rhythmically, and—it would seem—realisti-

137

cally. Given the first twenty minutes of this doll's-house entertainment, you could chart the next two hours with a reasonable accuracy, just as given the locale in the program notes you could always imagine the set.

Not long ago I happened to overhear two theatergoers chatting at random during an intermission. "Do you remember those Big Chief writing tablets," one was asking the other, "with red covers and sheets with blue lines on them?" The other did remember. "Well, they're still making them," announced the first, in a tone of mingled incredulity and triumph. It occurred to me on the spot that most of the three-act, one-set, mark-in-the-exposition and clean-up-the-loose-threads prose plays of the twentieth century seemed to have been written on Big Chief tablets. That's what those blue lines were for—to keep the creative hand from straying. It *is* incredible, though not necessarily a triumph, that the formula should have lasted so long; and it is not surprising to know that J. D. Salinger wanted to get out of there, or that Thornton Wilder did get out of there. ("Toward the end of the twenties I began to lose pleasure in going to the theater," Mr. Wilder has said; he'd begun to have a feeling that someone or something had "boxed the action" and "increasingly shut the play up into a museum showcase.") This, of course, is the theater we are now determined to pull apart, to reduce to shreds as the party favor is forever and unregretfully shredded.

But when a man has decided to show his heels to the neat, the plausible, the familiarly shaped, where does he go? If an old formula strikes him as dishonest and unlifelike, what would a new one look like? A playwright may be heartily sick of the theater of naturalistic illusion, of the acted-out pretense that a "slice of life" can really be sliced into precisely weighed portions and wrapped for the freezer, ready for instant use. He must still discover for himself, and display for his audience, not only the nature of the fraud he thinks has been perpetrated but a new way of coming at the rock-bottom truth that will be persuasively better than the stale crusts at hand. He is first obliged to destroy an illusion, and then to replace it with something else.

The job of destroying and replacing is going on now, rather violently in some quarters. And some of the violence is due to a fundamental disagreement about the nature of the task, which brings me to the second of the echoes that Salinger stirred in me. The noisiest and quite possibly the most influential response now being made to the challenge of a decayed stock naturalism in the theater is a response very much like Salinger's.

It is the effort to kill off naturalistic illusion by calling mocking attention to how it is made. In Jack Gelber's *The Connection,* the audience enters the uncurtained playhouse to discover unidentified personnel moving in listless preoccupation about the unready stage. In due time, it is directly addressed by a not very articulate representative of the management and awkwardly introduced to a not very confident author. Once the "action" has begun, and a variety of dope addicts are making fitful conversation by way of shutting out their pain as they wait for a "fix," a team of documentary filmmakers appears at the edge of the platform to photograph the proceedings for use at some other time. Between scenes, a home-movie projector flashes onto a wrinkled curtain a jumbled stream of rehearsal shots in which the same actors who are now realistically made up and costumed are seen at their ease, and in mufti.

The play is not real, it is written; we have met the author, and he is still lurking about somewhere. The action is not a continuity, not an unfolding narrative; it is subject to interruption at any time by photographers who are recording it in fragments which may, or may not, be put together later. The characters are not people, they remain actors: if we are not convinced of this as one of them circulates among us in the lobby at intermission time, we will have it rammed home every time the projector lights up to show us the players when they were only playing at playing.

This is not precisely the same thing as Bertolt Brecht's celebrated doctrine of "alienation," but it is related to it. "It must at all times be apparent to the spectators," writes Martin Esslin in his study of the German writer-director, "that they are not witnessing real events happening before their very eyes at *this very moment*," but that they are sitting in a theater where "the director must strive to produce by all the means at his disposal effects that will keep the audience separate, estranged, alienated from the action."

Nor is it necessarily and in all respects the identical atmosphere director Joan Littlewood and author Brendan Behan so lustily established in their jig-play *The Hostage*. But again the similarities are unmistakable. Should the story show signs of moving forward, it must instantly be aborted by an irrelevant song; an actor drops, or elides, his characterization in order to tell us, confidentially, that he is going to sing the song; the song itself is not content with being irrelevant, it must also outrage us.

Each of these violations of our most familiar model has a somewhat different end in view. *The Connection*, of which we shall speak more fully later, seems to want to shock us first with its theatrical unreality in order to make the theatrical reality which follows more shocking still. Brecht wished to alienate his audience in order to educate it; if he could persuade people that what was happening was not true inside the playhouse but was true *outside* it, he would have made them better socialists, or better Communists, or just plain better thinkers. *The Hostage* seems the disruptive ebullience of a man rather than a theory, an explosion of personality that means to be personal and in no way confined, a case of Brendan Behan going to his own head.

But they do have in common an iconoclastic determination to knock naturalistic form as we know it square on the noggin. They are sometimes despairing and sometimes merry as they go about their work and they may find themselves, when this first work is done, driving at last in assorted directions; for the moment, however, they share an eagerness to call into question the fundamental assumption on which our earlier drama rested, the assumption that we were to "suspend disbelief" when the curtain went up, that we were to try hard not to notice the part that canvas and greasepaint and long hours of rehearsing and rewriting might have played in all this. We are now asked to *notice,* to disbelieve, to stop short abruptly when we have begun to accept too much. The house is being taken apart for us; each of its supporting members is being held up to scorn in its impotent isolation; later on, perhaps, we shall put the pieces together in some other way.

And then again, perhaps we won't. There are indications that some of our doubters are not simply wrecking the house in order to rebuild it. Some, it would seem, are thinking of taking a still deeper plunge. It is possible to go beyond the dismantling of a shabby framework that was only regarded as being temporary anyway toward a profound distrust of all framework as such. It is possible, that is, not only to recoil from one tired shape that art has taken during a certain time in history, but to recoil, absolutely, from art.

Suppose, some of our writers seem to be saying, all art automatically falsifies? The merest gesture toward shapeliness, the tiniest tuck here or there in the fabric borrowed from life, the very orderliness of a progressive narrative or of a consciously tooled sentence—all, all are cheats. The moment you touch what *is* with the wand of style, the moment you arrange either words or events in such a way that the arrangement itself becomes attractive, a fraud has been perpetrated. Truth has been turned into artifice, and the architectural outcome cannot help being a lie.

The fear that every effort toward conscious art may prove

a liability, a prettifying fig leaf upon the naked truth or an arbitrary barrier between the artist and the actual impulse that roils within him, is with us—above and beyond the simple desire to wash away one tired formula. *The Connection* does not rest its case on occasional interruptions, is not content with reminding us that a playwright is loose in the auditorium. It wants also to insist that the playwright, that deliberate artificer, is a plain excrescence, however present he may be.

The playwright, we are told, may have initiated something —the idea for the evening, the first tick of the clock in a particular place, perhaps. But he has not been permitted to design its movement thereafter. The actors, given the playwright's first push, have been commanded to "improvise." They are not improvising, of course; Mr. Gelber has written down the things they are supposed to be making up, and we have subtly returned to the theater of illusion even while we are loudly denying its existence. But the denial is there. We are urged to believe that what we are watching is as free to be itself as the hand of the "action" painter, attacking a canvas before thought has spoiled its pure energy.

Finally, even the pretense to no pretense must go. In Jackson MacLow's *The Marrying Maiden,* the playwright proclaims that he has *not* written down the sequence. He has left it to the throw of the dice. Numbers are rolled at random by a master stage-manager and the actors must swing into movement not according to the dictates of a prepared text that can be read but under the immediate impact of mathematical whim. The theory, if I understand it correctly, is that the director has staged a certain number of ready responses which can be summoned forth by the players as the triggering numbers are called. The shape that any one evening may take can therefore never be premeditated; we are present not at something determined but at something still in the process of being "done." Calculation kills, and we must turn to chance to feel the warmth of the creative spark.

Chance is not Salinger's method; he seems to be aiming instead at total candor, at an unburdening that will relieve him not only of his memories of the brother he tells us he is writing about (the controlled selectivity of art would suppress some of these memories, and so tell a lie of omission) but also of the charge of having created a character who, coming to exist in his own right, will acquire an independent identity (and so constitute a lie of commission).

But whatever technical methods are marshaled to meet it, the fear of the lie is the bogey that confronts us; it accounts, I think, for two quotations that Mr. Salinger has called to the colors at the beginning of his nonstory, his antistory. From Kafka he summons the thought that "the actors by their presence always convince me, to my horror, that most of what I've written about them until now is false," in spite of the fact that it has been written "with steadfast love." (An immediate parenthesis adds that "even now, while I write it down, this, too, becomes false.") Deception creeps in between the muscle and the scrawl.

And from Kierkegaard he has taken the figurative notion that the management of art is like a slip of life's pen. Such a small clerical error may perhaps be "no error but in a far higher sense . . . an essential part of the whole exposition." Still, it is a fib, and a fib that forbids the author to correct it, as though it were saying in Kierkegaard's words, "No, I will not be erased, I will stand as witness against thee, that thou art a very poor writer." Something essential to art may make a dishonest man of the artist. For some years to come we may find a good many desperately serious men making public confession of such sins.

But there is a third and last echo to be accounted for here, and its sound has not the least trace of *mea culpa* in it. Moving directly against the almost maddened urge to kill all artifice is a fresh and cunning determination, on the part of certain sorcerers, to break with our weary formula and to get more "truth" into the work by doubling, tripling, and quadrupling the amount of artifice. More, not less, is the battle cry here.

If this seems an odd plan of campaign, a quick glance at Jean Anouilh's *The Waltz of the Toreadors* may serve as an intelligible map. Anouilh is every bit as fed up as his adventurous contemporaries with the familiar theater of apparent fact; I do not know that he has ever written a play that could properly be called realistic. He is also eager to explore a specifically contemporary content, to dig more deeply into our romantic despairs and our hardheaded idiocies than a conventional form, with its careful comings and goings and time wasted on cocktails, would permit him to do.

But his method of dismissing the torpid and limiting theater of naturalistic illusion is to substitute for it an alienated form that is even more formal than the old one. Instead of shooting for the declared formlessness of *The Connection* he imports and imposes upon himself the severely stylized, rigidly run, absurdly polished machinery of mistaken-identity farce. *The Waltz of the Toreadors* is set inside a burnished glass showcase borrowed from a Victorian aunt: the characters flirt at glossy cross-purposes, aborted twin suicides take place at the same comic moment, the rival in the living room is the old romantic's long-lost son. The façade is pure nonsense, erected according to unalterable laws.

We are delightedly aware that it is nonsense; and our awareness kills off, and gleefully mocks, the plausible theater we are tired of just as certainly as the "alienation" theater does. This is, we know, unreal—a preposterous conceit. It is also a frame. It is, on the one hand, an easy frame of reference: we recognize at once the artifice we are dealing with, we have our bearings, we know what moves to expect and how the farce will work out. On the other hand, it is a frame that, being so swiftly recognized *as a frame,* can be taken for granted and, in effect, dismissed. Because we know so well every foolishly overdressed nook and cranny of the silly house we have been invited to, we are free to give our full attention to what may be going on inside it.

Anouilh has been freed by the same stroke: having to give no more than impish lip-service to a predictable style, to a cheerfully prefabricated outline, he can fill the great empty space inside it with anything he likes. What he does do, now, is fill the bonbon box with sad and angry and wistful and wicked human emotions, all the more harrowing at heart for the strict and mindless gayety of the surface. Anouilh's box is not at all like the plausible "box" Thornton Wilder rebelled against, but is as gracefully decorated as Pandora's; it has also been opened.

The discovery of a new reality inside a deliberate archaism is not a trick to be confined to comedy, if *The Waltz of the Toreadors* can really be called a comedy. The Greek myths with which drama began have proved surprisingly suggestive to later and very different ages; in *The Prodigal* young Jack Richardson has again borrowed the trappings of the Orestean legend, narrative and even costumes intact, and used them as a pattern that is at once familiar and unreal, inside which vigorous new comment can be made. One rigs up the tent, for circus or for battle; an area has now been circumscribed, artificially, and its arbitrariness may still be mocked within its own boundaries; but it has become a shelter in which pressing and perceptive fresh work may get done.

Nor do all of those who are choosing to work inside a set of firm, even foolish, regulations feel themselves bound to adopt a regulatory pattern belonging to one or another time in the past. In the theater, Friedrich Duerrenmatt has sometimes thrown his weight on the side of antiform: in such a play as *Fools Are Passing Through* he causes his nightmare characters to ring down lecture-charts from the heavens in order to make sure that we are not lured into the illusion of continuing, believably imitated, life. He has sometimes shifted footing and used the stylized conceits of mythological farce: *The Jackass* puts on an ancient Greek mask and keeps it there. But, as we move with him to the other end of the bookstore and dip into his most characteristic novels, we find him beguiling us by seeming to observe the rules of a quite rigid, and wholly contemporary, genre. He uses the most conventional and commonplace of twentieth-century formulas, that of the detective story, to map out his terrain.

There is a nasty murder, somewhere in Switzerland. There is an aging detective, bitterly determined to ferret out the culprit. There is an investigation, there are many false leads, there is the thrill of a chase. And there is, as well, a solution to the mystery—in *The Pledge* and again in *The Hunter and the Hunted*. We are given a promise of form, we move for a very long while in the well-oiled grooves of a form, we are never absolutely denied the pleasures of that form. But the helpful shape contains a secret: Duerrenmatt has made a convenience of the convention (a convention has no other purpose but to be a convenience) and has performed its ancient and arbitrary gestures only to bring us the quicker toward an unexpected aberration, a shocking psychological insight, a snatch of highly personal philosophy. The silverware is what we are accustomed to; the meat it is used to cut is something else again.

Those who are straining mightily to keep artifice alive as a kind of mutually understood chessboard on which new games can be played are faced with sobering problems. They are severely dependent upon borrowed frames from the past, or frames from the present that are, like Duerrenmatt's detective-story gambit, so completely stylized as to constitute a rigging that cannot be mistaken for the naturalistic illusionism we are forced to abandon. Their problem is to arrive, eventually, at a fresh style that will be seen and accepted *as a style,* much as Restoration comedy must have been blithely and knowingly accepted by British gentlemen of the seventeenth century or as a performance by the Kabuki is still accepted by gentlemen of Japan. You will often find their partisans studying the calculated unrealities of the Kabuki, or of the Piccolo Teatro playing Goldoni's *Servant of Two Masters*, and wondering how so deliberate an artificing can be newly and indigenously arrived at for the twentieth century.

Those who are heaving their shoulders in the contrary direction have their problems, too. One problem, really. Forms can be destroyed by mockery. Form itself can be destroyed by inserting a quick cancellation of its virtues each time one or another virtue threatens to catch hold of an audience. But a dismissal of all artifice, and a distrust of all that is or may become art, at last tends to paralyze. If a "small clerical error" inevitably crops up whenever anything is transcribed from life to page or stage, and if this "essential" error is to be regarded as fatal, dare we ever transcribe anything at all?

I have been trying not to take sides in this running account of the contest to date, though I am naturally a side-taker and find such virtuous conduct difficult. But we are gradually being confronted with a choice between absolutes, and the time may come when we feel excited enough to cast votes. The rival positions become reasonably clear. At one end of the fraying rope the antiform team is crying, "Be honest, never lie!" in terms so uncompromising that every measure of control over the materials of life must be unconditionally surrendered. At the other the formalists are suggesting, with a faint smile and a shrug, "Lie, but lie in such a way that the lie is obvious and in no way deceiving; the scaffold of the honest lie will give you something to walk on, somewhere to go."

IN THE INTERESTS OF FORM

Jean Anouilh

AFTER SOME YEARS of educative theatergoing, I have learned to trust Jean Anouilh. This is not to say that M. Anouilh can be trusted to produce a perfect play every time out. What can be looked for each time, though, is a defined intention, a deliberate style, a particular shape—and sometimes a very odd shape indeed—for highly particular materials. What M. Anouilh does most often, it seems to me, is construct from crepe paper and other party materials an engaging little child's house, inside which adult things may happen.

The case history of Anouilh in the American theater has been a curious and instructive one. It has involved two different struggles, struggles which have crossed one another and sometimes crossed one another up. There has been the battle to produce him properly so that we should understand his intentions. And within this battle his own battle to realize his intentions has continued.

Reviewers are educable. All you have to do is take the poor things by the hand and show them. I mention this because I have never succeeded in dislodging from my head a small thrust imbedded in a program note toward the end of a confusing season. The program note was the work of Harold Clurman, who had directed the play at hand and who is himself a critic when he is not directing—a double-play which entitles him, fairly and squarely, to bite either of the hands that feed him.

The issue of the moment was the plays of Anouilh, and Mr. Clurman's not very veiled suggestion was that it had taken the reviewers of America an unconscionably long time to detect and to appreciate the special qualities of the French dramatist. On first acquaintance, they had been appalled. On second, baffled. On third, oddly interested. And then, at long last, light had dawned. (Mr. Clurman did not actually take us through these successive stages of enlightenment in his memo; but the evolutionary development from cretin to connoisseur was there to be clucked over by all who were paying attention.)

Viewed dispassionately by a visitor from Mars, every word of this must be taken as accurate. The evidence is there to be looked at. The first few American productions of plays by Anouilh found few if any reviewers suggesting that the man from Paris had promise. *Legend of Lovers* was a sizable debacle, and not many failures have been as total and as scandalous as the failure of *Cry of the Peacock*. If *Ring 'Round the Moon* was more assured in its manner, it seemed to possess no matter beyond a tinkle of earrings, and only bafflement attended *Mademoiselle Colombe* with its apparently gratuitous destruction of an innocence that was not interesting in the first place. The word, generally, was that however obvious the defects of a given production, the playwright himself would simply not do. Speaking for myself, I sat down to a sober and thoughtful Sunday piece in which I explained that the mood of the moment in France was patently unintelligible to the American mind and profoundly untranslatable for the American stage. Score for Junior: zero.

But attend. Not long after, a careless off-Broadway group that had not yet heard of Anouilh's disgrace ventured to mount his *Thieves' Carnival*. The mood was light, the manner mocking, the conceit engaging, and the upshot startling: the newspapers, quite forgetting themselves, liked it. It was hastily ventured in some quarters that they had liked it only because it was early Anouilh, which is roughly comparable to liking only the early Picasso, and that the dunderheads would be back in the trenches the minute they were exposed to a mature sample of the man's work. Along came a decently mature sample, *The Waltz of the Toreadors,* and the impossible happened: the play was hailed and, what is more, the playwright's reputation as a contemporary dramatist of the first rank was incontestably established. It was clearly time for a hallelujah chorus: the walls of ignorance had come tumbling down.

As I say, all of this is true. Mr. Clurman, in his quiet use of the needle, had neglected to mention only one thing: the small service performed by two extremely intelligent directors. In the case of *Thieves' Carnival* young Warren Enters had succeeded in understanding the play before inviting us all to see it: staged in the light of his understanding, the hitherto secret world of M. Anouilh was jovially illuminated. A big, bright, rose-colored light bulb was turned on right in our faces.

And it was, of all people, Mr. Clurman himself who drew for us the precise comic outlines of *The Waltz of the Toreadors.* This last play, as we've said, is a strange business. Deeply concerned with the fading powers of every human being, and with the gasping frustration that follows every attempt to reverse the tides of twilight, it expresses its bleak despair by means of the formalized nonsense of mistaken-identity farce. It would have taken no particular genius to have mismanaged the project utterly. Mismanaged, the play would have seemed preposterous in its intentions and unrescuable in its methods. "Anouilh is at it again, and why don't they put him away?" we'd all have muttered darkly.

It did take a considerable genius to find just the right balance of boredom and absurdity, of querulousness and quixotry, of fury and antic fun—and there was no chance of stirring the mixture "as before" because there wasn't any "before"; it was an original. But the key was found, the door was opened, and we all went in like lambs.

What I wish to suggest here is that the Anouilh record of rags-to-riches is not so simple a matter as the progressive awakening of reviewers with ten-ten vision. Nor is it a matter of the progressive awakening of audiences. It is much more a matter of vision before the fact, vision on the part of directors capable of penetrating scripts even as they read them and of helping actors to play them in such a way that the content will not be gracelessly concealed.

Maxwell Anderson once remarked that there was no play so perfect it couldn't be destroyed outright by an obtuse production, and those of us who have suffered with *The Importance of Being Earnest* before we were satisfactorily introduced to it, or who have seen productions of *As You Like It* that demonstrated beyond doubt the paucity of Shakespeare's talents, know perfectly well that Mr. Anderson was right. The Anouilh story does not consist of several beautiful early productions that were sadly unappreciated, but of several devastating nonproductions that took an author's name in vain. As the productions themselves began to grasp what the man was getting at, the reviewers—and I am proud of them—proved strangely able to see a church by daylight.

They were also at last in a position to attempt to measure the author's own success or failure in a given instance.

Thus *Time Remembered* displayed itself as a fragile piece of theatrical chinaware, complete with tiny, vagrant, worrisome cracks in the surface. In performance some time was required to establish that brittle, faintly disbalanced universe in which, as star Helen Hayes suggested, "art is stronger than nature."

But one of the characteristics of the artist, as distinguished from the tried-and-true craftsman, is that he is able to touch nature without smearing it. He puts his finger, let's say, on a pinpoint in time or on a delicate pressure-point of passion, and takes it away again while the tingle of contact is still in the air and before he has discolored the moment with his own blunt mark. He makes the world transparent without making it obvious. Everything hovers on the edge of definition, holding its breath.

In *Time Remembered* artist Anouilh held us transfixed, after a time, in a curious half-light where secrets can't be kept but where clumsy certainty isn't allowed a foothold, either. We listened to Richard Burton grope longingly back to a woman he had known for three short days but whose memory had chained him to her, even beyond her death. He was talking to a pretty young milliner who had been hurled at his head in an effort to shock him out of his prolonged reverie. He had difficulty in summoning up the precise inflections of the lost enchantress' voice, the particular inclination of her head as she extravagantly, yet demurely, ate the heart out of an orchid.

Still, little flashes of pleasure lighted up Mr. Burton's eyes. Images returned to him. A conversation in a canoe, spectacularly incoherent. A pet snake that had trailed her, companionably, across the floor. A habit of brushing into a dining room, eyes at half-mast, to sweep in apparent fond greeting toward an old friend—only to veer like a banking plane just as embrace seemed inevitable.

As we listened, we came to strange conclusions. The woman had been a monster, an empty-headed Circe who quite deserved to be strangled by her own theatrically knotted scarf. She had been useless, frivolous, phantom-thin in her gaudy graces. Yet we were not permitted to name her absolutely, to know her for a joke, to laugh at the easy irony of a romantic man mooning over a fraud.

The delight that played across Mr. Burton's face, and that absurdly warmed all the odd little things he had to say about her, was too real to be dismissed. There had also been, behind all the ephemeral nonsense of orchids and contemptuous eyelids, something inexplicably intelligent: perhaps only the kind of intelligence that knows how to make the world and oneself more colorful, perhaps only the kind of intelligence that knows how to make a fantastic attitude throb with life, but an intelligence that could nonetheless be helplessly respected and hopelessly loved.

M. Anouilh was willing to tell the truth about a flamboyant seductress; but he was not willing to make a fool of Mr. Burton. All sides of an enchanting daydream were honored: what had been silly about it in the past, what was silly about pursuing it now; what had once been completely captivating, what was ruefully captivating still.

We stood at the top of a teetering ladder, slightly dizzy and not entirely secure, looking at the whole landscape in a single bemused glance.

Mr. Burton was by no means alone in his intuitive feeling for the author's arrogant and winning determination to build a house out of playing cards that would, somehow, all have real faces on them. It fell to Helen Hayes to enact a moment in which we learned of the charmer's death by accidental, but deeply satisfying, strangulation. Miss Hayes was asked to show us that the lady could not have resisted a theatrical gesture, that if the perfect completion of such a gesture had meant pulling a knot too tight and too permanently, she would faithfully, firmly, have done it; and Miss Hayes showed us.

The moment, of course, was funny; but it was essential that it not be so funny as to bring the whole fairy-tale structure of morose Prince Charmings, sheltered parks, wistful milliners, and ivy-covered taxicabs tumbling down in a fury of farce. The balance was struck with the assurance of a hostess tapping a table bell for a servant she knows will come.

I have sometimes thought that Miss Hayes's voice is the happiest sound I know in the theater. There is a light, liquid, barely suppressed merriment about it that suggests—each time she bounds through a doorway—that she has just come from hearing the best news, the most amusing and exhilarating news, of her life.

In *Time Remembered* she used it to draw laugh after gratifying laugh out of a silver-haired duchess' addled but purposeful maneuverings: announcing that she was much too much of a coward to tell the truth and immediately bolting from the room to prove it; suggesting that she was emotionally unable to continue a conversation and interrupting it steadily thereafter; simply informing the gathering, in irrelevant but most agreeable confidence, that no one had ever seen her in her bare feet.

She also used it to draw a shadow over this amiable picture-postcard universe in which a shopgirl princess could be turned into a brand-new, down-to-earth queen. During the second of the evening's five scenes she leaned against one of Oliver Smith's stylized trees and, as twilight descended about her, spoke with mellow magic about the wasteful loss of love that eternally goes on in the world. There was no love lost at that moment.

Given the hazards that beset all theatrical production, it is never easy to put one's finger on the special conceit that may have spurred a playwright into impudent action; it certainly wasn't easy to be certain about it in the case of the obviously unfinished production of Anouilh's *Becket* which, with a roar of stars and a flapping of scenery, was offered New York.

But I am going to chance a guess about the play. It came equipped with a subtitle. This particular historical pageant was called *Becket—or, The Honor of God*. Now it is a very long time since anyone indulged himself in the old-fashioned, faintly juvenile habit of backing up the main title with an explanatory phrase calculated to show off the moral. And we might have to go all the way back to Horatio Alger, Jr., to find one as plain and pompous and clarion as this.

Why the subtitle? Put that bald and declamatory trumpeter's phrase alongside certain things that were seen to happen in the play. Laurence Olivier (Becket) and Anthony Quinn (Henry II) appeared several times on puppeteer's horseback:

they cantered into a boldly painted forest, dipping and swaying and brushing skirts against the floor, with merry-go-round beasts wrapped fancifully around their middles. Other tournament chargers, stripped from a tapestry or a grade-school exhibit devoted to King Arthur's Court, slipped and bobbled gaily against the inked-in skyline.

On a surprise visit to a peasant's hut—and all of those stories about incognito kings turning up in wayside places came instantly to mind—Mr. Quinn eyed a countryside wench he might have liked to take home. Upstage, and behind the king's back, the wench's sturdy brother appeared with a knife in his hand. Unbeknownst to the king, and with a flick of his virile wrist, Mr. Olivier disarmed the assassin, benevolently freed him, and concealed his own wound—looking rather like Robin Goodfellow during the bravura pantomime passage.

Some of the dialogue seemed to demand capital letters and a picture-book page to itself. "Do you love me, Becket?" for instance, sounded as though it ought to stand as a lone caption on an illustrated leaf. So did the king's tight-lipped remark, when he learned that Becket didn't love him, "I shall learn to be alone." And the dialogue that wasn't spelled out in such banners tended to be informal, chatty, history-made-familiar: "Do I have to shave?" fretted Henry.

There were other possible clues: quick charcoal sketches of the king's unhappy home life, of the turncoat villainy of the Bishop of London, of the pragmatic politicking of a Pope and a Cardinal (both of whom spoke in the pidgin-Italian of easy-laugh vaudeville).

Taken together, what these crayon-stroke humors and chapter-head declarations seemed to suggest was a handsomely illustrated Boy's Life of Becket (or "The Honor of God"), as though Anouilh had adopted a pleasantly remembered experience of childhood reading for his frame and then gone on to fill it, ironically, with subtler and more knowing psychological states.

Were the subtler states there, between the double-spread

155

color plates and the G. A. Henty rhetoric? They were. The loutish monarch who could see no real difference between dirtying his fingers at a meal and dirtying the new-fangled fork knew himself for the second-rate brain he was, knew precisely the values his cultivated friend Becket brought to him, and was able to mock himself wryly—with candor and good humor—as he slapped his thighs and roared, "Oh, Becket, I am subtle, I am profound!" It was fascinating that, in the agony of his estrangement from Becket and on the eve of arranging his old friend's murder, he should have been able to sum up the horror his life had become by bleating out, with a shudder, "Oh, Becket, I am bored!"

Becket caught us off guard, too, as he dallied, speculatively, with the psychology of the hair shirt, admitting at the last— and in his growing humility—that the only reason he didn't take it off was because he might then catch cold. Packing away his glowing Chancellor's robes and assuming a plain gray monk's gown, he instantly invited a horde of beggars to dinner. "A truly saintly man would not have done the whole thing in one day," he paused to observe. The playful format had pungent things inside it.

The difficulty with director Peter Glenville's mounting was that one was forced to do a certain amount of after-hours guesswork—coming to right or wrong conclusions—in order to tie its various, apparently disparate, tones together. Becket at prayer and Becket on horseback were not yet housed in a single play with the stamp of a clear style upon it. Henry's epithets in the vernacular did not seem to match, or deliberately to counterpoint, the ringing, overly-plain slogans. The point of the passage between Pope and Cardinal was quite obscured by organ-grinder accents: we could not imagine, on the spot, why these had suddenly turned up in this play. Even Oliver Smith's settings, enchanting as most of them were, tended to confound one another: a city landscape as busy as Bosch was dropped behind severe arches that seemed to have been devised for as formal a work as *Murder in the Cathedral*. Mr. Glenville, his designer and his actors had not laid firm hands on the dominating conceit that would permit so many strange, tantalizing, and counterpointed effects to fall comfortably into place.

I continue to suspect that one exists, in Anouilh's intention at least, and that someone will some day show it to us. For the playwright seems always to be saying: yes, I would like to use the theater to reflect actual truths of the heart and mind, but, while I am busy using it, I should also like to respect it in and for itself, for its shapeliness, its elevated proportions, its almost mathematical precision, for the incredible formal delights it possesses as its birthright and can—with sufficient persuasion—be made to yield.

The Complaisant Lover

Scarcely a line passes in Graham Greene's *The Complaisant Lover* that doesn't leave a carefully provocative aftertaste ("The trouble about marriage is, it's a damned boring condition even with a lover"), and yet the things that linger most flavorsomely on the tongue are the things that aren't spoken at all.

This reserve, which is the foundation of the play's good humor, insists upon its rights—the rights of insinuation rather than statement—in two entirely different, independently charming, ways. One of them has to do with the strange and subtly jocular shape of the entertainment. I treasure, among other things, a moment in the second act when four frustrated people are lined up across the stage as formally as though they were waiting to collect their unemployment insurance. They have come into a London living room one after the other, each in pursuit of an affection that is not properly his (or hers). An attractive matron is the pivot, a bland, blond chrysanthemum of a woman, interim mistress of a fellow who also keeps a bookstore, wife of a sheep-dog dentist whom she cannot wholly betray. (In fact, she cannot even bring herself to leave his bedroom. She'd move into the spare room, as she explains to her lover, "but he'd notice.")

Next to her, eyes fixed fiercely upon her, stands her lover, righteously demanding that she make an honest man of her husband by telling him the truth. His entreaties are useless, however, because Christmas is coming and how can a woman hurt a husband, even a dull one, before Christmas? Next to the lover stands a teen-age sprig of lilac, declaring and redeclaring her passionate availability. ("You're not in love with me, I know that. It doesn't matter so much, does it? There's always lust.")

Her entreaties are useless because she is so young, and besides the bookseller isn't interested in lust. ("Lust isn't very strong, Ann . . . there are twenty-four hours in a day.") And next to Ann stands a very small boy who has offered this girl both his heart and a stuffed mouse. Needless to say, the lad—last, forlorn member of the beseeching queue—is getting nowhere; neither stuffed mice nor underage males are at present in demand.

The situation is as stylized as a tumble of dominoes, a wink in the direction of that immaculately meshed clockwork, that wrong foot forward and swift spinabout, that keeps all French sex farce going. The familiar machinery is to be heard purring elsewhere, certainly in an Amsterdam hotel room where the lovers' four-day idyll is thoroughly at the mercy of a baffled valet, a beaming stranger who cannot be dislodged from the chamber, an unlocked door and the husband who unexpectedly pops it open. There is a whisper behind everything that is up-to-date about the play, a rumor of Pantalone and Pierrette and Arlecchino.

But it is the barest whisper, a sibilant secret that has almost been suppressed beneath Mr. Greene's concern that artifice should be made to seem as cozy and suburban as flowered chintz, as authentic as mother's shopping list. Here infidelity is a matter of dollars and cents (what part of the family budget can be reserved for a liaison?), of small talk and large cavities (the cuckolded dentist, even in the moment of distressed discovery, cannot help noticing that the lover has one atrocious filling), of plausible lies and omnipresent children (what may happen to an unexpected letter from Amsterdam if one's intelligent small child is a stamp collector?).

"It's unfair, isn't it, that we're dressed for domestic comedy?" asks the husband morosely as things threaten to get out of hand. In superimposing upon the outlines of an impudent comic valentine all the kindly paraphernalia of day-to-day living as well as day-to-day loving, Mr. Greene has cut for himself a perfect small crystal capable of throwing off differently tinted lights. For someone deeply involved in the sad and funny mixture, the contradictions between romantic dalliance and domestic devotion can seem almost the work of a tragic muse: the dentist becomes touching, without losing his essentially comic posture, as he faces up to the fact that he has bored his wife to a very real distraction. For those of us who hover outside the open triangle and gleefully watch it fold to an apex, the double vision—pathos over prank, the habit of love wrapping its warm cloak about a jolly escapade—suggests all sorts of things at once. It suggests that the truth is always terribly close to farce, and that farce is all too often terribly true. And our most special delight comes from Mr. Greene's power of suggestion, from the undercurrent of frolic buried deep within the plausible.

The author is adroit at implying rather than pronouncing—and at making our pleasure depend upon the tease of meaning just beyond the realistic surface—in another, more intimate and less structural, way. The husband, for example, is a responsible householder. In his methodical manner, between unstifled late-night yawns, he carefully checks each window and door, not to mention the wine cabinet, to make certain it is locked. As we follow him, amused, it *does* occur to us that he has now locked up everything except the one thing he is likely to lose: his wife. The thought is not stated; it is merely moving around in front of us.

And nothing is more to be relished than the lover's appalled, silent, knuckle-chewing dismay as, near the end of the contest, he listens to the dentist's astonishing proposal for the immediate future. The dentist has humbly, but firmly, suggested that he retain his wife on a routine basis but that she be free to join her bookseller for weekends or fortnights every so often.

Listening, eyes now narrowed in intense alarm, the bookseller is plainly horrified—not because the arrangement is so irregular, but because in its very irregularity his cause is lost. He knows that the woman for whom they are contending is a charming, middle-aged child, a gleaming innocent. He knows what happens to children when they are wisely indulged and formally given their way: they lose interest in their way, and start inquiring about the rules again. But he has come up against something more formidable still in a husband's stuffy, unexpectedly generous, presence. He has come up against the fact that it is terribly difficult to cope with virtue. Virtue is unbeatable not because it is virtue, but because it is dense, undemanding, utterly vulnerable. One's heart goes out to it. The victim hears his own heart and—not at once, perhaps, but soon, all too soon—that woman's heart going out to it. In the gift he is given, he hears his epitaph read.

We hear it as well, though there is no public announcement. Mr. Greene tickles our ribs, and slips a knife between them, with a quiet grace that is polite and perverse, sober and insouciant, plain as day and delectably elusive.

A Man for All Seasons

A Man for All Seasons is certainly a play for ours. By "ours" I mean the mid-century weather to which we have all been born, the very odd time of our very odd lives, the season in which the inarticulate sounds made by the "common man" have been revered as prophetic while the articulated intelligence of the uncommon man has been viewed as effete, academic, or merely fanciful. For it is dramatist Robert Bolt's most vigorous intention to put the common man back into his very common place and, by centering our attention upon a superb mind in motion, to restore wit to the world.

The restoration of wit may seem a curious objective for an intensely serious and fiercely penetrating examination of one man's conscience—the man is Sir Thomas More and his conscience tells him to defy the king he wishes to serve—but Mr. Bolt both uses and displays wit in what has become a very special sense. We all know what wit means, or have been telling ourselves that we do. It means clever riposte, sassiness with the salt of surprise in it, elegant insult or felicitous epigram; the adjective "wry" goes with it as smoothly as butter.

And, as a matter of fact, *A Man for All Seasons* is delightfully generous with the condiment as it is familiarly understood. Thomas More seems never to have been a malicious man, but he knew how to mock. With a few fragments of history, plus his own bristling intuition, the playwright lets More set his judicious jaw, smile mischievously, and send spears flying—both at himself and at the hapless souls around him.

It is gratifying to hear him put on a pretended temper as he listens to members of his family piously exchanging Latin salutations: "Latin isn't holy, it's just old." It is heartening to hear him silence his solicitous wife: when the badgering woman reminds him that even great men catch cold, he refuses to attend to such "dangerous, leveling talk." The gentle,

161

jolly irony with which More affects to notice the beginnings of a nimbus about the head of his "saintly" son-in-law is slyness to be savored. And humor stays with him to the end of his days and to trial for treason. Somewhat enfeebled by his long private struggle, and by the pressures of the cage that imprisons him, he is not too feeble to look hard at the perjurer who is betraying him and to see, hanging about the opportunist's neck, a bright new circlet proclaiming him an overseer of Wales. As though no amount of fatigue could suppress his impulse to level-headed merriment, More remarks that he can grasp a man's bartering his soul in exchange for the whole world. But for *Wales*?

The mind's delight in its own skillful play, for the sake of play, is constantly and joyfully in evidence. But something else, something curious, attaches itself to this same prance and scamper of verbal grace. The troubled central figure is to be heard insisting, during one of his soberest and most searching passages of plain thought, that "God made man to serve Him, wittily, in the tangle of his mind." One's expectations are jolted here, more forcibly than when a dry pleasantry catches us unawares in the middle of a moment of passion. For Mr. Bolt and his hero now seem to be defining the mind's most responsible activity as wit.

What are they up to? The question is enough to send a man back to the dictionary, where it is all too quickly answered. I confess to some surprise upon discovering that the association of wit with humor (with "clever, ironical, or satirical remarks") does not show up until we have run a finger down to the fourth acceptable definition. Everything before that, everything that must claim priority, gives over to the term all our powers of perception, our powers of intellectual precision, our common sense, our wisdom, our ability to place values in balance.

Obviously, in our peculiar time, we have got a few things backward. We do not think of wit as mind; we think of it as light-mindedness. The man who displays any special dexterity with the quicksilver of verbal coins is not so much pursued as a seer as he is suspected of shallowness. The notion that one kind of intellectual felicity might be related to another eludes us. In the process of turning a word around, and forgetting what its top half stands for, we may have downgraded not only the epigrammatic but also the meticulously and responsibly thoughtful.

Mr. Bolt downgrades neither. From the subtlety of mind that can phrase a quip (it is the task of opportunists to make "convenient" what a king is going to do anyway) to the suppleness of mind that can weigh even the temptation to martyrdom against the private need to speak out (some men "have to stand fast even at the risk of being heroes") there is a direct, fluid, ever-forward movement. Having established its respect for the infinite resources of reason, the play hurtles ahead to make reason exciting and thought extraordinarily moving.

It should be emphasized in passing just how moving an essentially intellectual struggle can be in the theater. If Paul Scofield, in the New York production, rarely betrayed emotion, he stirred it. There were perhaps only two or three times during his exacerbating effort to serve king and God and self simultaneously when his posture of easy, controlled strength shivered a little, letting the shadow of a tormented flesh fall across it. At one of these times—at the moment when he was being most blatantly betrayed—the actor's hands flew to his face. But they did not touch his face, or even each other. There was a suspended tension, a groan of mere muscle, as the clenched fingers hesitated, hovered before the desperate man's eyes, then slowly and forcibly descended to his mouth, hesitated again as though there were a cry to be stifled, and then fell to his sides, spent but triumphant. They had not been allowed to express defeat: what More knew conquered what More felt. The feeling itself, however, had not died. It had come out into the auditorium and invaded us.

Actors seemed to be thinking with the rapidity of lightning and with the force of a thunderclap. Words split the air not because they were shouted but because they carried long shafts of meaning with them. The headlong activity that stirred on the stage was not so much an activity of bodies: it was a thrust of souls making themselves belligerently intelligible. The coil of thought that spiraled constantly inward in an effort to touch, at last, the very core of personality had the clean and sweeping line of the great plunging staircase Motley had designed to encompass, and describe, the journey. The play looked as it reads: spare, pointed, piercing.

And, withal, kindly. The common man, of our own and every century, is kept in view by means of a knowing, impudent, hardheaded stage manager who hauls fresh costumes out of the hamper of time, whips the furniture about with slapdash efficiency, plays any small role that requires no hairsplitting, and in general gets through the world with a wink, a tickle, and a shove. The philosophizing of stricter, more stubborn men is not for him; he is philosophical about all that, trusting only such gratuities as he can hold in his hand. When he turns to the audience and offers us the pious hope that we will all die in our beds, he is insulting us and he knows it. It is men of compromise who die in their beds.

This jack-of-all-faiths has played, for a time, one of More's household servants. As More's fortunes begin to fail, he realizes that it is time for him to extract himself from that kettle of coming trouble. He announces his leavetaking. More, who knows all there is to know about him, tells him simply and with some honesty that he will miss him.

The sentiment throws our common man, momentarily. Is this some devious device for reclaiming his loyalty? Is it a joke, a parting thrust with a barb in it? Or—here he pauses a bit—could More possibly have meant it? He tries to puzzle the matter out. "What's in me for him to miss?" he asks, not without a whisper of humility and near-gratitude. Then he shrugs, leers cynically, gives up the effort to follow so intricate a mind, and departs. But More has meant it. Somehow, it is in wit that even charity is born.

The Tenth Man

Paddy Chayefsky's path in recent years has been admirably adventurous. Coming to the theater from television with a play that had the domestic commonplaces of television drama still clinging to it (*Middle of the Night*), he next gave himself the gigantic shake of a dog just out of water, sighted an inviting field no one had explored before, and raced into the rich seriocomic complexities of identifying a devil that had got into a twentieth-century basement.

To put this earthy exhibit into any sort of recognizable category we'd probably have had to go back seven or eight centuries to the medieval folk play, and even then we wouldn't have come close enough. *The Tenth Man* did have its medieval overtones, not because its story had to do with a girl possessed by a demon but because all of the people who were bent on exorcising the evil spirit were themselves so jovial, so vulgar, so pleasantly matter-of-fact. (Medieval drama is funny that way: you dip into it expecting to find a solemn piety and what you find is a rowdy candor.) Mr. Chayefsky's peculiar blend of simple devotion and sudden farce had, to a degree, existed before.

Still, there was a strange strain here that was shockingly unexpected and shockingly apt. To catch hold of the blowzy, friendly, Saturday-morning skepticism that crept through the play like the odor of burning fall leaves, it was not enough to remember a naïve and giddy folk form written in an age of faith. It became necessary to imagine the same jaunty frame of mind, and the same deeply religious impulse, applied to an age of doubt and anxiety and despairing disbelief. *The Tenth*

165

Man may have chosen to look Satan in the face; but it did so with the tart tones of the twentieth century, and with something of that century's gullibility, too.

Basically, Mr. Chayefsky had formed an image in which everything present, whether flesh and blood or brick and tin, contradicted its own nature. The action took place in a synagogue. But the synagogue was a derelict basement from which all grandeur had fled. The matter at hand was painfully serious: a girl was either insane or possessed of a demon. But more than half of all that was said about so serious a matter was funny.

Most of the Jewish neighborhood folk who were concerned with the exorcism were ordinary, realistic people. But in their swift descent into enthusiasm for the ancient and the occult, they became "more insane than the girl." The one clear mind on the premises belonged to a young disbelieving Jew who had been hauled in off the street to make up a religious quorum. He found it necessary to leave the proceedings in midflight to see his analyst.

Sanity and insanity, violence and vaudeville, mysticism and psychiatry, dignity and broad folk-comedy were meant to fuse into a single sound. And the sound was meant to be the sound of our curious world: a world in which superstition itself comes to seem far more sensible than the logical, unloving, self-destructive lives we lead.

This was a large order for Mr. Chayefsky to have given himself: to display, all at once, an age very knowing and very lost, an age that sees no future at all and still sees the humor of its sorry situation, an age that is as eager for spiritual experience as it is quick to make sport of the absurd endeavor.

Inch by inch this curious work got done. A young rabbi who had been fired from several congregations before inheriting his present seedy quarters in a Mineola basement picked up the telephone to give a colleague some timely advice: arrange raffles, run bingo games, encourage basketball. "You are a saintly, pious and spiritual man," he told his friend, "and you have no business being a rabbi."

The synagogue idlers, with atheists among them, were presented as homely, cheerful, caustic philosophers. "May my mother-in-law inherit a hotel with a thousand rooms," mumbled one fellow, "and be found dead in all of them." When a biology teacher brought his hysterical granddaughter into the dingy room, hoping that a religious ceremony would do for her what no mental institution had been able to accomplish, the first reaction of the sages clustered around an electric heater was an agreeable shrug: "When you've seen one exorcism, you've seen 'em all." If they did become energetically engaged in the proceedings, and if they were at last willing to scour the town to find a man capable of performing the necessary ritual, it was only because it had been such a long time since anything exciting, or foolish, or even sad, had happened to them. Against all reason, and with the animated eagerness of schoolboys, they joined in a vast and profound spiritual quest: as it turned out, they could not even find the Long Island Railroad.

It was because there were only nine more or less indifferent worshipers available for morning service that a necessary tenth man had to be lured in from the streets. He was, in Donald Harron's excellent performance, a lean and lonely fellow who had tried to destroy himself so often that his wife felt compelled to caution her neighbors not to worry when they detected escaping gas—it was just Arthur killing himself again. This "specialist in unsuccessful suicides" held constantly at his throat the knife of his own intelligence. He understood nearly everything he had been through: his absurd youthful rebellion against society, the infantilism of his having blamed his mother for all of his ills, the futility of living for the sex act alone. Confronted with the possessed girl, he was confronted with the leftover things he could *not* understand: love, the mystery of personality, a dimensional universe. As the girl urgently suggested that they marry, he simply pointed out with a sighing laugh that they would be coupling insanity with exhaustion. As the girl replied that they would then have achieved at the very beginning a state it normally takes many years of married life to arrive at, he could only stare at her, bewildered to find affection and worldly wisdom inhabiting the same soul. "Don't be saucy," he said.

The tone of the evening as a whole was one of saucy seriousness, as though the author had dumped Laurel and Hardy into the Third Book of Kings and told them to take it from there. One could only commiserate with those professors who would one day feel obliged, for textbook purposes, to give the play a precise label.

The Grand Kabuki

It should not be surprising that the New York theater has been more and more hospitable in recent years to visiting companies from abroad, especially to those companies performing plays of ancient or exotic design. The struggle toward form may be speeded up, or at least illuminated, by the shock of alien styles.

Everyone knows, for instance, that the Japanese theater is several hundred years behind our own. The members of the tradition-bound Grand Kabuki are still playing fifteenth-century Noh plays and nineteenth-century comedy-melodramas, rather as though our most popular actors were to occupy themselves permanently with *The Second Shepherd's Play* and *Uncle Tom's Cabin*.

While the Kabuki has certainly discovered scenery, it has not yet discovered realism. Choirs of musicians sit directly behind the performers, or kibitz over their shoulders from stage left, as they strike strings that seem to have been forged on anvils and chant those portions of the story that the playwright has neglected to put into dialogue.

When a refugee prince arrives at a barrier erected by his enemies, there is no barrier; the opposing parties recite at one another in voices "to make the heavens echo" over five or six feet of empty space. When it is time to show animosity, there is no swift, lunging anger in the Elia Kazan manner: instead, four separate knees begin to ripple as though the earth beneath them were in a state of seismic shock. And they ripple away from, rather than toward, their foes.

When a husband and wife are reduced to tears, their backs shiver against one another in a counterpoint that must have been agreed upon between them well in advance, and when the wife wishes to display a still greater anguish she gnaws strenuously on one corner of an enormous handkerchief.

The prince's guards are uniformed in what seem to be mobile pincushions, handsomely adorned with neatly spaced puff balls, while the principals of the party tack front for soliloquies like so many sloops in full sail: clearly none of them is ever going to get through a narrow defile in a crisis. And the brilliantly painted scenery, for that matter, is not so plausible as it looks. A magnificent river that crawls down a mountain proves, on closer inspection, to be composed of what seem to be seven adjacent strands of blue-tinted toothpaste.

The Kabuki, in short, continues to perform plays that are in that primitive, or slightly post-primitive, state that employs equal portions of ritual, choral chant, dance pantomime, frozen posture, stylized substitution for the most vigorous events, and earthy chitchat. (It is odd how familiar and casual a folk form invariably becomes, right in the middle of so much elaborate artifice.) To add to the feeling of childlike experiment, the players continue to delight in navigating the stage on built-up heels that must be nine or ten inches high.

Now it is probably true that all this clinging to costumes that look like generously filled Easter baskets and to formalized maneuvers that resemble witch-doctor incantations has in one or another way kept the creative impulse of a country from maturing as much as it might have. Though I am unable to read Japanese, I have a dark suspicion that Japanese drama has not yet turned the corner that Shakespeare turned (and that we have since somehow lost the map to). Literature is probably not its strong point.

But I have been seriously struck—thunderstruck, almost— to find myself moving with the Kabuki players into an interior life that was very nearly more real for being less so.

Consider a certain moment in a short play called *Tsubosaka Reigenki*. A blind old man has begun to suspect his wife's fidelity, whereas the devoted woman has merely been stealing away so often to say prayers for his speedy recovery. Penitent, the husband climbs a cliff and hurls himself into the valley below. Dismayed on discovering his body, the wife does the same.

This is, however, a Japanese miracle play, and a kindly white-and-gold goddess is at hand not only to restore the terribly loyal couple to life, but to restore the chastened man's sight. It is one of the pleasant formalities of this severely stylized theater that the chandeliers in the auditorium should burst into daylight at the very moment the aged hero pops open his eyes.

Still, the real illumination has come shortly before. The Kabuki is so rich in color, in costume, in teasing pantomime and impulsive dance that one can easily revel away a couple of hours, intent upon the surface texture, without even hoping to become emotionally embroiled in so rigid a form. The particular miracle of this little miracle play is that it does draw you through the painted-glass faces and the veil of the unfamiliar, deep into the heart of things.

It is impossible not to become alarmed and excited as the drums beat out their "hurry music" and Nakamura Kanzaburo XVII, as the sightless fugitive, jabs his staff against the broken rock of a mountain, scrapes his way in increasing panic, and then sways in irresolute despair over the yawn of a canvas cliff. It is surprising how much emotion is generated as Nakamura Utaemon VI, a skilled male actor playing the forlorn and misjudged wife, turns his head gravely from side to side and passes his hands through the empty air in rhythmically precise, and utterly evocative, sorrow.

The compounded theatrical elements do their magical work. Though everything is strange—two plaintive voices at the side of the stage deploring what is happening, a percussive series of clacks punctuating the growing tension—each device brings its primitive force to bear on an experience that is not in any superficial sense realistic but that digs at recognizable emotional roots just the same.

There are some things that are realistic in our sense. The actors' eyes, let's say. When an enormously gifted performer named Onoe Shoroku II beats his lord and master with a bamboo stick in *The Subscription List* he does it with four swift, solemn passes past the gentleman's ears that are clearly going to do damage to no one. This is simply the sign for a beating, and—given the violence we have had quite enough of, locally—the sign will do.

But when the formal exercise is over, something else happens. The servant has beaten his master, who is presently in disguise, in order to help him escape from a foe. Now that this helpful, but utterly unthinkable, deed is done, the servant falls to his knees in humble petition for pardon. And the apprehension that steals over the slave's appalled countenance, coupled with a look of pain for having injured the leader he loves, is instantly, absolutely intelligible. The external gesture makes a shape in the air like a twirled sparkler on the Fourth of July; but at its fiery point—in the eyes of the actor —there is real heat.

During any visit to the Kabuki, one may notice what at first sight seems an odd principle of stage decoration. Somewhere in the background, and in sizable proportions, scream bold concentrations of primary colors: flaring draperies in green and red stripes, swelling and dipping landscapes in hues to put a man's eye out.

Against these declarations of visual independence move the actors, often robed in the palest of pastels. What is odd about the tug-of-war is that you look at the pastels. The big splashes wear themselves out somehow, and you are left with your attention glued to a figure in a decidedly retiring shade of blue.

The actors themselves often work on something of the same principle. Nakamura Kanzaburo XVII, for instance, sits modestly on the floor of an imperial palace during the second scene of *Chushingura*, adapted from a puppet play of 1748. He is severely puzzled, at first, for the governor is teasing him about his wife and offering him veiled insults. During this early exchange he is as placid and self-contained as a small mountain pool.

Fairly spectacular things have been happening around him. A temple has been dedicated, a variety of flashing helmets have been raised aloft for inspection, the governor has declared his secret passion for the poor fellow's wife. In a moment or two, swords are going to leap from their scabbards and it is going to take a whole retinue of guards to hold the innocent husband down.

But between such explosions of spectacle and such unpredictable outbursts of emotional fire, the performer has taken great trouble to create around himself a stillness. The man taunting him has leered at him, slapped at him, all but overwhelmed him with his looming, challenging presence. And what we watch, once more, is the stillness, the clown-white control of a bewildered face, the faint flicker of alarm that is so infinitesimal we double our concentration for fear of missing it.

Nakamura Kanzaburo XVII does seem to me an astonishing man. His facial responses, when they come, are subtly and disturbingly mixed. Though he is beginning to feel both fury and humiliation, the corners of his mouth turn upward in a miniature spasm that is not unlike one of the comedy mannerisms of the late Harry Langdon. Yet with every controlled tremor, and every dart of his expressive eyes, the devices of folk comedy are made to express both mortal terror and intolerable pain. It is as though the two masks of the theater had again blended in one countenance.

The same player plays yet another trick on us in *Kago Tsurube* or "The Courtesan" (which I continue to think of as The Case of the Pockmarked Lover). When he appears with his face a veritable flowering garden of ringed indentations, one's first reactions are irreverent: I know I murmured to myself that when it comes to pockmarks, the Japanese don't kid around. But that is what they are doing, really. The disfiguring splash is as colorful, as formal, as vividly oversize as the heels and headdresses parading by.

To what purpose? Because what signifies a disease has been turned into a pattern, we are swiftly able to dart past it— past all that is unattractive about it—into the yearning heart of the man behind the mask. In a very short time we are charmed by this fellow, sympathizing with his wistful passion for a woman well beyond him, smiling at his foolishness and wishing him luck. The artifice of the make-up, far from being a barrier, has removed one; we are escorted the more quickly into the emotional interior.

Compare the case with the astonishingly accurate make-up used by Jason Robards, Jr., in the final scene of *Toys in the Attic*. Here the facial damage was quite real enough to be terrifying. It was also real enough to get in our way. We were so fascinated with it, so convinced by it, and so appalled at its actuality, that we were scarcely able to hear a word Mr. Robards was saying. Our concern for his state of mind was almost obliterated by our concern for that face.

It is a curious thing that reality itself should ever become a veil, that instant recognition should interfere with our in-

173

volvement. But it would seem to do so. When we see quickly familiar people in quickly familiar settings doing completely detailed things, do we give such ready assent that our minds go slack, long before we have done the kind of cooperative work that would embroil us more fully? When we say, "Yes, that's right" as we look at a glossy, just-so surface, have we begun to rest in the surface—and condemned ourselves to a superficial pleasure—instead of being forced to dig to get nearer the whole truth? Does an unrealistic surface stir us to a profound imaginative effort that we would otherwise not make?

Pantalone, Harlequin, and Friends

One of the most attractive things about the Piccolo Teatro di Milano is the way the actors behave off stage. The actors give us an opportunity, in their celebrated production of Goldoni's *A Servant of Two Masters,* to see both off stage and on: a gay central trestle takes up no more than the heart of the acting area, leaving all sorts of room for the idling performers beyond.

Thus Pantalone, having finished waggling his chin whiskers at a disobedient daughter and a quick-on-the-draw son, bolts through a slit in the raggle-taggle back curtain and then pauses to refresh himself from a company wine cask, keeping an appreciative eye on the new scene that is going on. Whenever Arlecchino is about to get a good clout from one of the two masters he serves, a helpful soubrette appears on the sidelines to make a nice, loud thwack with a slapstick by way of accompaniment.

A downtrodden super whose duty it is to thump his staff three times loudly at the beginning of each act, and whose particular misfortune it is to splinter his staff in two the third time he tries, can be seen—if you are not watching the on-stage action too closely—morosely examining his shattered emblem of office in the wings. When the second-act curtain goes up, he isn't even there to do his job. The entire ensemble, still primping before mirrors and practicing drawing their swords, are caught napping. The communal gasp of horror that escapes them on noticing the audience is a gasp to be remembered.

But perhaps the most delightful of the incidental improvisations this Italian troupe has dreamed up by way of reacquainting us with the busy and buoyant style of the *commedia dell' arte* is a bit of business that appears just a little later on. Pantalone, nearly apoplectic, is having a ferocious set-to with his pompous friend, the Doctor. They are already at something better than white heat. The actors who aren't working at the moment, fascinated, begin to inch in from the dressing rooms. Their expressive faces take on the animation of the two yammering masked figures (Pantalone leads with a great black hooked nose, the Doctor wears a sort of eighteenth-century mudguard).

In a moment the company's fingers are restlessly itching, their knees bobbing forward in a go-get-'em rhythm, as they urge their colleagues to greater and greater heights of sputtering invective. The whole thing becomes a breathless countdown, until at last the unstrung old men seem to leave the planet in a great streaming arc, their tongues clacking excitedly to the whirlwind end.

Wouldn't it be pleasant if our own actors spoke this rapidly, especially since we already understand English? The crackle of consonants and the whooshing rush of vowels, together with all of the antic footwork that makes each syllable a fresh excuse for a scissors-step, are exhilarating in themselves. And I haven't even mentioned the almost blessed absence of pauses.

But the best fun, and the fastest, lies in the cross-legged impudence of Marcello Moretti's variation on Harlequin. In his diamond-patterned costume, and with his nervous feet angled in opposite directions, this inspired buffoon constantly suggests that if you could just close his ankles together he'd shoot straight out ahead and pick up something for you.

The Moretti showpiece comes, of course, in the famous sequence in which he must serve two dinners, in adjoining rooms, at the same time. I cannot pretend to have counted the morsels that fly by, or to have identified every course on the express-train menu accurately. But I will swear to a tureen of steaming soup delivered by Arlecchino on his back, to a plate of pastrami delivered by lateral pass, to a gravy boat riding in peril on the gentleman's neck, and to a most excitable aspic. The shiver of the aspic causes Moretti to shiver; Moretti's shiver gives the aspic a fresh case of fidgets; together, they make the theater no place for a man whose own nerves aren't steady.

But they do make the theater a place in which pure artifice may be honorably housed. I had also supposed that Molière's *Les Fourberies de Scapin* was pure artifice, as much a stereotype as anything ever turned out by a major playwright at the height of his powers. (Shakespeare's *Comedy of Errors* is an early work; Molière had already written *Tartuffe* and *The Misanthrope* when he permitted himself the sheer abandon of this nursery-tale romp in which a descendant of Harlequin plays every kind of trick on the bumbling fathers of some impetuous, and nearly idiotic, young lovers.)

I had supposed, too, that Scapin himself—the Harlequin figure—was plainly and simply a clown, a clown so much of the seventeenth century, or perhaps so entirely out of time, that he could never reasonably have been related to the twentieth century.

Robert Hirsch, who is now performing the role in the company of the Comédie Française, has other notions. He isn't a beatnik, precisely, even though the way he shades his eyes from the unwelcome sun and the way he scratches his untidy black hair when driven to thought do stir echoes of that most contemporary clan. Nor is he, I suppose, a pure existentialist; it seems doubtful that he would bother to wake up and live, or savor a moment for the moment's sake, if someone wasn't kicking him in the ribs.

But he is, of all things, an outsider. He belongs to the disengaged. He is so much of the twentieth century that the latest pretzel-bends of iconoclastic philosophy cannot conceivably be news to him. What he seems like, as he shudders and pleads and sheds crocodile tears, is a tragic hero born into a time when there is no longer any tragedy at all. Because he can believe in nothing, and feel nothing, the only way he can share an emotion is by mocking it. He is fascinating.

He begins, to be sure, by indulging himself in all of the tricks and turns and staggers and backbends of the jolly fools we know. He can throw one hip out of joint, walk on cat feet, lift one leg higher than his shoulder for no good reason, squint and blink and fold himself up into a boat most skillfully.

Slipping down a flight of stairs with his heels clamped together, or running his tongue along a menacing rapier, he is close to the gay and circusy stylization that Jean-Louis Barrault has made familiar to us.

But there is, significantly, no clown-white paste to cover his face, there are no arching eyebrows to say that we are merely skylarking tonight. And the really triumphant moments are not moments of vaudeville at all. They are moments of calculated, almost savage, madness. They come when he deals with a raging, stomping, spluttering old man by raging even more loudly, stomping even more furiously, spluttering even more volubly than the old tyrant can. He is imitating the human condition, not participating in it.

They come, again, as he moves from a mock tragic posture —knuckles clasped against forehead like an insincere Hamlet—to a passionate entreaty that is as intense, and as full of urgent twitches, as the most earnest lab study ever done at the Actors' Studio. This is followed, directly, by a nervous exhaustion, a twittering of fingers and a desperate catching of breath, that says only one thing: see, I didn't mean it—but I used all the right muscles. Rarely has sincerity been so kicked in the teeth.

If Molière is served without omission or distortion, our own century can hear—in M. Hirsch's brilliant mating of dexterity and denial—the sound of its own voice.

ANTIFORM

A Confrontation

Plays like *Sunday in New York* and *The Apple* serve each other right.

Sunday in New York, a sentimentalized Broadway farce by Norman Krasna, is precisely the kind of echo-chamber exercise that drives intelligent young theatergoers to complete despair; it also drives them off-Broadway to any event which promises that it will be in some way unconventional. For almost from the time that the first line is spoken, a sense of ghostly presences, pale mechanized shades of the tried and true, stirs to haunt us.

Mr. Krasna is entirely capable of writing an efficient farce, when he has an idea for one, and for a brief time in the second act he has an idea for one: the fact that two fellows, one of whom is pretending to be the other, answer the same questions simultaneously proves to be funny. But virtually everything else in the comedy seems to be there not because the playwright has thought of it but because he has learned, from other men's experience, that it tends to "work."

Thus the pert ingénue establishes her problem for the evening by expressing her conviction that she is "the only twenty-two-year-old virgin alive." It seems that no one will marry her, or even date her for very long, without bedtime compliance on her part; since she is a good girl, the discovery that "virginity went out with silk stockings" distresses her. We are now in a position to scoop the cream off three established, sure-fire conventions in quick (no, slow) succession.

The very bandying about of the word "virginity" has a lively, cash-register ring to it, though only in a theater so immured in its own conventions as never to have noticed how casually the word is used elsewhere; a superstition persists that this is being outspoken. As we move from a lavish use of the term itself to the question of "should she or shouldn't she," we are in clover: we can make prolonged debate, sassy and iffish, of the very materials that served an earlier, clearly remembered comedy so successfully. And in the course of passing from "should she or shouldn't she" to the breath-taking tensions of "will she or won't she," we glide, with the dance steps all marked out, into the two-bathrobe tease that has defined the shape of seventeen other, equally well-remembered, confections. It is not necessarily anything against any earlier play to say that it employed these doodlings; everything depends, in a way, on how early it was. But Mr. Krasna comes late, with his own hands empty, prepared to do, do, do what others did, did, did before. His comic structure does not rise upon a set of familiar gestures, it rests on them.

Small wonder that those who have ears to hear, and even very short memories, rush off to the likes of Jack Gelber's *The Apple*, an invention that strains every nerve to defeat our expectations rather than trade on them. We are reminded, upon arrival, that our theatrical responses have all become dulled by the trivia in triplicate we have been watching in Broadway playhouses (and not only in hand-me-down comedies, but in routinely formed serious plays as well). "Hokay," snaps the master of ceremonies with a flick of his derby and a swivel of his red-and-white belt, "let's everybody take a deep breath and start off alive."

We are not going to be permitted to live long, for what Mr. Gelber most wishes to show us—in the process of shocking us alive—is how dead we are. (A paradox? Of course. The avant-garde likes best of all to play with the ambiguity of "Wake up! Don't you know you're dead?") The audience is promised "some destructive scenes" and these scenes will "make you forget just how warm your body is." One of these scenes hurls a drunk to the aisle floor of the playhouse with a heart attack; we watch the man try to force himself up off the floor into life again, crying out his belief in his continuing identity, as a loudspeaker at the back of the auditorium intones over our shoulders, "It's cold, it's cold." Another shows us a gasping spastic trying to drink a cup of tea; another shows us a homosexual turning, in the middle of a conversation, into an oversize fly with one arm in a sling. When someone dances to the blare of a lunchroom radio, he usually dances with a dummy.

Well and good, or at least fair and fair enough. Our habits of thought, and especially those habits of thought that constitute our knowledge of ourselves, have grown stale and sterile, and in that degree false. When a girl leers across the edge of the intimate platform and urges, "Come over to our side, you're not doing anything important," the invitation is in part generous and the insult is in part just.

But. In the course of putting a blowtorch to the theater's familiar patterns, and in the act of trying to rub our nerves raw enough to restore us to consciousness, Mr. Gelber slips into a form of sleepwalking of his own. His touchstone is the unconventional: everything must conform to it. It is not enough that he say something disturbing; he must also disturb the process of saying it, even the possibility of its ever being said.

Scenes must not stand in a meaningful relationship to one

another: that is too customary. Scenes themselves must not be permitted to disclose, or contain, their meaning: that is what scenes have always done. Instead, a man leans across a table and asks a woman, "What's the name of this town?" The lady replies, "New York City." The man pulls a gun. "You're wrong!" he cries triumphantly, and shoots her dead. Blackout. Multiply the blackout by no given number, for there is no way of multiplying an infinite series of unlikes, and the nonresult is the play that isn't there. The play dare not be there, dare not express itself, dare not communicate the disturbing thing it dare not say: if it did it would be doing one familiar thing. The trap is now sprung. Because he has denied himself the right ever to choose the conventional, Mr. Gelber has put himself at the mercy of the *merely* unconventional. And to be merely unconventional is as empty an act as Mr. Krasna's. It may have the further effect of defeating itself by sending patrons of *The Apple* right back to *Sunday in New York*.

Perhaps there are two brief notes that should be appended here. The terms "convention" and "conventional" are widely regarded, at present, as dirty words. They aren't. A convention isn't a bad thing. It happens to be a good one. It is nothing more than a convenient temporary agreement between author and audience as to what artificial devices shall be used this evening, this year, or this half-century in order to organize the almost unmanageable sprawl of life itself. Some such agreement is necessary or the work could not get done. These agreements do wear thin after a time, and must be exchanged for new ones. But the thinness has not come about because a useful convention helped to frame a play. Weariness has set in because the convention *became* the play.

Note Two: It is curious how quickly the unconventional play develops inverted conventions of its own. Almost all avant-garde theater, just now, is surprisingly alike. The devices are very nearly sanctified: actors arising from the audi-

181

ence, repeated use of what are thought of as gutter words, action interrupted by outsiders or by the actors themselves taking the case to the audience, symbolic properties and costumes, decayed locales, conversations composed of *non sequiturs,* themes having to do either with the inability to communicate or the uncertainty of one's identity. The range does not so much widen as narrow into an increasingly recognizable path. Is the instinct toward convention a permanent one that will not be denied and that will display itself maliciously and upside down, even in its hoped-for absence?

And, if so, may not the better experimentalists be better off searching consciously for what is freshly conventional rather than for what is thoroughly, desperately, perhaps futilely, shapeless?

The Connection

The inverted recurrence of a convention, persistent as crabgrass, may be better seen in Mr. Gelber's more widely admired experiment, *The Connection.* The effort made here, I think, offers quiet testimony to the author's real concern with a kind of truth rather than with assorted kinds of trickery. The effect it achieves—that of unendurable delay followed by mindless relief—is undoubtedly the effect it intends.

In performance at The Living Theater the direction and acting arrived at a lifelike rhythm so absolute that the players became inseparable from the "junkies" they were impersonating. Various sensitively composed still lives, such as two vegetable derelicts huddled in torpor over a portable phonograph, had so much atmospheric finality about them that they could be sustained, paralyzed and paralyzing, for minutes at a time.

But the evening produced in me a sensation of moving forward in order to go backward.

Everything that is successful in *The Connection* belongs to a form known as naturalism, and is an extreme example of it. The drug addicts who are waiting in pain for a "fix" wait for just about as long as they might have to in life (an hour and a half by the clock). While waiting, they fill the nerve-torn time as they would in a perfectly real pad: they read, they sleep, they listen to music, they fidget, they break open boils. When the fix comes, and they surrender to a sensation that deprives them of all other sensations, they close their eyes, stretch on the floor or cot, and leave us. Nirvana is more or less permitted to run its course, without the interruption of familiar dramatic incident or any "expressionist" effort to explore a subjective state of being. The surface of this small world is recorded with detached fidelity, and a voice at the back of the auditorium can repeat, hypnotically and with considerable justice, "That's the way it is . . . yeah, that's the way it is."

Now the early naturalists—from Zola and Hauptmann and Gorki onwards—were eternally distressed by what seemed to them the irrelevant demands of the theater. How could they be expected to come closer and closer to the untidy and often desultory "facts" of life when curtains had to fall, and climaxes were expected shortly before curtains, and literary habits kept trying to creep back into the day-to-day language of peasants?

Anything that was in any way "formal" about drama tended to give the lie to the utter identification with reality for which they were hoping. Since drama itself is a form, the effort ultimately wavered, lost energy as an all-out credo. Zola had wanted to deal with nothing but facts, but how was any man ever going to turn an actor into a fact or a stage into an attic without admitting into the work a compromising degree of artifice?

Mr. Gelber knows his theatrical history. Though he clearly still wants to reproduce the texture of a certain kind of life as though it had never been tampered with, he seems to be aware that the promise of total formlessness—the promise of shape that varies not at all from the actual shape of life—is a fiction and perhaps a fraud. His solution here is to admit to the fraud, to advertise it. By bringing the "author," the "management," and two documentary photographers on stage, he calls our attention, as we have seen earlier, to the presence of artifice, as though—knowing that it has never successfully been pushed under the rug—it might now be killed by exposure to the light. Form is not concealed: it is mocked.

Mr. Gelber would like, really, to laugh form out of existence, the better to get on with the real business of clocking, to the second, the shuffling, scratching, wearying "way it is." The naturalism itself would have satisfied the most resolute of Mr. Gelber's theatrical grandparents. Actors suck their teeth, hide their trembling hands, and eat real pineapple with patient restraint. The language studiously avoids any attempt at literature. (On opening a boil on the side of one man's neck, another faithfully asks, "What is all that green stuff, man?") Because these men listen to jazz while they wait, the audience listens to jazz while they wait—four or five times an hour for four or five minutes at a time. (Mr. Gelber now achieves identity with life: real musicians really play, without interference from author or actors.)

Of the two forcibly joined elements—the clinical observation, and the mocking insistence on fraud—the naturalism comes off about as well as it always has in good hands: that is to say, it is impressive and unsatisfying. The cavalier artifice does not work well at all: for the most part it seems coy, sheepish, and unassimilated.

But it does not in the least concern me that the "improvised" elements should frequently seem arch. What bothers me is the essential position that shape itself is a fake and had best be exposed for what it is so that it can be the more easily dismissed.

This is an echo, of course, of that distrust of art we have

mentioned; it repeats the conviction that whatever is organized must thereby be falsified. It has led—not only in
experimental drama but in other media as well—to a notion
that truth is never to be found in meditation, and certainly
not in premeditation, but only in what pops out on the spur
of the moment, only in what is wholly or at least partially improvised. A craftsman can lie, but a reflex cannot.

I would like to stress one of the reasons why this disturbs
me. In the case of *The Connection*, when all that is unwritten
is taken away—the long, suspended silences in the theater,
the itching choreography, the experience of physically enduring the passing time, the half hour or so of jazz—is there very
much left beyond some intentionally ordinary lines and a
road map for the director? The distrust of art, on the grounds
that art distorts the truth, may in the end leave us with very
little to hold in our hands.

Overtones

I often find myself thinking about the two different theaters
in New York: the one that I see, and the one that you see. On
the whole, we do not quite inhabit the same world. For at
least half of my own theatergoing season is made up of plays,
the lion's share of which appear off-Broadway, that open without having aroused any advance interest (no "names" are
connected with them), that behave rather peculiarly while
the curtain is up (perhaps a woman keeps saying, "Oh, heck,
there's that telephone again," although the telephone hasn't
rung at all), and that vanish after a night or two without
having penetrated the public consciousness in the least. A
reviewer's image of the contemporary theater may in large
part, or at least in substantial part, be composed of just such
experiences: they belong to his habits of thought when he is
thinking about the stage. For the public at large such experiences do not exist at all.

There are several strange things to be said about this dramatic underground. One is that it represents the work of new playwrights. Broadway itself always offers us at least a few new writers each season, but the real invasion by newcomers takes place off-Broadway and it is an invasion that generally fails without having established so much as a beachhead. The writer announces himself, betrays himself as the evening progresses, and then backs away without having left even the minutest mark upon history.

The other characteristic of this half-world is the determination of dozens and dozens of plodding young enthusiasts to make us hear something more than the glib conversational exchanges that so often echo the banter of life without seeming to notice that beneath the banter there are bruises and contusions. These eager adventurers are on the hunt for overtones, for meanings beyond what is merely being said, for the philosophical implications that may be hidden in our ordinary conduct and deserve to be hung on the line for airing. They really do mean to enrich drama, even at the risk of impoverishing themselves.

Granting the genuineness of the effort, is there any one thing most such innovators are doing wildly wrong just now, is there any one patent misconception that might account for so much quick failure? I think there may be. Those of us who spend a great deal of time attending first performances of plays that rarely play third performances have become accustomed to a certain kind of "overtone." Let's say that a young man is making love to his boss's wife, on a bench at a bus station. In the middle of his declaration, "I adore you," he sneezes violently. He doesn't have a cold, nor is he sitting in a draft. The sneeze is there to make his passion seem routine, artificial, insincere. Or let's say that two men who have virtually sealed themselves from the world in a loft obtain their morning newspapers by reaching for them without opening the door. The base of the door is an irregular scallop, a ripple of free space. The door has not been cut into for this purpose, or for any purpose that is spoken of. It is shaped in this way in order to say to us, the audience, that no sealed room can be absolutely sealed: the world will slip in somewhere.

Or, to go back to that woman who is constantly answering a telephone that hasn't rung—when she isn't answering the telephone she is feverishly playing cards with a man who isn't there, begging him not to let her win. She is neither insane nor the victim of mild hallucinations: she explains to her daughter, quite intelligently, that her card partner isn't there. She is simply frustrated, and, at the end of the play, can tick off the theme in so many words: her companions "are only shadows—inventions against our incredible loneliness."

Now not one of these contrivances is unclear: we get the point and are not the least bit interested in charging the author with obscurity. What is the matter with them all is that they are not truly interesting: they are bald, flat, and dull. For they are overtones bounding about in a vacuum, overtones that have not come from tones. There has been no initial happening from which a secondary significance might be derived; the secondary significance has been handed us right off, and is all there is to the play.

Perhaps I can make this a bit plainer by mentioning an odd, though interesting, instance of parallelism I happened to come across in the literary review *Odyssey*. Charles Chaplin's work was being compared to that of a Peruvian poet, and in the course of the discussion much was made of a fondly remembered passage from *The Gold Rush*, that in which the snowbound tramp ingeniously devises for himself a Thanksgiving dinner by boiling one of his shoes: the shoelaces become spaghetti, the boot nails become chicken bones, and so on.

In this sequence essayist Xavier Abril has discovered a good many allusive symbols. The transformation of shoelaces into spaghetti is, by implication, nothing less than Christ's multiplication of the loaves, just as a later passage in the film becomes a new parable of the Last Supper. "The artist confirms the value of the old myth by adapting its concept, adjusting it to the social truth of our era without repeating, as in Holy Week, the tired picture of the outworn legend." The sequences offer us, above and beyond their narrative value, intimations of the "tragic and miraculous."

Farfetched? As one who has, in his lifetime, seen *The Gold Rush* some ten or fifteen times, I must confess that not once in the ten or fifteen times did these overtones occur to me. Still, the suggestion is instructive, not for what Chaplin may or may not have had in mind, but for what he certainly did not do.

Whatever was in his head when he was making the film, he did not offer us implication in place of plot. First things came first. First, an actual man was actually hungry in an actual place. Driven by a real hunger, he was forced to consider the real possibilities. Having considered them, he acted—fantastically, perhaps, but not without cause. In the course of acting, he was marvelously and immediately entertaining: there was never any need to look beyond the business of the spaghetti and the chicken bones for the substance of the moment, because the substance of the human condition was being so deeply, so thoroughly, so satisfyingly demonstrated. Secondary significances? Now you can name any you like, find any you look for. The basic and essential work, the creation of a hard core of happening in time and space, had been done.

The man who offers us his afterthoughts, his symbolic conclusions, his deductions from an event without first taking pains to display the event in all its natural fullness and self-justification is a man chattering on and on about someone we have never met, or a place we have never been to. As a matter of fact, the very same parallel which critic Abril has plucked from a film of so long ago appears in a contemporary work for the Theater of the Absurd. In Arrabal's *The Automobile Graveyard* there is again a figurative Last Supper, a meal of peanuts hastily consumed by three jazz musicians gathered about an abandoned crate. But we do not know the musicians except as self-conscious prototypes, we do not understand the pressures that account for their haste (why are the police after them, and what do the police signify?), we are given no real reason for their need to dine exclusively on peanuts. What they do is in itself gratuitous, a mere accommodation of an idea revolving in the outer space of the author's head.

In a sense, too many of our new playwrights are in too much of a hurry. They want the meaning of a meal before the meal has been served, as they want to take the measure of a man before the man has been encouraged to breathe.

The Ambiguity of the Theater of the Absurd

Oddly enough, ambiguity is a quality that has often been admired in the theater. It is not a quality anyone can let alone, even when he professes to admire it: confronted with it, the most understanding scholar and the least subtle member of the audience will instantly begin to wrestle with it in an effort to pull apart its superimposed uncertainties and reduce them to simple, separated propositions. The character of Hamlet, we say, is ambiguous. Is Hamlet a man of action or a man incapable of action? More than three hundred years of grappling have not resolved the issue; neither have they quieted the demon that keeps urging us to try to resolve it. The implications of *King Lear* are ambiguous: whose fault is it that Lear's children treat him as they do? Alceste, Molière's misanthrope, is ambiguous: in demanding that society behave more honorably than it does, is he right, is he ridiculous, or is he both right and ridiculous? Even the forthright Antigone, useful as she may have proved in our own time as a symbol of private conscience versus the totalitarian state, is not so uncompromisingly defined in her Greek beginnings; as Sophocles drew her, doesn't a shadow of intractable personal pride fall across, and faintly corrupt, her defiance of Creon, and isn't Creon's position in some degree defensible? We do probe as though it were essential to us to know the answers.

Yet even as we probe, and cannot stop probing, we recognize that the very mystery that bedevils us, and has so far defeated us, is in some measure responsible for the greatness of the play. We grasp what T. S. Eliot is saying when he suggests that Shakespeare was never able to discover an "objective correlative" for the emotions he felt about the Hamlet he was drawing, and we find the coined phrase useful to us in our other literary work. But insofar as Mr. Eliot's analysis suggests that *Hamlet* is, as a consequence, something less than a fully realized play, we will have none of his reasoning. We have an experience of *Hamlet* that tells us it is fully realized; even as we return to our habit of gnawing at the text to see whether or not we can dispel its apparent inconsistencies, we know ourselves to be fully satisfied. It is curious that so many of the plays we elevate to the very highest rank should have this eternal elusiveness about them, and more curious still that recognized masterpieces which speak their minds more openly—as *Macbeth* does, as *Tartuffe* does—should seem, in their clarity, less substantial. Clarity is, after all, a virtue. How do we dare, then, cling so passionately to, and reserve our deepest homage for, these several-faced conundrums from which an ultimate clarity is presumably absent?

We dare for several reasons, no doubt. One is that we sense an ultimate clarity in them, an intuited clarity of the core, that untouchable center—infinitesimal and red-hot—which sends its rays outward in intangible wave lengths to lave, with the same slant-of-light, a half-dozen surfaces which in themselves appear irreconcilable. This is a great deal like saying we "know" an intimate friend whose oddities of behavior baffle everyone else; our intimacy, so existential as to constitute a breathing in and out together, has enabled us to give assent to what we could not possibly have named. Another reason is that plays which can be known only as friends are known—by radar, through confusion compounded—seem to us closer to the conditions of life. Here we discover in the concrete what we could never have defined in the abstract; we stand face to face with a multidimensional reality across which a complex of veils is constantly playing, throwing now this side and now that into surprising relief. The dance of veils, with its illuminating relief work, implies a solid behind it; the combined sensations of evanescence and solidity correspond nicely to the yes-and-no, now-you-see-it-and-now-you-don't lives we lead. The degree to which a play is ambiguous, but knowable in and through its ambiguity, is often the measure of our affection and respect for it.

In what sense is this also true, or should it be true, of that most deliberately ambiguous of all theaters, the avant-garde form that has come to be called the Theater of the Absurd? Certainly the plays of Samuel Beckett, Eugene Ionesco, Harold Pinter, N. F. Simpson, and Arrabal have not at once capitalized upon our instinctive admiration for the indeterminate, though satisfying, image. Mr. Pinter's *The Caretaker* was given an impeccable production on Broadway, not off, and met with an enthusiasm in the press that ought to have guaranteed it substantial audiences for a lengthy run. The production did not find those audiences; the preinterested attended for a few moderately lively weeks, though never in sufficient numbers to fill the theater to capacity, and the houses dwindled thereafter as rapidly as though the work had been received as a near-failure. Such examples of the form as have achieved "long" runs—Jean Genet's *The Balcony*, and the double bill of Samuel Beckett's *Krapp's Last*

Tape and Edward Albee's *The Zoo Story*—have generally done so in off-Broadway playhouses which restrict their capacities to 299 seats. Nor can the relative reluctance of audiences to expose themselves to a new ambiguity be attributed to the strangeness of being asked to accept a duality of meanings. *Hamlet* and *Antigone* were instantly successful; whatever was ambiguous about them did not operate as a barrier.

At the same time, and just as certainly, the form cannot be dismissed as a mere temporary aberration, irrelevant to the atmosphere in which audiences as well as playwrights live: it has already demonstrated too much fecundity for that. In a few years—ten at the most—it has not only captured the loyalty of talented writers during their most productive time of life, it has leapfrogged its way from country to country and from continent to continent so energetically as to suggest that a degree of universality is in it. It is apparently not to be shaken off as easily as German expressionism was shaken off, or as the theatrical explorations of an e. e. cummings were shaken off, forty years ago. It is a theater of ambiguity with the power to proliferate, though not with the power to compel the large-scale assent that has sometimes welcomed a degree of obscurity in the past. Allowing for the fact that genius commands where talent moves tentatively, and acknowledging the fact that Beckett makes no claim to be Sophocles, is there nevertheless some essential difference between the uncertainties we grant *The Misanthrope* and the uncertainties we resist in *The Caretaker*?

The Theater of the Absurd, which is likely to retain that generic label now that Martin Esslin has effectively formalized it in the first full-length study anyone has made of a fairly diversified school of playmaking, is so thoroughly soaked in ambiguity as to seem, upon acquaintance, composed of nothing else. The mathematical formulas upon which the universe may be thought to rest, numbers themselves, are ambiguous in Ionesco's *The Lesson*:

". . . Here are three matches. And here is another one, that makes four. Now watch carefully—we have four matches. I take one away, now how many are left?"

"Five. If three and one make four, four and one make five."

The words with which we describe to one another our knowledge of the universe are ambiguous in nearly all such plays, as they are in this Joyce-inspired passage from Beckett's *Waiting for Godot:*

". . . the practise of sports such as tennis football running cycling swimming flying floating riding gliding conating camogie skating tennis of all kinds dying flying sports of all sorts autumn summer winter winter tennis of all kinds hockey of all sorts penicillin and succedanea in a word I resume . . ."

Whenever we wish to use words as tools of reason, as soldiers in a syllogism designed to prove one or another proposition about the universe, the proof also becomes ambiguous. Arrabal's *The Automobile Graveyard:*

"What a brain! And you know how to prove things, like the big shots?"

"Yeah, I have a special method for that. Ask me to prove something for you, something real hard."

"All right, prove me that giraffes go up in elevators."

"Let's see. Giraffes go up in elevators . . . because they go up in elevators."

"God, that was great! . . . Suppose I asked you to prove giraffes *don't* go up in elevators."

"That's easy. I just prove the same thing, but the other way around."

If the insubstantiality of digits, words, syntax, and logic tend to make all communication between people at the very least ambiguous, people are ambiguous as well. An old couple, married or not married, childless or parents of a son, speak constantly at cross-purposes in Ionesco's *The Chairs:*

". . . Where is my mamma? I don't have a mamma anymore."
"I am your wife, I'm the one who is your mamma now."
"That's not true, I'm an orphan, hi, hi."
"My pet, my orphan, dworfan, worfan, morphan, orphan . . . We had one son . . . he's gone away . . . he was seven years old, the age of reason, I called after him: 'My son, my child, my son, my child.' . . . He didn't even look back . . ."
"Alas, no . . . no, we've never had a child. . . . I'd hoped for a son . . ."

Critical actions performed by the characters may mean one thing or another. The climax of Beckett's *Happy Days* is reached when a husband, in frock coat and top hat, crawls on hands and knees to the foot of a mound of sand in which his wife is buried to her neck. A revolver is "conspicuous to her right on mound." With painful effort, the husband attempts to claw his way up the mound. "Oh I say, this is terrific!" cries the wife, certain he is coming to offer her one last kiss. During a pause, doubt crosses her mind. "Is it me you're after, Willie . . . or is it something else?" She does not look at the revolver; Willie does not reach the top of the mound; the play ends without our knowing whether Willie wished to kill himself or kiss his wife (or kill his wife).

The new play of ambiguity is apt to take place in "A bare interior" or on a stage possessing "No decor" during "A late evening in the future." The printed instructions to the stage director may be optional: "The clock strikes as much as it likes." There is ambiguity before the curtain has gone up, ambiguity in rehearsal: "He either kisses or does not kiss Mrs. Smith."

Now the open meanings, the choices among several or many possible meanings, we are cataloguing here are obviously different from the fluid ambiguities of character and

narrative implication we so highly prize in certain plays of
the past. At first sight the difference may seem a mere matter
of quantity. Hamlet possesses a few ambiguities that are titil-
lating in a world composed mainly of plain statement; here
everything is unnamed, down to the last detail of stage management, and nothing is at any time defined, spelled out,
clothed, made plain.

Curiously this is not so. While vast portions of the familiar world are being steadily atomized in the avant-garde play,
and while the familiar tools that help us deal with it are being cumulatively mocked, certain aspects of our residence in
the universe are being spelled out in such bold, crude letter-
ing, are being cast in concrete in such a dense and literal
way, as to make the dramatic statement seem close to simple-
minded. For instance, environment may generally be left
vague. But the effect which a given playwright thinks environment may have on us is not left vague at all. It is bill-postered.
Suppose it is a playwright's intention to show us that, no matter how free the human animal thinks it is, the human animal
is irretrievably earth-bound. Is there any ambiguity, or even
any slight subtlety, in presenting us with a woman choked
in sand up to the neck? It would be difficult to conceive a less
elusive or more literal illustration of thought. Suppose one
wishes to dwell upon the ruthless discard into which the aged
or maimed are thrown. In *Endgame,* Beckett deposits an elderly couple in ash bins, downstage left. In *La Parodie,* Arthur
Adamov causes street cleaners to sweep one of his principal
figures, who has been run over, into the garbage. Plainness
could not speak better for itself. Suppose a dramatist wishes
to convey to us the notion that our once-efficient world has
broken down. When he composes his stage of a disconnected
stove, a frame without a picture in it, a rusty lawn mower, a
collection of empty suitcases, a rolled-up rug, yesterday's yel-
lowed newspapers, a toaster with a broken plug, and then
covers the litter over with a noisily leaking roof—as Pinter

has done in *The Caretaker*—he is leaving very, very little to chance.

Ironically, there is far less ambiguity—and, indeed, far less complexity—in each of these illustrations than there would have been if identical attitudes had been incorporated into much more conventional plays. It is possible to suggest that a woman is earth-bound even while she is moving rapidly and gracefully about an expansive living room; as it is possible to imply that the elderly are being discarded even when they are being coddled or that the world is showing a fissure although the kitchen sink is functioning. We should not see the "truth" as readily, of course; we should have to dig beneath the surface for what is not at all obvious; catching a hint of the interior content, we should have to be willing to continue to look at the play on two levels, although it is generally the Theater of the Absurd that asks for attention at two levels; from the dramatist's point of view, the play of concealed comment, of secret texture contradicted by surface texture, is much harder to bring off—its very activity is, in its nature and in the manner of nature, so ambiguous. By contrast, some aspects of avant-garde drama seem rigidly fixed, not fluid but frozen.

There are other things that might lead one to question the degree of ambiguity actually present in what is sometimes called antidrama. The length of the plays is one of them, the recurrence of themes another. Logically speaking, whatever is truly ambiguous ought to require a longer time for its development than whatever is truly plain. Either "yes" or "no" can be said more rapidly than "yes and no." The exploration of shifting colorations, of faces looked at now in this perspective and now in that, of meanings so chameleon-like that they can only be identified after they have been seen against every kind of foliage, should take longer to record than a snapshot does. Yet it is the avant-garde play that most often seems a snapshot. Some examples of the genre take as little as eight minutes to play. Though Beckett, Ionesco, Pinter, and Genet have all written full-length plays, only those of Genet seem to demand the running time allotted to a conventional evening in the theater. Most of the work of most practitioners of the Theater of the Absurd is either in the one-act form or otherwise marked by brevity; playwrights are notably slow, in some cases confessedly reluctant, to move beyond miniaturism. Urged on, they have developed a somewhat standard defense. "What *is* a full-length play?" becomes the riposte. "A play has achieved its full length when it has said what it has to say," even if it has said what it has to say in twenty or twenty-four minutes. Some of this clinging to the short form may be due to the newness of the genre and to an understandable fear that experimentation, in a too rapid advance, may betray itself by borrowing from conventional sources; some of it, though probably not much of it, may be due to a conviction that audiences are not yet supple enough to be able to endure prolonged exposure to persistent ambiguity.

What the tendency toward brevity cannot help but suggest, however, is that the premise upon which the play rests possesses neither the complexity nor the many-sidedness requiring an extended examination under a variety of lights and shadows. Prolonged investigation of the material, instead of thickening its substance by discovering fresh layers, would apparently lead only to dangerous repetition. (Thus Albee's longish *American Dream*, interesting as it is, is not more interesting than the very short *The Sandbox*, which it resembles; it runs the perfectly obvious risk of belaboring a theme that has earlier been delicately, and adequately, intimated.) Somehow the new ambiguity is an ambiguity that leaves relatively little room for maneuver; somewhere inside it is a knot that resists being unraveled.

Equally strange in a form professedly devoted to an infinity of meanings is the prevalence of a handful of repeated themes. The difficulty, or the impossibility, of communication between

197

people is demonstrated so often—in *The Zoo Story*, in *The Caretaker*, in nearly any play by Ionesco—as to become a badge of the genre. The encrusting effect of conformity, of habitual response in thought and behavior, of automaton-like devotion to false ideals, is not the special insight of *Rhinoceros* and *The Apple;* it appears so frequently that it constitutes, in itself, a kind of conformity.

Closely related to the repeated theme of encrustation is the equally repeated theme of loss of identity. People make so many conventional gestures that they forget, or never have time to discover, what a truly personal gesture might be: "You don't know who you are until you're dead." And when the interior emptiness that is loss of identity is coupled with the exterior pressure of encrustation—when our habits and the universe harden about us—we find ourselves in the "zero" world that Samuel Beckett creates again and again (as do his imitators). Imprisonment in a chair, in a room, in a sandbank becomes the familiar point of departure; the act of waiting, for nothing that ever arrives or for something that proves not to have been worth waiting for when it does arrive, becomes the familiar line of tension; either gibberish or a view of the void becomes the not unexpected summation of the essentially static situation. Having seen Beckett's *Endgame,* and having watched an old man climb to a window, put a telescope to his eye, and report that he sees "Nothing . . . nothing," one is entirely prepared to follow a young man as he goes to a window, puts a telescope to his eye, and reports that "there's nothing out there to see" in the youthful Arthur L. Kopit's *Oh Dad, Poor Dad, Mamma's Hung You in the Closet and I'm Feelin' So Sad.* Echoes scamper from play to play, and sometimes coalesce to make a single play a kind of counting-house of themes. But when one has counted off the problem of communication, the problem of encrustation, the problem of identity, and the problem of the surrounding void, one is surprised to discover he has more than five fingers left over.

There are obvious reasons why these should be special themes for our time: what is puzzling is that there should be so few of them in a theater that has carefully arranged itself for a maximum flexibility, for an endless openness to overtone.

Perhaps it is the combination of these last two odd qualities—shortness of form and familiarity of point—that creates a further impression of essential literalness rather than far-ranging ambiguity in much of the work of the avant-garde. The Theater of the Absurd is generally theater in a state of shock; it also means, by its methods, to shock those who attend it. But there are occasions when its shock is not the bewilderment of the adult confronted by too much that is eluding him but the shock of a child who has just now noticed the obvious and is shrilly calling it to our attention in brief, agitated, reiterated rhythms. For example, the excited insistence that words lack absolute meaning takes on, after a while, just such a tantrum tone. When one is first exposed to a play in which the words slip and slide into one another, blurring their identities until they begin to lose touch with any possible referents, the verbal sleight-of-hand may provoke mild amusement. When one has been exposed to dozens of such plays, and heard the shocked discovery announced dozens of times in unabated wide-eyed clamor, a reaction may set in. "Yes, yes, of course," one is apt to respond, "it is true that words are arbitrary and artificial constructs, mere mechanical agreements, which do not in any absolute sense either contain or describe their referents. They are at best conventional, and, lacking an unbreakable link with the realities they are meant to signify, they are always unstable. But hasn't everyone always known that, and why so much fuss just now?" If the arbitrariness and instability of words had not always been perfectly evident, no one would ever have been tempted to make a pun. A pun, of course, is mankind's playful admission that the words he makes use of are notoriously slippery. It is doubtful, indeed, that without this awareness anyone could have conceived the possibility called poetry. For poetry makes its whole effect out of the absence of an absolute value in words: if the word "fire" signified only and absolutely the specific chemical activity of oxidation, Yeats could not so much as write "a fire was in my head." Puns and poetry are discoveries of the dawn, not of late last night, and they remind us that what many new plays trumpet in headlines is not in any real sense news.

As we begin to notice that the proposition is not altogether novel, we notice something else: the statement of the proposition is not really ambiguous. If a playwright were to write a sentence that seemed to mean one intelligible thing and actually meant another, *that* would be ambiguous. But if he writes an unintelligible sentence in order to say that words are unintelligible, he is being utterly straightforward. The line "such caca, such caca, such caca, such caca, such caca, such caca, such caca, such caca, such caca" does not give us a choice of meanings. It confines us to the single, simple, unsupple assertion that there is no meaning.

Thus, though we may feel the world slipping from beneath our feet as we first make acquaintance with the Theater of the Absurd, not everything in the form is fluid. What is being said and done is often being said and done absolutely: a woman is absolutely earth-bound (we are given no opportunity to believe otherwise), words are absolutely without meaningful content (we are not led from an illusion of content to a discovery of vacuousness but are handed the vacuousness right off). What is said and done absolutely can, as a rule, be said and done quickly: plays tend to be short. And because absolute assertion tends to close in on itself, instead of putting out tentacles toward possible alternatives, it does not tend to mate with other subject matter but to repeat itself: a few propositions, close to geometrical postulates, are repeated from play to play.

What sort of theater is this that it should, in spite of what we feel to be intangible about it, insist upon a fixity, a precision that is almost bald, at certain of its extremities? It is, in essence, a philosopher's theater, rather than a poet's, for it is the philosopher who needs to make as rigid as possible the external terms in which he clothes his thought. Because the philosopher's thought is insubstantial—in the sense that it is an immaterial idea darting this way and that in his head—he is under great pressure to freeze the formulas in which he attempts to record his thought as absolutely, and as unambiguously, as possible. Each term in his hypothesis must mean one thing and no other; the center of his syllogism dare not be undistributed; he does not wish to be guilty of "loose thought." The philosopher deals in defined, and hence hardened, concepts.

The poet, historically, does not work in this way. He begins not with an immaterial concept but with a material fragment of nature, with something embodied in a ready-made musculature of its own. He starts with something concrete, however mysterious its inner sources of energy may be to him. Because it is concrete and has its own sources of energy he is able to throw over it a loose-fitting robe, a garment that partially conceals and partially reveals. The looseness will suggest something of the form beneath it; but it will not constrict it, not bind it, not keep it from moving under its own laws and displaying itself in its very freedom.

A philosopher's theater cannot let its terms be uncertain: these must be fiercely exact so as to lead us, without error, toward the nub of the play's thought, toward that interior pinpoint upon which its theorem rests. We move by plain paths —along which discarded people repose in ash cans and earthbound women are bound in earth—to the pith of the matter. But, much to our consternation, it is precisely here that we come face to face with a genuine ambiguity, perhaps with the one true ambiguity of the Theater of the Absurd.

What—behind the bold assertions of the surface—do the

plays mean? The philosopher-playwright has spoken bluntly of the slipperiness of words and of the binding force of encrustation, and we have heard him; but what is it he wishes to say about these things, what is his attitude toward them? Two obvious and incompatible answers present themselves at once.

One is that we have foolishly allowed ourselves to fall into our present state and need to be jolted out of it. We have let our hearts harden, and have not tried to communicate. We have used words carelessly, or without awareness of their inherent imperfection, and have frustrated our efforts at communication. We have permitted our habits, and our conventional social responses, to form crusts about us; we conform to a mold without realizing that it is a mere mold. Behaving by rote, speaking impersonally, and failing to engage in relationships that will help define us, we have forgotten who we are, mislaid our identities. We had better look at these things—hard—before the world breaks down; only by admitting to them, and hopefully correcting them, can we keep the world from breaking down.

The other answer that can just as readily be given is that, so far from being responsible for what has happened to us, we are just now waking up to the fact that nothing we can do, or nothing we ever have done, is capable in the least of affecting the essentially irresponsible, incoherent, and immobile nature of the universe. However things are, that is the way they *are*, and forever will be. Communication is impossible; we are fools to think we might achieve it with our pitiful tools. Encrustation is inevitable; it was in the beginning, and the sand can only drift higher. Identity is an illusion: it exists only on the driver's license that is somewhere in our wallet, and the wallet is lost. It is no use knocking one's head against the universe to prove that one has a head; the universe is not there. The situation cannot be rectified, only recognized.

The avant-garde play of the present time does not give one

or the other of these answers: it gives both, or neither. The two positions are maintained, or refused, simultaneously. This ambivalence is not simply something we feel as we sit in the playhouse, an ambivalence that might be resolved if only our minds were quicker or the playwright clearer. It is in the work; in some documented cases it is in the playwright. Esslin, for instance, quotes Ionesco to just such cross-effect. Ionesco has explained, on one occasion, that the "clichés, empty formulas and slogans" of social life and social thought must be "relentlessly split apart in order to find the living sap beneath." Not only is there a living sap to be found, but finding it and naming it is within the competence of man and his tools for communication: it is merely "difficult to make oneself understood, not absolutely impossible."

On another occasion Ionesco has carefully defined the meaning of his play *The Chairs*. "The subject of the play," he tells us, is "the absence of people, the absence of the emperor, the absence of God, the absence of matter, the unreality of the world, metaphysical emptiness. The theme of the play is *nothingness*." Mr. Esslin, on his own, concludes that *The Lesson* is "a demonstration of the basic impossibility of communication."

It is the yes-no of these two mutually contradictory positions, I think, that most often unsettles us in the theater, sometimes whetting our appetites for more and more of the destructive work that is being done, sometimes defeating us utterly. So long as we seem to see the destructive work as a clearing away of rotted superstructures, with the promise or at least the possibility that new foundations may be laid, the appetite surges. It is not merely time for new theater forms, and away with the tired ones. It is time for examinations of conscience, and the exploration of fresh terrain, at every turn of our lives. We cannot afford to be echoes now: we must know what we *do* think, and why. We are aware that we stand at the edge of an abyss; the play that reminds us not only of the abyss but of the fact that we are standing there, *alive,* still capable of acting meaningfully if we will only stop acting mechanically, is a play we are apt to give ear to.

Listening with this one ear, we seem to hear prospects for the future. Mr. Esslin's hope that "some of the elements of the Theater of the Absurd can be combined with those of the conventional well-made play to produce a very fruitful fusion of two different traditions" stems, in part, from the hint that the avant-garde may be functioning as a wrecking crew in order to open the ground to rebuilding. The same note was struck by producer Richard Barr in announcing his plans for a festival of Absurd plays. These plays offer "a distorted picture of a world that has gone mad" in order to "break the old mold of language and narrative sequence in the theater and to emphasize its mystery and truth."

It is this same hopeful instinct that leads one to pursue an obviously honest writer along paths that one fears may be blind alleys. Let us say that Harold Pinter wishes to speak— not in a play but in a short story—of the chilling abstractness and indeterminateness of our lives, of the ease with which identity blurs and roles are reversed. And let us say that Mr. Pinter is such a conscientious craftsman that he will not only try to find a narrative situation in which indeterminateness may be felt as something actual but will also try to use words in such a way that their own abstractness reinforces the abstractness of the situation. Form and content are going to fuse. Now one may believe, as I do, that the natural lair of poetry is deep in the concrete, and that the effort to strip dimension, solidity, the fact of flesh from it is an effort to turn the sound of music back into the silence of mathematics. One cannot know how far Mr. Pinter can push his possibly perverse search. But neither can one know what unlooked-for, elliptical results may come, quite profitably, from using what are said to be the wrong tools. Because Mr. Pinter is in earnest, and because the "right" tools are patently rusty, one reads on, fascinated:

When we began, I allowed him intervals. He expressed no desire for these, nor any objection. And so I took it upon myself to adjudge their allotment and duration. They were not consistent, but took alternation with what I must call the progress of our talks. With the chalk I kept I marked the proposed times upon the blackboard, before the beginning of a session, for him to examine, and to offer any criticism if he felt so moved. But he made no objection, nor, during our talks, expressed any desire for a break in the proceedings. However, as I suspected they might benefit both of us, I allowed him intervals.

The story proves to be readable; its conclusion, a few pages and one dissolved world later, is most effective.

Still, one gropes one's way through a world that has grown faceless—a world in which there is not so much "chalk" or "blackboard" as there are "times," "intervals," "allotment and duration"—on the assumption that space is being emptied out so that one day it will be clean enough to receive and house a face again. The assumption is not necessarily valid. Mr. Pinter may be saying that there are no faces, only "intervals" of a certain "duration" in which "proceedings" take place.

We may be looking into the *nothingness* Ionesco asks for, or part way into it. If this is the case, all of our talk and all of our wistful dreaming about a meaningful future that is to come when the present debris has been blasted away—whether in the theater or in life—is nonsense. There is no future. There is not even a present. In order to force us to face up to the "truth" that the present is not present and that meaning is not meaningful, Ionesco insists that in any production of *The Chairs* "the invisible elements must be more and more clearly present, more and more real (to give unreality to reality one must give reality to the unreal), until the point is reached— inadmissible, unacceptable to the reasoning mind—when the unreal elements speak and move." At this point, "Nothingness can be heard, is made concrete."

Should this point be reached in actual production, no appetite can stir: there is *nothing* to stir it. If the audience mind has successfully joined the playwright in an act of cerebration which denies the value of the act of cerebration, if it agrees that the playwright has finally communicated the impossibility of communicating, it has indeed reached "zero," the ultimate impasse. It has contradicted the equipment that permits it to recognize contradictions, it has denied the premises by which it can know premises, it has canceled out the possibility of making any sort of response because there is nothing to respond to and the very act of responding would be gratuitous, irrelevant, insane. When and if the play achieves Ionesco's stated objectives for it, the audience mind can only clap down over itself, subside into black silence and never be heard from again. When the play does not achieve this objective, it must be dismissed, of course, as a failure: any response it now provokes must be negative, irritated, dissatisfied.

A question thrusts its way in here. To the best of my knowledge, no one has yet come newly mindless from such a performance. *Can* the play that means to arrive at nothingness succeed? *Is* it possible to communicate the impossibility of communicating? If the experience cannot, in fact, be realized, then the play is unproducible to begin with. There are indications within Ionesco's own work that this is the case, and that Ionesco—in his interior consistency—is aware of the problem. When he writes in a stage direction that "the clock strikes as much as it likes," he is waiving the possibility of any two performances of the play producing exactly the same effect; he is saying that a defined goal is unreachable. But he goes beyond this waiver. When he writes that "He either kisses or does not kiss Mrs. Smith," he is abandoning the possibility that the play, as he wrote it, can be produced at all. For in production the director and actors must choose one of the two alternatives: in performance Mrs. Smith will either be kissed or she will not be kissed. Performance in the flesh, in the concrete, does not allow for the act and the nonact simultaneously. The "identity of contraries" in which the form of antidrama frequently confesses belief is not realizable on the stage. To the degree that the playwright wishes to illustrate that contraries are identical, he is helpless, bound to fail; he mocks himself, and calls attention to the absurdity of attempting to be truly absurd, by writing stage directions that can never be followed.

But there is an escape hatch. The play is performed anyway, with Mrs. Smith either being kissed or not being kissed. The playwright's reached-for nothingness is being compromised by somethingness, just as in Beckett's "zero" world it is only the characters, looking off stage, who see nothing; on the stage we always see something, even if it is only a character who claims to see nothing. It is in the indecisiveness here, at the heart of the play, that we feel, face, and wrestle with ambiguity. We do not know what the playwright means to say, or what we are meant to think, or how we are meant to respond. If the playwright means to say that nothingness *is*, and that contraries are identical, he is not showing us that. If he means to say that we are behaving contrarily, and so seducing ourselves toward loss of identity, then that is another matter —but does he? The play hovers between two poles, seems to embrace both and neither. It refuses to reveal the content of its core either because it cannot (in the case of a genuine belief in nothingness) or because it will not (perhaps the playwright who means to clear ground against the future is fearful of seeming too affirmative).

Faced with an actual ambiguity at the core, our responses can only be ambiguous. When they become more strongly defined than this, as they sometimes do, it is through emotional impulse rather than through intellectual grasp. Sometimes we come from an Absurd play thoroughly enraged, perhaps because we suspect that we have been flirting with nothingness that is meant to be genuine and is not, perhaps because we feel we have been victimized by untalented opportunists who have made the irrational features of the form an excuse for self-indulgence. And sometimes we come away somewhat pleased, having been touched by the enforced death of the grandmother in *The Sandbox* or by the grotesque arms stretched around a boxful of memories in *Krapp's Last Tape*, or having found ourselves unexpectedly moved to laughter by the butcher's ever-growing skyscraper (one entire floor devoted to "used meat") in *The Red Eye of Love*. In these cases, however, we are trusting a response without quite being able to justify it, going on faith: we say to ourselves that *because* we responded in this way or that, the play itself must mean this or that. In one sense, this is a good enough way to react to any art form (it is spontaneous, unprejudiced, uncluttered by excess baggage), though ideally one might wish to feel emotionally and intellectually satisfied at one and the same time. But in another sense, and because it contains a blind spot, it can be enormously treacherous. For instance, I now cannot be certain what I think of *Krapp's Last Tape* because I have discovered that the gesture that moved me most and seemed to me of greatest significance in performance—the stretching of those arms about the very memories Krapp had spent an hour reviling—seems to have been an invention of the director and does not appear in the published text.

Anyone who has listened to the laughter that greets so many avant-garde plays knows that it is, for the most part, an insecure laughter. Titters come from here and there in the auditorium; not many minds are reached at once. One can hear the uncertainty: *was* that last line or bit of business intended to be funny in its grotesquerie, or was it an open door to Hell as chilling as any Hieronymus Bosch ever designed? If I laugh, will I be advertising myself as a sophisticate, a man in the know, or as an uneasy boor, a man incapable of reading the handwriting on the stage? In general, the writers of anti-drama are eager to encourage—in their comments about their work—the thought that laughter is in order. Nothing is commoner than the suggestion that what is happening on the stage bears some relation to the methods of the Marx Brothers or of old-fashioned burlesque comedians, just as there is a Spanish avant-garde play entitled *Buster Keaton's Walk*. The hopeful comparison is not new. Twenty-five years ago W. H. Auden and Christopher Isherwood wrote a stage direction for their *Ascent of F6* asking that the principals "jump on each other's shoulders . . . and behave in general like the Marx Brothers," and it may be significant that the direction occurs, in this early and most interesting effort to reimagine the possibilities of theater, at the very moment that the play falls apart. For the invitation to respond to what is merely irrational as we would to the Marx Brothers is never wholly accepted; the parallel is simply not acceptable. No thunderclap of laughter unifies the audience, instantly and unselfconsciously, as it does when Groucho is at his best, and for a very clear reason. The Marx Brothers were newsboys of the incongruous, waving headlines that shouted their misbehavior. But the delights of incongruity are only possible in a congruent world: there must always be a recognized pattern for Groucho or his brothers to violate. The elegant Margaret Dumont was such a pattern, standing starched and indignant in defense of all the proprieties while Groucho behaved so improperly. The humor is in the irreverence for what is reasonable, the fingers snapped at a world essentially coherent and stable.

The Theater of the Absurd, in its central ambiguity, is without such an anchor. There is nothing in it that may be regarded as coherent and stable, no pattern of expectation from which a delinquent may depart, caring not a fig for it. Were Margaret Dumont to enter this world, she, too, would have to be treated as unrooted, irrelevant, unreal. Now, instead of having one delightfully displaced person in collision with another who is clearly placed, we are confronted with simultaneous instabilities. Between them, they are incapable of producing a firm comic effect because there is nothing in their relationship that is incongruous. Whatever they do to or with one another is merely arbitrary, as it is arbitrary for a Fire Chief, in *The Bald Soprano*, to enter a living room in which he is neither expected nor unexpected in order to tell a joke that is not a joke.

Irrelevance is funny because it is irrelevant *to* something. Arbitrariness, lacking a point of departure, produces a mixed, timid, tentative response. If there is something disingenuous about the antidramatist's hinting that we may well respond as we do to the Marx Brothers, if he often has the air of asking for an openness of reaction he has not in fact earned, it is because he is not prepared to be open with us about the nature of what we are watching. We see the surface gesture of comedy, and begin to try to laugh; but we are not certain that behind the gesture there is the substance of comedy, and so rein our laughter, waiting for clarity. If the author is razing the present world in order to rebuild, then his purpose is satirical and hilarity may be appropriate. If, on the other hand, his purpose is to deny substance altogether, which means in passing that he must deny the substance of comedy, then laughter can only be the frightened and hysterical response of an idiot. It is often assumed, especially by the uninitiated, that those who laugh gaily at the Theater of the Absurd are those who understand it and that those who sit glumly in its presence are those who cannot for the life of them make out what is going on. The reverse may well be the case, indeed is bound to be the case if the dramatist is genuinely bent on achieving "nothingness." In this eventuality the man who sits in despair is the man who understands, and the man who laughs readily is the man who is missing the point.

But just now it is not possible to make such distinctions, any more than it is possible to find an audience responding with any degree of uniformity to the Absurd symbols set before it. For at the moment nearly every playwright of the school is keeping his own counsel as to the ultimate significance of his ultimate symbol, as to the precise intention of his philosophical thought. In the innermost recess of the play, there is not so much a bedrock of conviction as one more veil. The play may be saying "Stop this nonsense" or it may be saying "Stop, all is nonsense." For reasons of professional caution or of private uncertainty, in fear of being found out or in fear of misrepresenting the truth, the philosophical dramatist avoids committing himself to a defined philosophical position. He chooses not to make the choice at the heart, to blur the last alternatives, to make the kernel itself ambiguous.

Thus he has in effect inverted the methods of those who have gone before him. Molière, the poet, keeps his character elusive at the surface: we watch Alceste behave now this way, now that, most contrarily. But the tension of his surface contrariness leads us to his identity. By the time he leaves us, we know that we know him; we know that the man moving away from us down the loneliest of roads, hurling imprecations over his shoulder as he abandons us forever, is a real man. The movement has been circuitous, but its path has been determined by a center. The antidramatist, philosophical precisionist that he is, restricts his terms at the surface as firmly as Beckett restricts his heroine to a home in the sand, or as Ionesco restricts his hero who does not become a rhinoceros (there is no choice here; the last man on earth yearns to become a rhinoceros and *cannot*). But as we mine the explicit surface to see where the mother lode is, we do not come closer to a subterranean reality, we become more and more aware that there may not be one. The philosopher has carved his road markers absolutely and then, in a coquettish gesture that may have been born of irresponsible prankishness and may have been born of real pain, refused to say what they mark the way to. There is, or is not, a reality at the end of the road.

THE COMPETITION: MOVIES

As THE THEATER struggles to remember its name, those of us who are interested in it cannot help casting a weather eye at the rival forms around it. What problems of identity are they having, and what luck?

Now I am not one who is given to imagining conspiracies where there are no conspiracies. I am perfectly well able to sit listening to people chatter on about the intolerable state of the stage, or the moribund state of criticism, or the decline of acting as a conscious craft, without coming to the conclusion that "they" are out to get me or the institution that occupies my nights. On a certain spring evening, though, I wondered. It seemed as though everyone I met was determined to whisper in my ear, with an insidious glee that would have done credit to that sly fellow in *Faust,* a single message. The message was that movies are not only better than ever; they are—at the moment—infinitely better than the stage.

One knowledgeable friend, barely able to eat his dinner for the excitement of his convictions, kept waving his fork at me as he demanded an answer to an unanswerable question: where, in the contemporary theater, were we to find the equivalent of the elusive—yet perfectly controlled—imagination of Ingmar Bergman? (The question was unanswerable because Bergman's mind does indeed seem to me to be as unique as his manner, and because, being hungry, I was trying to eat my chicken with wild rice.) A little while later I found myself in the company of an intelligent writer who had been a reviewer for the theater and who had given it up. He had discovered that he would rather go to the movies, including some of the latest American movies, and so he had. Beginning to feel like a passenger on a leaky ship watching the last lifeboat bobble away across the waters, I remembered that only that morning I'd read in the newspapers that producer

Robert Whitehead—who should surely have a good word left in him for the art he serves—had bluntly announced that it was easier to find an audience for a serious movie than for a play. Not a funny movie, mind you, nor a spectacle in which Spartacus goes down at the Alamo before the massed assault of the entire Yugoslavian army. The audience would rather go to a *serious* movie, leaving the stage without its last shred of dignity.

Put all of these ominous opinions together with some exceedingly ominous facts—the fact that the number of plays produced on Broadway declines annually, the fact that more than 90 percent of all off-Broadway productions fail to find audiences to support them—and you've got a landscape with very depressing figures. Is it time, I asked myself, to give up the ghost and go to the Criterion?

The curious thing is that the more I listened and the more I learned, the less depressed I became. This was, no doubt, sheer perversity on my part. But the very recent shift from a long-lasting apathy toward films to a genuine enthusiasm for films offers, in an upside-down way, a real note of hope for the theater. In the sixties, films *are* better. They are better because they became so bad.

I don't suppose I have to run over the latter-day history of the form that was long and successfully dominated by Hollywood. Everyone knows that the day came—after years and years during which everybody in pictures got richer and richer—when the handwriting on the screen became plain as doom. The box office fell off, as the theater box office continues to fall off. The formula that had always worked refused, peremptorily, to work at all. Major studios which had turned out sixty or seventy films a year—and you'd better have a formula if you're going to do that—were forced to slash their schedules to a mere twelve or fifteen. The patterns of success had become patterns of boredom, and an industry disintegrated.

It was just this disintegration that opened the door to imagination. If an old rule of thumb no longer attracted audiences, then something new would have to be attempted that wasn't a rule at all. If the masterminds who once rode herd on dozens of films a year, driving them like so many duplicate sheep to the marketplace, could no longer perform this massive miracle, then some one man would have to be permitted to make just one film per year. If absolutely nothing could be described as tried and true, then everything would have to be tried.

It was through the cracks in the foundation that fresh quality crept in. Fissures had opened through which independent minds, given free rein now that there was no alternative, could wriggle and squirm and prod and poke and gradually arrive at their own maturity. And the bored audience—precisely because it had become so bored—was ready for them. An audience surfeited with marshmallow was ready to risk the shock of an anchovy; it might even wrestle with an artichoke. It is, in fact, the people who have become passionate about artichokes that we are hearing from now.

Naturally, there is no guarantee that the millennium will follow directly upon catastrophe, and we can't be sure that the theater's present hour of groping is the hour before dawn. But it may be. What I believe—perhaps I should say what I hope—is that the decay of the usual, and the falling off of business as usual, will have the same revitalizing effect upon the stage that it has had, perforce, upon films. "Perforce" is the key word. When there is no point at all in imitating models that no longer make money, what choice has the playwright but to be himself, and chance everything?

AND TELEVISION

FOR TWENTY-FIVE YEARS or more everyone kept explaining that the art of the motion picture was still in its infancy; suddenly, in the fifties and almost without warning, it seemed to be dying of old age. Television is in its infancy just now; I wonder if a premature senility is just around the corner.

I am not in the least concerned, in these remarks, with the youthful indiscretions that human concupiscence is always ready to visit upon any art that is also an industry: quiz scandals, poor programing for children, that sort of thing. Any medium can ride out an incident of corruption. What it cannot ride out is a corruption of form.

The birth, maturity, and death of any entertainment medium is a fascinating, sometimes exhilarating and sometimes saddening, process to follow. And we must all of us face the fact that forms do not necessarily find themselves. No natural law protects a Johnny-come-lately in the arts, guaranteeing it a period of ripe maturity before it breathes its last. It is perfectly possible for one or another kind of promised delight to lose its way before it has quite learned to walk, to walk thereafter in the wilderness with a limp, and to grow old without ever having grown straight.

Let me explain. I have done some work in television, and I have been fortunate in being able to do it in the company of some of the most intelligently creative people I know. On one occasion I was part of a project that most of the newspapers found adventurous and far-seeing: the recording on magnetic tape of a program staged entirely "on location." Until that time most taping had been done in studios, under pleasantly controlled conditions. But the scenery, the caves and bridges for such an extravaganza as *For Whom the Bell Tolls,* had looked like studio scenery, and the venture I was associated with—an hour-long dramatization of H. L. Tredree's *The*

Strange Ordeal of the Normandier—was about to try for
something else: for an on-the-spot atmosphere that would remove all traces of hothouse fabrication. Tredree's factual
narrative had to do with a maritime disaster of World War I,
the harrowing last days of a British tramp ship pressed into
service without adequate equipment and left, powerless, to
drift through hurricanes while most of her crew died of fever.
It was decided to move cast and cables over to Bayonne, New
Jersey, where an old destroyer might be used for a stage and
where fire ships might pour tons of water over listing actors
in a believable simulation of hurricane seas.

After three days' work the tape was completed, and on the
following Sunday afternoon I was able to watch it in my living
room. It had flaws: the splicing together of pieces of tape was
a new and difficult technique and wherever splicing had been
necessary the image "rolled over" on the television screen;
some sequences seemed to have been shot through dirty wire
mesh; the louder the gale, the less intelligible were the Cockney accents. It had virtues: authenticity, spectacle, speed in
the making and speed in the viewing.

The newspaper notices, as I've said, were generally admiring. The telephone calls that flowed in after the program were
congratulatory. And I was still in shock.

What I had watched on Sunday afternoon wasn't a television show at all. It was a 1933 British movie.

My relief that so vulnerable a project hadn't ended in patent disaster kept me from arguing too heatedly with the television professionals I met during the next few days. When I
did express doubt about the quality of the program, it was
generally assumed that I was being prematurely captious
about the mechanics of tape. In time, I was assured, the
shaky photography would grow firm, the sound would spruce
up, and the splicing would glide by with the grace of the river
Clitumnus.

There can be no doubt that these assurances are valid. If
the program I had seen had been recorded three years later,

instead of at the dawn of a new method, it would certainly have been clean, supple, and superbly convincing. It would then have looked like a 1962 British movie.

But is there anything really wrong with a television show's looking like a British movie, or an American movie, or a movie of any kind? I think there may be. There is, first of all, a practical problem: a form is straining every nerve to compete where it cannot compete. The most generous of television budgets, after all, demands that a tape recording be completed in three to four weeks at most. And a program assembled under these conditions, barring that odd act of genius on which no one can count, is probably not going to duplicate the quality John Huston will achieve, given six to nine months and five to eight million dollars, filming the same materials off the west coast of Africa. The practical problem, however, is not half so important as a problem that pops up the minute the practical one is solved. Suppose the unlikely happens, the accident of genius intervenes, and the completed entertainment truly succeeds in competing with its wealthier and more experienced rival—what, then? It will then have become its rival. It will have ceased being itself.

Of course, television may be without a self to worry about.

It is conceivable that television is not a form at all, but simply a convenient device for channeling other forms into millions of homes. In this case, it is no more than an impersonal instrument, like an artificial hearing aid or a pair of bifocals. Its "live" shows are stage shows, dramatic or musical, faithfully transmitted. Its films are films, somewhat reduced in size. Its tapes are films of a quick-mix kind, photographs developed in the camera without a side trip to the laboratory. If these things are so, there is no reason under heaven why the medium should not appropriate every gadget that is available to it, refine each gadget until it purrs, and content itself with marketing all things to all men and no one particular thing to anybody.

If I am not wholly convinced that television is an anonymous delivery boy incapable of a creative act of its own—a funnel without a face—it is because I have, at one time or another, seen something happen on the home screen that could not, within reason, have happened anywhere else. It is an accident of time and place that I stumbled upon the first of Agnes de Mille's essays on choreography for "Omnibus" before I had ever seen a Leonard Bernstein seminar in music: Mr. Bernstein is the man who shaped the curious combination of intimate discussion and massive illustration that has so handsomely served a few of his contemporaries. Watching the de Mille show, I was thunderstruck—not so much by the quality of the program, which was superb, but by my own realization that there was nowhere else in the world I could go for this.

Though it was something of a lecture, I could not look for it in a classroom: there is no classroom that could accommodate, or afford, the scale of the illustration. Though it might have been called a concert-with-comment (Mr. Bernstein subsequently arrived at just such a mixture in his "preview" evenings at Carnegie Hall), I could not hope to find my experience duplicated, in just this way, in an auditorium: here I had a mobile camera to reach out for, and stress, accents. Though the mobile camera was essential to its uniqueness, I could never expect to see its like in a motion-picture theater: the motion-picture theater, like the legitimate playhouse, is essentially and properly devoted to narrative. What I was watching, I told myself, was an entirely new form: the visual essay. And because television had managed to arrange its resources in such an individual way that no rival medium could claim, or even aspire, to offer precisely the same experience, television had, for me, aquired an identity.

Thereafter I knew what sort of program I could not afford to miss. I could miss the westerns, and catch them at Loew's. I could miss the dramas, and see better on Broadway. I could skip the news analysts, and read Walter Lippmann. But I could not miss the "visual essay" and expect to make up my loss.

The combination of values was not merely shrewd, or ingenious. It was native to the instrument for which it was designed. The essay was possible because of the intimacy and ease of a situation involving a few listeners in the relative quiet of their homes: good essays are usually "casual." And the scale of illustration, the freedom of the essayist to summon up a veritable universe of dancers (or to bring the Philharmonic in for the afternoon), was possible because millions of such intimate situations had been created across the country, quite enough to encourage someone to pay for all the prancing examples. The special contradiction that gives television its hitherto unheard-of character—a mass experience that is also a solitary experience—had here fashioned a dress to fit, had made a gesture completely in accordance with its own most complex and private nature. It had expressed itself.

Such self-expression, and assertion of identity, has not been confined to a handful of programs devised by Leonard Bernstein and Agnes de Mille, Edward R. Murrow or "Camera Three." It has appeared, with a quite different set of habits, in such an experiment as the "Project 20" recapitulation, in still photographs, of the life of Abraham Lincoln. In *Meet Mr. Lincoln* something uniquely suited to a curious new medium once again caught most of us by surprise. What we were looking at was neither a motion picture nor a parlor scrap book. One of the two or three basic laws of motion pictures is that the separate images must move; these images did not move. They were, quite simply, the forever-frozen snapshots made by Matthew Brady and the rigidly carved caricatures made by a dozen political cartoonists put back to back. But neither did they constitute a pictorial album which we should have to leaf slowly and so lose the relationship of one image to another. A curious combination of apparently opposed, even contradictory, values took firm imaginative hold: the quiet, close-up, concentrated attention we might give to a treasured picture in the privacy of the study, unexpectedly heightened by the meaningful arrangement and the fluid visual and vocal rhythms made possible by the use of sound film. The experiences—the one intimate and reflective, the other busy and constructed—fused to produce a wholly unfamiliar effect, as though a mountain had been seen moving a little. Between the authenticity of the record and the bursting energy with which one portion of it shouldered another for position in the frame, an absent man breathed.

There is also a sense in which television, used in a certain way, has succeeded in making present men breathe. Most of us have seen newspaper photographs of most of the prominent men and women of our time; most of us have heard them speak in newsreels. But as candid as the news photos may have been and as familiar as the newsreels may have made these voices, we have still only known such men and women publicly, at a good bit more than arm's length. What television, with its strange public-private atmosphere, suggests at once is the possibility of meeting them at armchair length, of overhearing in our living rooms people who would not normally be found in our living rooms.

This is not mere opportunistic happenstance; it is a principle derived from the nature of the tool. That it is a valid principle is attested to by the recurring—and each time surprisingly fresh—excitement stirred up when a Mike Wallace, an Edward R. Murrow, a Jack Paar or a David Susskind makes use of the mixture. The mixture is that of public figure and private tone, of exceptional event and our matter-of-fact view of it. Whether we have attended to Sean O'Casey on his own back steps or to Senator Wayne Morse beating Mr. Wallace at his own game in a smoky studio, we have a habit of describing all such experiences as "conversation," and for very good reason. If we are not yet free to converse with the person, the person is clearly conversing with us: his deportment is special, and is a distinguishing mark of the form for which it is assumed.

Much as we may enjoy Phil Silvers romping his way

through the rogueries of Sergeant Bilko, we are wholly aware that what we are enjoying is, in essence, a filmed short subject and that we should enjoy it quite as much in a movie house—perhaps more, since our laughter would be encouraged and increased by the laughter of so many others around us. Television becomes television when the door is opened to Mr. Silvers' apartment and Mr. Silvers, person to person, turns out not to be Sergeant Bilko. We do not need the movie house, or the presence of hundreds of companions, for this; indeed, the intimacy would become false and embarrassing in more massive circumstances, as it does whenever Bing Crosby or Greer Garson addresses us directly from a very large screen on behalf of some charity or other, or as it did when Cecil B. de Mille chose to introduce us to his new film.

The visual essay, the rhythmic album, the invitation to drop in on a casual conversation—these are the idiosyncratic traits by which television, as television, has come to be recognized. There is no reason to suppose that there are not more such traits waiting to be uncovered in a form that is still quite young. No one can say what imaginative resources, what quirks of personality, may lie hidden waiting a test of strength.

The danger is not that television is limited in its own right, but that it may never discover what its own right is, that it will never subject itself to proper tests of strength. When the living is easy no muscles are flexed, and the living is very easy just now. A television professional can go to sleep counting money so long as millions of feet of old film keep rolling down the Hollywood hillside. If the old film supply begins to run dry, he need only buy up the studios that once turned it out and arrange for experienced personnel to begin turning out new film, millions more feet of it. The old film can not only be turned into new film, as *The Thin Man* and *Dr. Kildare* and even *Rin-Tin-Tin* have indicated, it can also be turned into "live" or taped ghosts: with new costumes and new faces *The Bells of St. Mary's* can be made to ring out forever. Too much from the film vaults? Try the stage. *Winterset* and *Harvey,* and, next thing you know, *My Fair Lady* are on the wing. These can also be imitated. "Originals" can be written that not only observe all the laws of tidy stage dramaturgy but observe them so well that they can thereafter be trucked across town onto Broadway. Should both Hollywood and Broadway threaten to run dry, there remain the public libraries: not all of Jane Austen, not all of Hemingway, not all of Conrad has yet been triple-spaced down one side of television manuscript-page. How soon are we likely to run out of literature?

Most treacherously of all, these things can be well done. Audiences—lazy audiences, temporarily indifferent audiences—may well be grateful for each brilliant instance of mistaken identity. After all, an excellent adaptation of *The Turn of the Screw* saves them the trouble of reading Henry James, at the same time that it is saving television the trouble of being something other than Henry James. There may be quality in the work, and a thankful letter in the mail. Television is free to sit complacently under the landslide of borrowed materials because it knows, as it sits, that there is gold in those tumbling hills.

Nevertheless, sitting under a landslide is still one way of committing suicide. Death by being drowned in goodies may be a comfortable way of going; but it is death. That patient, sometimes admiring audience is an erratic and elusive beast, possessed of uncanny right instincts: in some restless intuitive way it eventually realizes that it is not grappling with the real McCoy and it goes on the prowl to see if it can find out where McCoy lives. While it is never possible to say with finality, "These are the *right* things television should do," because not all of the right things have been discovered yet, it is perfectly possible to say, "These are the wrong things," and to forecast the time of the prowl.

The rule of thumb is negative, but simple: whenever a form spends its time doing what another medium can do as

well, or better, it is headed straight and swift for the bone-
yard. Boredom is coming; the surrender of audiences to media
with more distinctive personalities is coming; failure at the
heart, followed by failure at the bank, is coming.

All of these notices from the sheriff have been handed to
rival media, at one time or another and in one degree or another. We are accustomed to saying, nowadays, that motion
pictures lost their stranglehold on the mass imagination because television came along and was both handier and free.
Did you know that at the very time that the movies were presumably capitulating to television in the large cities, motion-
picture attendance fell off to precisely the same degree in
mountainous areas where there was no television? Competi-
tion always makes inroads; but the size of the dent depends
largely upon the vulnerability of the form that is attacked.
The dent in this instance was enormous: in a three-year
period Chicago alone lost two hundred movie houses. The catastrophe reached such proportions, I am firmly convinced,
because the art of film was at that moment at its most vulnerable. It had spent eight to twelve years steadily refining processes calculated to deny its own best nature.

Example. When films first broke on the world, let's say with
the full-scale achievement of a D. W. Griffith, one of their
most persuasive and hitherto unexperienced powers lay in
the absolute reality of the moving image. The camera is a scientific instrument, not a paintbrush: its special virtue is accuracy, actuality. Thus, when Griffith organized a pan shot
beginning with a mother and child huddled in terror on a
mountain and then moving slowly to a raging battle on the
plain beneath, we were left breathless by a juxtaposition in
scale—from the individual to the group, from the passive to
the active—that was, quite literally, taking place before our
eyes. Our belief in the medium had begun with actual railroad trains roaring down actual tracks right at us, with actual
ocean waves breaking somewhere near our feet. Griffith

223

moved from simple documentation to high imagination, from fact to fiction, from present to past; but he took us with him because he used his camera as a faithful recorder of something that was really and truly going on; he did not abandon his camera's ability to state visual facts.

It is quite a long time since we have had such a shot, not because Griffith had no competent successors but because his latter-day successors have forgotten first principles. The same shot today would begin with a reasonably real close-up of mother and child, perhaps compromised slightly by a color camera that is not as accurate about color as black-and-white cameras were accurate about lines and shapes. It would then begin its pan toward the valley. As the valley began to come into view, something else would come into view: a thin, fuzzy, indeterminate line indicating that we were now being confronted with a "process" shot. We would realize, as we invariably do, that we were looking not at one picture but at two, or rather at two halves of a picture: one shot in a studio, no doubt, and the other shot on location, both to be matched up —almost—later on. The foreground would have a clear texture, the background a grainy one. Now the imaginative ground plan, the meaning of the shot, remains; what has been stripped from it is its power to delight as a record of an actual event, an actual contrast, an actual movement through space. We are not looking at something somebody filmed; we are looking at something somebody faked. Hollywood has removed precisely what thrilled audiences in the first instance; and Hollywood is surprised to discover that audiences are disenchanted.

The use of the easy way, the substitute way, the unnatural way inevitably and instinctively leads to a loss of faith.

The other substitutes for the sense of actuality in which a rich and fat Hollywood indulged itself are well known to us: the dubbing of voices, for instance. It was one thing to hear Maurice Chevalier animate a song he was singing; it is quite another to attempt to sit through a *Carmen Jones* in which Harry Belafonte and Dorothy Dandridge are going through the motions but are not singing. The image before us is fragmentized, our minds turn this way and that, the picture before us is anything but a true one—it is not even all of a piece.

I have mentioned color, though it may be the least of the ready-mix deceits that have disimproved films in the guise of progress. All art forms make use of conventions, which are tacit agreements between the makers and the viewers. Black-and-white photography was such a convention; it was agreed that one whole aspect of visible life could be eliminated in return for an astonishing fidelity to all that was left. Color, however, as we now have it, blurs the original fidelity without adding a true fidelity of its own. Color remains, at the moment, an artifice comparable to what goes into bottles of lime and cherry soda, a substitute that is a stylization: it works wonderfully where the thing photographed is already a stylization—in Disney's cartoons, and, to a slightly lesser extent, in poster-hued musicals. Its addition to a dramatic film almost invariably reduces our confidence in the truth of what is happening: it is not in itself "true."

CinemaScope—and the other large-screen devices—came into being not as a result of some director's inspiration toward the betterment of the medium but as a result of a box-office decline presumably brought about by television. In one sense it offered an intelligent response to the unhappy situation: it tried to be what television could not be—vast—and so to reassert its identity. Unfortunately, for a time at least, it neglected to weigh in the balance those aspects of its identity it might lose in the adaptation to a new panoramic shape. It was, for one thing, brushing perilously close to the shape, and the acting techniques, of the legitimate theater's present proscenium arch. There was the terrible danger that the elongated rectangular image would look like a stage set; that the director would begin to manage his actors as though they were in a stage set, asking them to slog across the entire frame at a realistic rate; and that both of these duplicated effects would be imposed without a corresponding gain, without benefit of the theater's very special virtues—dimensional actors seen in the round, actors emphatically present.

Much more alarming, however, was the loss—and it is still not made up—of the right of what film theorists call montage: the rapid-fire, vividly subjective placing and cutting of camera angles. The wild rhythms that once hurtled us from close-up to long shot, from terrified eyes to advancing truck to neighbor's glance to bird's-eye view, and all in a blinding rush, were much too wild and much too rhythmic to be applied to this enormous canvas. We should grow dizzy trying to grasp so expansive an image at so rapid a rate.

Another of the most characteristic tools of the motion-picture-maker was now being blunted. Because the camera can be anywhere, it comes under the obligation to be everywhere, and in the twinkling of an eye. But the camera eye was no longer twinkling: it was staring long and hard, and from right to left, and the experience was far less lively. To run the last two reels of an antiquated classic like Lon Chaney's *The Hunchback of Notre Dame,* in which the editor who wielded the scissors seems almost to have been a sadist in his genius for whipping film in our faces, is to rediscover a secret that Metro-Goldwyn-Mayer has long since forgotten: it is to make fresh acquaintance with a medium unique in its laws of composition and almost frightening in its capacity for a highly personal passion.

The history of motion pictures is cluttered with fat years and lean, years when film knew what it was and years when it was trying hard not to know. Griffith himself had a literary turn of mind and liked to suffocate his more pretentious work with exceedingly literary subtitles. But it did occur to many men, and quite soon, that all such borrowings were excrescences—inferior as film, inferior as literature—and the time came when there was praise not only for Chaplin's economically worded, infrequently used subtitles but for F. W. Murnau's effort, in *The Last Laugh,* to produce a masterpiece that should have no words at all.

The earliest talking films are intolerable today because they were not films but photographed stage plays. The earliest CinemaScope films, beginning with *The Robe,* are already nearly as intolerable because they seem to be high-school pageants shot by a home-movie-maker who could find no more than three possible positions in the auditorium. The more creative film directors are now working furiously to overcome the uncharacteristic stasis imposed by an unwieldy frame. In *The Bridge on the River Kwai,* for instance, David Lean tackled the problem, brilliantly, in two ways: he used montage, particularly long-shot montage, as frequently as he dared; and he explored such untapped advantages as the boxcar shape might possess, making great capital of picking out a distant, tiny figure in the upper right corner and bringing him not simply across the frame but toward us at the same time. The struggle, at this moment, is to see whether the identity of film can be preserved in a size and shape that tend to deny that identity.

The sickness or health of a form is not easy to determine at moments of crisis. Sometimes a fever must break before the outcome can be known. There have been times when an actual malady has been mistaken for new vitality, largely because of its novelty. There are times when the patient seems to be doing nicely, though he is only being cheered by loyal friends: a medium that has once earned affection will, in its decline, continue to profit from that affection until such time as the old loyalty is all used up. Irrelevant circumstances cloud all diagnoses. By and large, though, I think that a chart showing the relative popularity of motion pictures over the years would prove a quite accurate indication of the degree to which the motion picture was or was not engaged in honoring its very own temperament.

The legitimate theater has not escaped the penalties of failing to answer to its name. Its most notorious lapse, in our time, took the form of a scenic binge, a drunken holiday on heavy-laden turntables, during which it tried very hard to do everything Hollywood could do, worse. An awakening is upon us: as we have seen, the theater is urgently embroiled in an effort to rid itself of its schizophrenic tendencies and to reassert those personality quirks that it alone possesses. Contact between living actor and living audience is being stressed; reliance upon words, rather than pictures, is increasing. The stage is learning to say, "Never mind everybody else, what am I?" and it may catch more flies with character than it ever did with stolen honey. It has, of course, been through all of this before. When we read that a certain ancient Roman version of the Agamemnon story presented its audience with a Clytemnestra preceded by six hundred mules, we can be fairly certain that drama was being diminished donkey by donkey, and that the theater engaged in such practices might just as well have given up the ghost, then and there, to its rivals, the gladiators. Embracing a rival is like running on a sword.

A form in false-face, in borrowed finery, is a form that will one day fail to be recognized. The quality of the finery will not save the day; neither will the skill with which the mask is worn. Behind the trappings lies a nonentity, a wax dummy, a clotheshorse. We shall pass it in the shopwindow without a second glance; in our homes it will be something to stuff in our closets.

A form can have the impulse of life, and then be aborted—just as whole cultures have stirred and then, through a failure of ego that became a failure of energy, subsided without leaving any firm signature on the desert. It will be interesting to see whether television becomes a mere convenience to be replaced by more convenient conveniences, or whether it makes a stubborn little place for itself in the memory of man.

PERMANENCE

I HAD JUST COME from *The Bridge on the River Kwai* and was carrying on not about the panoramic camera positions but about the quite unexpected intellectual complexity of its narrative: the business of locking men of principle, but men of contradictory principles, in a great battle of antlers.

The man I was chatting with, a fellow who'd done some writing for the theater and perhaps may do more, was in a still more lyrical mood. He not only granted the film's virtues but doubled them. Then he sighed, wistfully. "That's what I'd really like to do," he said. "Get a great idea, translate it into great images, and then stamp them all down where they'd stay, where they'd be so perfect and permanent in their own form that my work could forever be seen just as I made it, always the same, always getting the same response."

This was where I reneged. I felt immediately alarmed, not because I feared a working playwright was going to go galloping off to that medium that has for so long swallowed working playwrights, but because I knew that he was kidding himself, that his reason for going—if he went—was a boobytrap.

Film isn't a more permanent medium than the stage; the stage is more permanent than film. The very durability of film is what kills it.

I'm not thinking at all of literary values, of the fact that a manuscript by Shakespeare does outlive a screenplay by John Emerson and Anita Loos (and John Emerson and Anita Loos wrote some dandies, back in 1918 or thereabouts). I'm thinking exclusively of *performance,* of the far greater survival value of something that is wholly gone than of something that is half-gone.

This may sound like a verbal trick; let me clarify. I never saw John Barrymore's *Hamlet.* But John Barrymore's *Hamlet* is as firmly fastened in the indelible roster of theatrical memory as Joe Jefferson's *Rip Van Winkle*, David Garrick's *Richard III*, Charles Macklin's Shylock, or Will Kempe's clowns. Each performance is here to stay; it can never be challenged, and it can never be erased. We own it as an indestructible sovereign in the theatrical treasure chest.

Not long ago I attended a screening of John Barrymore's film *Dr. Jekyll and Mr. Hyde*, made in 1920. The performance isn't there any more, though the film is. The Barrymore face is familiar; not all of the acting is the prisoner of time; the movement through space is precisely what Famous Players Lasky made it so many years ago. But I cannot possibly savor what I see. I can only observe it as a visitor from the moon; total detachment has asserted itself between me and an image that was sensitively constructed for another man in another time and another place: indeed, on the basis of what I notice now, I am inclined to doubt that John Barrymore could ever have been all that good as Hamlet.

But I would be wrong to doubt it. Any performance, every performance, is a curious collaboration between the weather of men's souls and an actor's awareness of that weather. He draws a line that is the kind of line his colleagues in the auditorium expect to see, understand, and are prepared to accept as illuminating for them. When he draws it, if he is a good actor, it *is* illuminating; it showers heat lightning over a terrain composed of geographical assumptions with which we are all familiar. It takes place in a moment, it is of the moment, and it is absolutely valid for that moment. It happened when we were there.

The difficulty with a film is that it continues to happen after we have gone home; and when we come again a few years later—down a new street, with new eyes, with our notions altered and our responses differently attuned—the bond between us has been savagely shattered.

Indeed, we are now in the greatest danger that we shall be led to conclude that the experience hadn't been much in the first place, that we were—in our innocence—wrong. We weren't wrong; we were only wearing another skin, one that the actor knew about and knew how to penetrate. The memory is truer than the record.

I am not saying that *all* old film is disenchanting: with a not very strenuous effort of the historical imagination it is possible to adjust quickly to, and take fresh delight in, some of the work Chaplin and Keaton did thirty or forty years ago. (I hope it will hold out longer still.) Nor am I really trying to say anything we haven't known; when film was a brand-new toy Sarah Bernhardt was eager to try her hand at it because it promised her immortality. It has been clear for a very long time now that her perfectly genuine immortality resides not in the two terribly remote films she made but in the still tantalizing presence of the legends handed down to us. The issue was clear from the beginning, almost.

But here it is, cropping up again in all of its longing and all of its forgivable error.

Dear writer, actor, director: if you want to build a castle that will be remembered and loved forever, be sure to build it of sand.

AS WE WERE

CONVENTIONAL THEATER

POISED MIDWAY between the blandishments of pure show business and the lively arrogance of an iconoclastic spirit that professes not to care what happens to show business so long as it is free to speak its piece are the men and women who have spent twenty or more years working out their own theatrical destinies within what must, by this time, be called the "conventional" theater. Their work is serious work, or means to be; but it takes the familiar realistic theater as its point of departure, departing—when it does so—with an exploratory patience rather than in a bring-the-house-down hurry. In the light of what is happening, their methods sometimes seem old-fashioned, or at least relatively conservative; when utterly conventional plays of twenty years ago are revived we are frequently appalled at their obviousness of manner; yet there is a surprising amount of vitality in the old stage still when it is served by craftsmen who approach it with care.

Miss Hellman

When Lillian Hellman returned to the theater after a nine-year absence (with *Toys in the Attic*) she offered us a suggestive image. An old maid sat cross-legged on a piano stool, halfheartedly fingering the keys of a piano that had so faded it looked like ancient milk chocolate, and wondered why she was no longer able to wear pink. Pink had once looked well on her, but, as she observed, she herself must have changed color as she grew older.

Listening to her, and to the plain, penetrating truths that were coming out of a tough-minded sister who moved with familiar purpose about a memory-stained Mississippi house, one

235

was suddenly aware that there are some things that do not change color as they grow older. Spare, clean prose is one of them, and Lillian Hellman writes it.

During the nine years of Miss Hellman's silence, a good many fashions had altered. So many, indeed, that it had become a commonplace to hear the conventional American theater described as the particular product of three men: Williams, Miller, and Inge. I confess I had always found myself restive whenever this triumvirate, and only this triumvirate, was mentioned. Where, I wanted to ask, was Lillian Hellman, whose body of work exceeded Miller's in volume and at least Inge's in force? Was our temporary forgetfulness due to nothing more than our handy habit of grouping everything in threes? Or had the near-poetry of Williams and the shock-tactic virility of the melodrama of the late fifties left the lady who once possessed a whiplash tongue far behind?

It hadn't, as we now know. The very special pleasure of *Toys in the Attic* lies in its cool, resolute reaffirmation of certain primary virtues, in its calm reminder that lucidity and control are qualities to be prized and that language painstakingly whetted to a cutting-edge has the same power to slice deeply into flesh as it did when Regina Hubbard was a girl. Nothing is blunted; if anything, the blade has become finer as perception has grown deeper.

Curiously, *Toys in the Attic* is a play about the failure of growth through a failure to change, a dark and despairing playground on which eternal children wither and die. The ghost at the piano, having long since reared her younger brother, has never surrendered the moment of their closeness: so long as he lives, even if he lives as a moving corpse, she will find ways of keeping him a dependent, grateful, loving small boy.

The boy, married and ten times a failure in the world beyond his sister's front porch, has refused to surrender a youthful dream: a dream of one day storming into the warm, musty living room with a splatter of gifts, a fistful of cash, an over-flowing expression of his gratitude and devotion. He is the fa-vored child proving at last that all the favoring was worth it, and proving it at whatever wild cost to his marriage, his fu-ture, his standing as a man. His adult years have shown him no other goal; and the combination of his forever-sustained childhood and his sister's forever-enveloping mother-lust do more than make a disaster of the present—they also now in-vert and degrade whatever was good about the past.

The sense of past and present, of love and greed, of gayety and suppressed terror, is sustained in each poised, precarious phrase Miss Hellman engraves: the author has heard some-thing in her mind, and she has trusted it to grow between syl-lables (with the characters not quite looking one another in the face), letting it drift onto a veranda bordered by a wrought-iron terrace as though the heart and steel of the dra-matic materials could be persuaded to coil as subtly, as im-perceptibly, and as firmly as the design on the trellis does. When a high-living neighbor who allows her Negro "fancy man" to wait for her beyond the fence in silent, stalking pa-tience brings her velvety rustle of voice and parasol into the garden, the atmosphere of sickly hothouse and onrushing na-ture is gently insinuated. "It is very vain of flowers to compete with the Mississippi," the visitor murmurs. When the same woman turns an alert eye on her daughter to rap out a wise, "Shame on you, Lily, you're looking for pain," or when she shrugs her reserved shoulders to observe that "this climate puts mildew on the truth," the syllables seem to belong to a person even as they are, with subterranean stealth, moving the play proper to its landslide destination.

The work is not perfect, any more than its people are pleas-ant to know. Miss Hellman's method here is indirect, allusive; sometimes an area is circled, prior to descent, too long. More disturbing is our degree of detachment from the figures in the web; emotion does not often stir. This is mainly due, I think, to the fact that the boy-man who is destroyed does not reveal much capacity for becoming a whole man. As he is eaten alive, we suffer no sense of loss. Was there something worth saving, if love and innocence and generosity had not been so devouring? Because the eternal child seems to have no other seed in him, we watch his destruction impassively. The play charts his helpless course with hypnotic assertiveness; but it does not offer us the alarm and troubled sympathy of regret.

No matter. *Toys in the Attic* binds us to it with a cold, serpentine grace that is born of a clear head, a level eye, and a fierce respect for the unchanging color of the precisely used word.

Mr. Inge

What of Williams, Miller, and Inge? Miller has been largely away, making promises. Inge has been with us and not with us, warmly with us in *The Dark at the Top of the Stairs*, remote and troubled in *A Loss of Roses*.

The former is a touching example of one of our commonest theater experiences: the memory play. In performance almost the first thing you noticed about designer Ben Edwards' long, rambling, old-fashioned Oklahoma living room was the alcoves: the dim recess where a swinging door opened and closed silently, the tiny back parlor where the player piano lurked behind fringed drapes, the empty space that surrounded the front screen door and seemed to lead off to nowhere. There was also, to be sure, a wildly steep staircase that shot bolt upright to the dark at the top of it, but it was the private nooks and crannies that counted most.

For this was to be the kind of play that a child might have overheard as he passed, hastily or idly, through the corners of his parents' lives. Whenever a youngster with a mop of yellow hair sprawled over his forehead and a lower lip set in a stubborn indifference barged swiftly in or out of his elders' universe, all inflections changed.

Eileen Heckart, as an aunt with bobbed hair and jade earrings that rattled as rapidly as her tongue, might very well have been whispering a fast, scandalous confidence to the boy's broken-hearted mother. But the entrance of the child became a warning for skyrockets to go up, for Miss Heckart's scratched-slate voice to strip gears violently and bellow open into whooping affection. This child, like all of us, heard one tone at the threshold, another as he was sighted, still another as he vanished again through the portieres.

And it was the remembered, mysteriously rising and falling, heard and not-heard universe of oddly behaved adults that Mr. Inge and his director, Elia Kazan, had caught with such accuracy in the half-light. Not that the children's roles were dominant; they were simply ears that listened, legs that shuffled perplexedly, eyes that stared in incomprehension and occasional hysterical defiance as a mother and father fought over a party dress, as an aunt painfully refused to take the family into her own household, as lonely voices in the kitchen cried out during an all-night rain.

Thus the loss of a later play by Mr. Inge was not to be taken lightly. We had come to expect from the playwright a friendly sympathy for likable slatterns, a feeling for the fears that badger quite recognizable families, even a mildly poetic awareness of the dreams that torment tough-minded people who spend their lives thumbing rides on the roadside. If Mr. Inge's mood had most often been rueful, it had always been warm. If the voices overheard in parlors and bars had always had a commonplace twang to them, their very commonness and familiarity had helped to stir our affection.

But *A Loss of Roses,* the author's fifth play and first failure, was neither familiar in spirit nor touching in effect, and its difficulties stemmed, I think, not from any momentary fatigue on the playwright's part but from a growing tendency in the

conventional theater. The tendency, which is also a temptation, is for the dramatist to work in an ever narrower range,
and with an ever softer and more indulgent touch.

The softness of *A Loss of Roses* may have derived from a
conviction that the satisfactions of the flesh are sufficient.
The play dealt with a son's unnatural attachment for his
mother, and with his temporary transfer of that attachment
to a blowzy, not quite bright, tent-show actress who was old
enough to serve as a mother-image while remaining a legitimate object of sexual desire.

If the edgy and secretive guerrilla warfare that went on
between these three small-town people did not interest us for
very long, it was probably because Mr. Inge had nowhere
suggested that anything more powerful was at work than an
aberration of the senses.

When the son moved impulsively toward his mother for a
good-night kiss or bolted rebelliously away from her rigid refusal of warmth, the confused drive inside him was wholly
physical; it was perfectly plain that neither her revival-
meeting character nor her dinner-table conversation had inspired any part of the strangled affection he felt. The issue
was not at all psychological; it was steadfastly, and simply,
sensual.

The mother, unfailingly alert to every gesture that disturbed the tranquillity of a fatherless home, responded in
kind: nothing passed between these two to suggest any tan-
gling of minds over the long, lonely years; only an unlucky
proximity and a physical resemblance between dead father
and demanding son lay at the root of the contest.

When the actress-interloper bustled about the Kansas living room in cascades of tight black fringe and then suc-
cumbed in astonishment to the lad's importunities, the flare
of passion that overtook them, and the disillusionment that
followed, were both crises of nerves, mutual cries for comfort. The drama was skin-deep.

That the sting of the flesh is a powerful force in any man's life, or in any man's play, is surely not to be denied. That it should be thought to constitute a spectrum broad enough and varied enough to sustain an entire evening at fierce dramatic pitch is perhaps another matter. A surge of sensuality takes on genuine importance and complexity in the theater when it begins to engage, and challenge, the total personality, when the mind and will are pressed into the struggle, when the dramatist lays open not one layer of surface response but cuts resolutely into human tissue until a cross-section has been exposed. *A Loss of Roses* seemed to attempt no such penetration; it halted, rather, at the actress' straightforward but dramatically inadequate warning that she was "emotionally immature"; and the preoccupation with immaturity made us squirm rather than sympathize.

Mr. Inge's play faltered further in its symptomatic confinement to a narrow and clinical range of observation. "I never heard of such people," murmured the mother in mild protest as she listened, more or less placidly, to an account of the lively and indiscriminate sexual activities of an acting troupe. The point of the line, of course, was that she had indeed heard of them and had chosen to ignore their existence. The line was also meant to remind the rest of us that the things that were taking place in *A Loss of Roses* do happen, perhaps more frequently than we like to think.

But even as we acknowledged the truth of the inference, we were restive: if the twilight world of the seriously abnormal is real, it is also restricted. It is restricted emotionally, because of the emotional paralysis of its figures. It is restricted intellectually, because development has, in one way or another, been arrested. We may be quick to grant that such imprisonments of personality take place, and that otherwise attractive people suffer for them; but we are slower to concede that they occupy quite so impressive a place in the scheme of things as they have just now usurped on the stage.

In our own busy and complicated world we have come to enjoy a somewhat busier and more complicated field of vision: we are bound to the foolish, sinful, nearly normal people we know as we cannot become bound to these honorably drawn but palely loitering wraiths of the half-world. I suppose it must always be remembered that the so-called disturbed personality is not more complex than its presumably healthy opposite, but simpler. It is simpler because the obsession that deforms it tends to become self-centered and single-minded.

As a result, one's experience of a merely clinical play is always a little like navigating a bleak and endless alley in the company of people who deserve and rather querulously demand assistance but do not become the more winning for their crying over odd compulsions. We feel, as we watch, that what is truly pathological requires treatment and understanding, but not necessarily our presence during the therapy.

The Mirror

There is a distinction to be made, however, between what is neurotic or immature and what is violent or ugly, just as there is a distinction to be made between the merely fashionable posture of self-pity and the fact that savage pressures exist.

Too often the lines that may be drawn between these things are blurred, all troubled visions are lumped together under the single epithet "depressing," and a great hue and cry is raised against dramatists generally for failing to report the first crocus.

Contemporary playwrighting tends to view the human condition as though it were entirely scrofulous, the outraged insist, and isn't it time for a brighter-eyed craftsman to say a kind word about our nobler traits? Nobler traits do exist, surely, even in New York City, and wouldn't it simply be playing fair to devote an evening or two to rounding out the picture?

The complaint is understandable enough. It isn't much fun —nor is it profoundly moving in the tragic sense—to stumble night after night into a nest of badly reared vipers, there to be told almost without interruption that the situation is hopeless, hopeless. An enormous number of our most successful plays do wear a morose, as some wear a twisted, countenance. The playgoer who has done his best from nine to five, and who goes right on trying to construct a decent world from five till bedtime, may well be forgiven his impatience and his disbelief as he is forced to look at intricate patterns of corruption each time he visits Broadway.

Score one for the complainers. I am myself obviously somewhat impatient with the drama of neurosis, not so much because I am looking for uplift and light, but because it seems to me—almost in the nature of things—to be minor drama. The true neurotic is generally a victim of forces he does not understand and therefore cannot subdue or even do intelligent battle against. Barring a god from the machine who will rescue him, whether that god wear a psychiatric beard or some other life-saving symbol, he is a tormented and baffled victim of circumstances quite beyond his personal control.

Since he is also, by definition, ill just now, he tends to remove himself to the observation ward. By this I mean that because he has effectively isolated himself from the rest of us, who fancy that we enjoy a sort of minimum health, he has made any real interplay between us impossible. We can watch him behind glass; but because he is imprisoned in a snarl of nerves, inhibitions, and impulses that is unique rather than common, we no longer share with him a common tongue or a common pattern of memories and drives. We can try to understand what has happened to him, and we can be perfectly well aware that it might happen to us; but until his private knot is undone, we cannot really communicate with him, nor he with us. "Universality" is an easy word to toss around. But it does have a meaning, and the plays we cherish most are cherished precisely because they speak so intimately to so many.

Dramatically, then, the "sick" play is a small play, incapable of embracing the normal range of human experience; it is, at best, a second-best kind of theater. But to say this is not to end the argument. There are private neuroses. There are also vast public temblors that menace all of us.

I am haunted, whenever I hear hopeful partisans of the theater urging the theater to put a better face on things, by the image of an ugly woman improving the situation by smashing all the mirrors in her house. That the stage is a mirror of something actual in the society around it, and that it arrives at its most potent images through some kind of intuitive contact with the deepest fears or beliefs or doubts or aspirations underlying the social structure in which it lives and breathes, is a saw too ancient and familiar to require repeating. But there is no need to focus attention on the theater alone. Listen for a very few moments to a piece of music composed, let's say, by John Cage; go to any gallery you like and take the temperature of the paintings; you will, in the end, be surprised that the theater is so little—rather than so far—advanced in the preoccupation with dissonance and the insistence upon disintegration. The difficulty does not originate on the stage, or in any of the arts; it is in the air, sending out signals to which artists, of whatever quality, respond.

Disturbed as I do sometimes find myself by the morbidity that so often filters across footlights, I would say that there are two serious dangers inherent in the demand for a deliberate lightening of the playwright's outlook. One is the danger of outright falsification, the invention of a jollier world which bears about as much resemblance to life, to speech, and to persons living or dead as does the average television commercial. If the cheerfulness is not there, and must be invented, how is the playwright to keep it from turning into vitamin-enriched fantasy?

The second danger is that of smashing, or at least taking down, the mirrors. The woman does not get less ugly for removing the record of her ugliness; she only succeeds in concealing from herself the facts. It is possible that some of our sagas of disenchantment—the preponderance of such sagas certainly suggests this—do record facts. The facts need not be literal; they may be of a deep-seated, almost unacknowledged, psychological and spiritual kind. Should this be the case, the suppression of mirrors would constitute an appalling act of self-deception. If the canker is there, and widespread enough to set so many artists into simultaneous motion, it had best be looked at. It isn't likely to get itself corrected, or even worked over, so long as the evidence is being tidied away.

A word about the nature of these mirrors, and the fact that the reflections they give off are often less (or more) than literal. All of the arts, drama included, have a habit of putting on false whiskers.

That is to say, almost the first thing any born novelist or dramatist or poet does is to find a disguise, a disguise for himself, for his characters, and for his story. If, in his incessant prowling of the main streets and back alleys of the contemporary world he shares with the rest of us, he comes upon a trait or a tendency or a yearning or a fear that strikes him as new, real, and significant, he does not simply write his observation down; that is work for the editorialist or the essayist to do. Nor does he, as a dramatist, simply arrange to have his discovery acted out, more or less literally and with the maximum fidelity to what he has seen and heard; that is the province, let's say, of the filmed documentary.

He takes a very different tack. He casts about him for an image—an imagined, and hence not quite factual, structure that may possibly be bolder, bigger, stranger, and more curious than the hint he has taken from life but that will in any case be somewhat different from it. Wanting to say something about the spiritual agony of modern man, he may find it necessary to set his action two thousand years before modern man was born. Wanting to say something terribly serious about a destructive sentimentality that eats at the heart of the twentieth century, he may decide to people his vision with clowns and make them nineteenth-century clowns into the bargain.

Whatever he has seen must now be seen in a new focus; whatever he has heard must, somehow, be translated into another language—even if it is only the equally contemporary language of another part of the forest. (Don't be fooled; all of those "Southern" plays and novels we've been digesting aren't really about the South. They are about all of us, disguised as Southerners.)

Why bother with such an elaborate process of rearrangement, distortion, and magical sleight-of-hand when a plain mirroring of the facts in their original context would get a man praised for his timeliness? The playwright does it, of course, instinctively; it is the odd way his mind works. But his mind works that way to a purpose, for a reason. The magnifying glass and the Coney Island mirrors are brought into play because the dramatist is looking for certain things he wants badly: for distance, for detachment, for the chance to see his material clearly and to make certain it has form. He is, in a way, testing the truth of what he has observed by trying to discover whether it will support another, though related, structure; and he is trying to clarify that truth for the rest of us by sharply divorcing it from the confusing continuum of our untidy, and sometimes unintelligible, lives.

Thus I am by no means certain that the exotic ring, say, of Tennessee Williams' *Sweet Bird of Youth* or *The Night of the Iguana* is wholly without value as a contemporary sounding board. I suspect that Tennessee Williams consistently fascinates us because his absorption with evil strikes us, in a dim and deformed but possibly deeper-than-journalistic way, as an echo of the evil we hear in our streets.

Indeed, I doubt very much whether any entertainment can be vastly successful without, in however devious a manner, implicitly touching a contemporary nerve. The business of having meaning for the moment is not entirely the province of the reporter and commentator; it is also the province of the myth-maker, the compulsive conjurer behind the borrowed beard.

Mr. Williams

Tennessee Williams has had so many successes that he is in constant danger of having each new piece of work judged on parlor-game principles. The curtain is barely up on opening night before certain leading, and possibly damaging, questions come to mind: is this his best play, or his third-best play, or just a bit better or a bit worse than *A Streetcar Named Desire?* The temptation to begin cataloguing the play before we have listened to it is almost irresistible.

The surprising thing about Mr. Williams' successive assaults upon the nervous system of the theater is that again and again they halt all such speculation like a blow in the face. Now it is extremely peculiar that this should be so. *Sweet Bird of Youth,* for instance, picked up a good many familiar threads where the author had last left them knotted, and thereby seemed to insist on comparison. The hero was a "criminal degenerate" in search of his lost innocence. The heroine was a woman of faded powers and shabby pretenses. The world was sharply divided between those who had had luck with sex and those who could do no more than look on enviously. The shape of this world was dictated by "corrupting" forces that denied love to the young, drove them to their hashish comforts and perverse rebellions, and then penalized them mercilessly (in this case by symbolic castration) for the sorry deeds they performed. The accent was Southern.

Yet we had no sooner been exposed to the evening's initial images—actor Paul Newman flinging back a great transparent curtain to light a cigarette and nervously measure the vulnerability of the woman he was traveling with, actress Geraldine Page pummeling an enormous pink pillow in an effort to shield her ravaged face from the light—than a sense of fresh and independent energy swept over us.

This assertiveness, and our feeling of having been caught up in an unrehearsed experience, came from a variety of sources. Geraldine Page's playing reverberated like an anvil— and like an anvil that had not been struck before. The performer had previously made her reputation, and the reputations of quite a few imitators, by a finger-at-the-forehead shyness, a capacity for gathering a hundred tiny, compulsive, and impotent gestures into one quivering human frond.

Here the line was as clean and as firm as something out of Sousa: all blare and polish and gaudy power. Miss Page, as a former movie actress who was now down to an oxygen mask and street-corner pickups, made her way to the edge of the stage, flung an arm heavenward in a poster stance that throbbed with abandon, and thundered out the story of her decline. ("It's not that I'm old—I'm just not—*young!*" she screamed, eyes blazing with an accusing fury that somehow succeeded in implicating us in her misfortunes.) We felt responsible, involved, rather as though we owed her a prompt explanation.

Still, the strongest voice remained that of Mr. Williams. *Sweet Bird of Youth* had unmistakable flaws: the evil that infected this world uniformly was nowhere defined; sex as a panacea was, as always, much too simple a proposition; the interest we were asked to take in the hero seemed out of proportion to his stature, and we sometimes felt an urge to ask him for his credentials; the political demagoguery on which the second act focused threatened, in its sheer clatter and its calliope pitch, to hustle us away from the heart of the play.

But in spite of all the charges that could be justifiably lodged against it, the play spoke up for itself, hacked at its materials as though no one had yet noticed their existence. Mr. Williams' own eyes seem, year after year, to grow wider in astonishment at the bizarre world he sees about him. If the vision that confronts him is in some ways a questionable one, in some ways a murky one, it is also a frighteningly tangible one: you could reach out and touch it if you wanted to, and your finger would come away burned. The author's intentions as a craftsman are clear: to advance upon each new exploration of human behavior and theatrical boundaries with something like an amateur's fierce enthusiasm to get everything down, and to get it down hot.

Sweet Bird of Youth was thus quickly popular, and quickly attacked. There are times, however, when an attack upon a play can amount to a profound compliment to its author.

Many things were said: that the political second act was the *real* play and should have been developed, that the personal story of the first and third acts constituted the *real* play and that the second should have been omitted, that director Elia Kazan had destroyed the play by removing some of its morbidities (an incest motif that had appeared in the original text was no longer stressed), and that Mr. Kazan had destroyed the play by magnifying its morbidities (the gross face of a demagogue bellowing race hatred from a sound track was thought to be the director's flashy personal addition to the saturnalia).

And somewhere behind all of the pained, groping, often self-contradictory nagging, a genuine uneasiness was asserting itself, an uneasiness that insisted on a hearing. It was not, even then, a dissatisfaction wholly inspired by, or wholly concentrated on, this particular play. The very fact that no two testy objections ever quite tallied with one another, that no two challengers ever quite agreed upon the general form they wanted to see the play take, suggested a broader and deeper concern: a concern not for the shape of *Sweet Bird of Youth* but for the shape of Mr. Williams' career.

The debate continues, I think, because a demand is rising, a demand that should—for all that is impatient and dismissive in it—be decidedly flattering to the playwright.

What people seem to be saying to one another is something like this: Mr. Williams is so good—so powerful in his instinct for the abrasive scene, so naturally skillful in his use of the theater, and at the same time so sensitively equipped that he is able to back up rude passion with near-poetry—that it is now time for him to become better, almost time for him to become great. The itch among Mr. Williams' erstwhile fans is an itch toward perfection, toward maturity, toward masterpieces, and—burden though it must be for the playwright—the attack may be read as a tribute: we know what Mr. Williams can do; when is he going to do more?

What more do both his admirers and his detractors want of him? From the sound of things, I suspect that they want tragedy—which is to say, an ordered and meaningful arrangement of the vice, the violence, and the failure he is so extraordinarily adept at making vivid. Perhaps the word that still recurs most often in connection with *Sweet Bird of Youth* is the word "melodrama"; there is a feeling abroad that the horrors we have been offered are in part cardboard horrors, calculated pieces of stage machinery, piled-up gimmicks geared mainly to the production of gooseflesh. The feeling has been summarized, with very sharp teeth, by Gilbert Highet in a magazine article: Mr. Highet paused to imagine Seneca, that Roman apostle of the senseless blood bath, giving Mr. Williams a few juicy tips toward an even gorier future. Beyond the most brilliant melodrama, the winds seem to say, lies something more important; Mr. Williams seems capable of it, but not yet willing to reach for it.

What holds him back? Possibly the refusal to assign responsibility for the savage events that take place. In *Sweet Bird of Youth,* as in several earlier plays, the evasion is double. The hero is presented to us as guileless, an innocent who has played no part in his own corruption. He may not *seem* to us altogether innocent: he has, after all, bequeathed to the ingénue the disease that disembowels her. But we are assured that he is without flaw, the victim of an otherwise universal venality which overpowers him.

Turning to the patently corrupt society about him, we find it no easier to name the source of the omnipresent cancer. Evil is explicitly present, and all of the remaining characters are stained by it. But how or why these "guilty" people first acquired the stain, why they should not be thought as helpless and as victimized as the hero, precisely where the virulent source of infection truly lies, are matters that consistently elude us.

Because responsibility for the damage is unthinkable in the hero and untraceable in the community, we are left without an intelligible cause for so many shattering effects: we do stand perilously close to the gratuitous blood bath.

We are also faced with a small but persistent problem of belief. There is a story going the rounds that a young Texan who took his wife to *Sweet Bird of Youth* listened carefully to Paul Newman's final plea for understanding ("I don't ask for your pity . . . just for your recognition of me in you . . .") and then murmured, with an earnest frown, "I don't think there's any of him in me, and I *know* there ain't any of him in Alice."

Close identification with either side of this two-faced universe becomes difficult. The world we move in doesn't seem quite so filled with monsters born to the role; we suspect that the disagreeable people we meet have helped make themselves that way. And utter innocents seem to us not to have been born at all; we cannot feel that we have ever met one, or ever been one. Further, we do not really know what to make

251

of a man who behaves corruptly while inviting us to regard him as blameless. Corruption is inveighed against; but its nature is unclear.

Where so many impressive and tantalizing but ultimately undefined figures cannot lead us is to a sorrowing acceptance of their fate as just—to a rounding out that is clear and necessary. (It never was necessary for Mr. Newman to wait, at the end of the evening, for the castration that threatened him; he was innocent—why not run?) Tragedy is both comprehensive and coherent: it embraces everything, including all of the demonic postures Mr. Williams' characters love to strike; and it places them in some purposeful and profoundly lifelike relation to one another. The guilt and the results of the guilt become one—not two, or some hazy, unreadable number.

I don't think that Mr. Williams' critic-enthusiasts are really asking him to give anything up, not even the curdling of the blood he manages so effectively. I don't think they honestly object to anything that is there—who would be so ungrateful? They are urging him to find, in his superior resources, the last ounce of accuracy that is missing.

If *The Night of the Iguana* does not resolve the issue, it nevertheless commands respect for the gamble it is.

The truly creative act is always a gamble. Where the journeyman playwright will protect himself by organizing his material neatly in advance, snipping and basting so that no telltale seam will show to embarrass him, carefully measuring the cloth he is capable of cutting and never risking the stroke that may expose his limitations, the man who means it is always throwing away the pattern on the chance that he will be able—this once—to catch lightning in his hand. Without prefabrication, he plunges into the formless, hoping that he will find life itself at its core, and hoping against hope that life itself will then give birth to a form no one has seen before. As the heroine explains in *The Night of the Iguana,* she has made certain unexpected and possibly dangerous gestures toward a mercurial and half-mad defrocked minister because, where people are concerned, she is willing "to draw to an inside straight." In writing the play, and in respecting the equipment that is his, Tennessee Williams has done almost nothing but draw to inside straights. It is astonishing, in an unpredictable game, how often the right card turns up.

It turns up infallibly wherever the wraithlike but strongwilled central figure is in question. I do not think that Mr. Williams could tell you, in a sentence, the name or the nature of the demon that inhabits this woman so entirely that she cannot—now or at any future time—make room in her mind or heart for further guests. He can show you her placid, overriding authority: she takes possession of a shabby room in a Mexican mountain hotel for herself and her near-senile father with the unyielding, though graceful, imperiousness of a mother superior accustomed to ruling convents.

He can show you the knot of her will: her voice betrays no apprehension as she informs the proprietress of the hotel that she intends to pay her bill by "passing among the tables" of the dining veranda offering to sketch the portraits of the other residents. He can show you the suppressed warmth, the leashed radiance, that glows within a composed façade but is forbidden to display itself or to spend itself: the self-possessed heroine is drawn to the dispossessed minister as a circle of cloud is drawn to a hilltop, eager to embrace and conceal it— and then to move on as though the brushing of shoulders had never been. And he can make the sound of her rigid soul ring with bell-like clarity through the mists of what-might-have-been. "What will I do?" she asks herself. "Stop, or go on," she answers firmly and without self-pity, "probably go on."

The showing, and the striking of a true tone, are not only enough, they constitute the exposed nerve of artistry. This artistry was aided in production, it is true, by a performance from Margaret Leighton that was so intangibly spun and so mysteriously self-contained as to cause one to dismiss as mechanical exhibitionism most of the work that is done weekly on our stages. But the first discovery was Mr. Williams', and it is one of his rewards for having risked failure. He has composed for us a portrait which owes nothing to calipers, or to any kind of tooling; it is all surprise and presence, unanticipated intimacy. It is found gold, not a borrowing against known reserves.

Mr. Williams has not here been vouchsafed every reward he might have hoped for. Very often a vein is struck, a dark corner made to blaze with light: in the chill, bitter, defensive humor with which the minister spells out the transgressions that have destroyed him ("statutory rape is when a man is seduced by a girl under twenty"); in the shrill, single-toned animal outcry of a child who is not loved; in an old man's woolgathering gasping out of a poem he has struggled for years to complete.

Yet these human absolutes, born of their own authority and owing nothing to the niceties of routine craftsmanship, again fail their author in one respect: they do not evolve, in their interplay, a stable design that will explain their coming-together on this particular occasion or their parting on the morrow. They are incontestably alive, but they are independents all, ready for any play but unable, through mutual effort, to define the shape of this one. The minister possesses no active dimension; he can only be eaten alive by the hotelkeeper. The hotelkeeper skirts the psychological struggle, biding her time and waiting for whatever bones may be left.

The effort on the part of the playwright to hint at a meaningful structure through the symbol of an iguana that has been tied up beneath the stairs until someone is ready to eat it is vague, perhaps halfhearted. Though the symbol is relatively unobtrusive, it clarifies little: when the iguana is freed of its bonds (ugly as it is, it is "one of God's creatures") we seem to see it in contrast to people who cannot be freed of theirs; but why no hand can free them, or why they are unable to free themselves, remains an unanswered question and a perplexing one. To say that "we all have just so much and no more in our emotional and nervous bank accounts" would seem to avoid the issue with an attractive phrase.

Mr. Williams' gamble, then, does not end in total triumph. *The Night of the Iguana* is, in effect, a dream of immobility from which the dreamers never wake. Still, a dozen, even a hundred, other playwrights might have rounded the sleep to a tidy awakening, straightened the bedclothes and brushed everyone's teeth until an orderly world was populated with good little soldiers, and never have stumbled, in nightmare revelation, upon the translucent life that appears from nowhere on a vine-tangled veranda to assume tangible substance. We go to the theater month after month and become accustomed to plays that are put together; then Mr. Williams returns and reminds us what it is to watch poetry in the process of finding itself.

The Miracle Worker

If it is sometimes difficult to make ugliness palatable, it is even more difficult to make goodness persuasive.

All audiences love to have their emotions stirred in the theater, and all audiences hate to have their emotions stirred too easily. The greatest danger author William Gibson faced in telling the story of Helen Keller in *The Miracle Worker* was that of arousing the quick, instinctive resentment of people who might come to feel that they had opened their hearts to a setup.

The materials for too many tears, too easily drawn, were there. The child Helen Keller, deaf, dumb, and blind, was at once an object of pity. We were apt to be on guard, determined not to surrender our compassion too swiftly, when we met her. Annie Sullivan, her twenty-year-old nurse and teacher, invited very nearly the same obvious sympathy: she was orphaned, unlettered, the victim of half a dozen operations on her own eyes. The spectacle of these two misfits, cut off from the kindness of the rest of the world and from each other as well, moving in sorry circles toward a moment of communication that might never come, was in one sense irresistible; in another sense it was the very sort of patent bid for pathos that generally causes us to set our jaws, stiffen our backs, and defy The Little Match Girl herself to make us cry.

Mr. Gibson won our consent to the harrowing adventure, and then our open surrender to the full-throated chords it dared to sound, by one right stroke of craftsmanship. He did not deal tenderly with images that were already rich in wistful appeal. He dealt roughly with them.

The most direct question posed during the earlier stages of the evening, as a harassed family tried to cope with the small inarticulate monster that moved among them, was spoken by one of Helen Keller's parents to the other.

"Do you like her?" was the question. It was not answered, though the silence, of course, constituted an answer in itself. Love, perhaps, was possible, in some dim maternal way, for the pale, spastic creature whose fingers went flying like thousand-leggers over the faces around her, searching out frantic identifications. But honesty forbade the pretense of liking. Patty Duke played the near-animal who crawled like a frightened crab across an Alabama front yard to hurl a stolen key into a well and then pound herself fiercely on the head as a sign of secretive delight. And she played with a taut mouth drawn back from defiant teeth, with hands that were quicker to strike than they were to receive caresses, with a directionless energy that was doubled by a despair she could not understand.

Nor was any sentiment wasted on the problems Anne Bancroft faced when, as the inexperienced Annie Sullivan, she settled down to the task of breaking a fierce, unintelligent

256

will. "A siege is a siege" said this indestructible battering-ram, rolling up her sleeves and lunging at the locked fortress with a ferocity that might have distressed Attila. There was a long pantomime passage in the middle of the second act during which Miss Bancroft was determined that Miss Duke would eat her dinner, eat it with a spoon, and thereafter fold her napkin. Miss Duke was ready to kick, scratch, bite, tear chairs to splinters and the tablecloth to rags before any such eventualities took place. No known holds were barred, no shreds of flesh spared; the sounds were the sounds of bodies grunting under impact and of furniture cracking under assault; two naked wills wound up on their knees, like dogs panting twice before moving in to the kill; the holocaust was total, not merely physical but spiritual.

When it was over, Miss Bancroft quietly reported to the waiting parents, "The room's a wreck but her napkin is folded." And there was almost more strength in the quiet statement than there had been in the desperate donnybrook. Miss Bancroft's command of her own powers was absolute; and when she touched us she did it not by begging but by the assertion of a rigid, almost brutal, rectitude.

Certain questions of art may be raised about play and production. Should Mr. Gibson have carried along with him, from the television original, a subjective sound track native to another medium? Hadn't he compromised his own honesty by casting six children who were actually blind in one very short sequence in order to introduce, through their attractiveness, an appeal that had nothing to do with the quality of his writing? Had he drawn too steadily not on what was pathetic in his materials but on what was artificially dramatic around them, stretching some of his family tensions beyond the point of profitable return? I think he may have done all of these things, though without essential damage to what was, and is, essentially important: the excitement of watching a mind wrenched, by main force, into being.

257

The Shade of Eugene O'Neill

A question that has been asked again and again in the past few years, and is bound to be in the air for some time to come, is this: Will the present revival of interest in the work of Eugene O'Neill prove permanent, thereby placing the American dramatist in the "great" line of playwrights who are likely to be produced so long as actors are able to climb up onto boards?

My own reluctant guess is no. The thought seems ungracious and ungrateful, even as I put it down. After all, we've returned to O'Neill after something like twenty years and found him genuinely stimulating. For all the wear and tear of his theatrical demands upon us, we continue—in the presence of *The Iceman Cometh, Long Day's Journey into Night* and *A Touch of the Poet*—to sit spellbound, unable to wrench ourselves away even when the writhings and the repetitions seem intolerable. An authority asserts itself, we listen to its commands, we obey. The man's personal power is a simple fact.

But we are still within his reach, historically speaking. He can talk to us of twentieth-century man, in twentieth-century accents, and we can hear him. The discovery that American elms sheltered something more than genial family picnics is our discovery as well as his; disillusion, in whatever sodden circumstances, is familiar to us. Freud is our neighbor, too: the man who doubts himself within the Yank who boasts is almost the dominant creative image of the years since 1920. This is a shared world, and it remains—for the time being—intelligible.

What is to prevent this intense vision of a particular age and its hard-won self-knowledge from reaching out to touch other, and presumably different, ages? Why shouldn't O'Neill illuminate an American state of mind for posterity in the

258

same way that Euripides has gone on illuminating a Greek state of mind? Other playwrights have been bound, and in a sense limited, by the special assumptions of their cultures: Orestes resolves his soul-struggle by appealing to a theological court that has virtually no meaning for us; Shakespeare wants us to follow a tragedy that depends heavily upon our literal belief in a ghost, or in a band of witches. The plays survive anyway.

They survive, however, by virtue of the one quality that is indispensable to long-distance transmission: language, the kind of language that transcends the idiosyncrasies of time, of jargon, of provincial expression. Language isn't the only quality a close-to-permanent play must possess: the play had better have a story that still interests us and some characters who tantalize us by their variety and dimension. But language is the vehicle that conveys these things, and if it is going to carry them over any considerable span of space or time—and on into the unknown future—it must have timelessness in its bones from the beginning.

The audiences that came into Shakespeare's theater didn't speak blank verse to the ticket-taker; the blank verse was a deliberate elevation on the part of the author, agreeable to his customers but pitched at such a height that we can still see his landscape from the poetic mountaintop he scaled.

The Greek who was given a free pass to the day's entertainment didn't join his friends in an early-morning choral ode; Aeschylus fashioned the ode, unlifelike as it is, for less realistic and more enduring purposes.

When the means of communication is sufficiently detached from the specific inflections of an age, it acquires the curious power of illuminating the age, even of preserving certain of the age's least universal and least likable eccentricities. Shylock isn't a character we should care to draw today, for reasons of our own. Richard III isn't a character who can be believed in historically or—for that matter—theatrically. We

259

are still urging both these fairy-tale monsters onto our stages because the words they speak convey them totally: as the contemporary myths they were, and as the defiantly enduring imaginative achievements they are.

Great plays survive because they are great in every way; but we know their greatness only through the still-living language that is our single point of contact with them, the channel through which they reach us. If Eugene O'Neill eventually becomes a relatively important transitional name in the history books rather than a continuing voice on an actual platform, it will be because the voice itself was admittedly incapable of the larger effects it strained after.

The once-realistic slang is already unacceptable to us; the balance of O'Neill's language, adequate to the purposes of hammer-stroke twentieth-century melodrama, lacks those overtones that promise to keep a chord humming in the air long after. We shall continue to admire O'Neill, I suspect, just so long as we continue to share the general shape of his life and his thought: we still need a man who can produce a sound that is sufficiently rich, precise, detached, and elevated to make another time share it.

THE PERILS OF DOING WHAT
COMES CONVENTIONALLY

THE THEATER that is most familiar to us is still capable of making a firm fist. It is also capable, when it is merely going through the motions, of making a wondrously empty gesture. Oh, let's not be so polite. It is capable of making a perfect mess. I record a few messes, lest we forget.

The Tumbler

A week before director Laurence Olivier brought *The Tumbler* to Broadway he gave an interview in which he expressed his disapproval of that method of staging plays in which the director, for days and days, discusses with his actors their motivations, their past histories, their souls. Sir Laurence was all for getting actors on their feet and making them act; at the time these possibly intemperate remarks cheered my soul.

Seeing *The Tumbler* made me reconsider. Shouldn't Sir Laurence have discussed this play with somebody—the actors, his agents, his mother? Surely the teensiest bit of probing would have convinced everyone within earshot that there was absolutely nothing in it, whereupon a group of competent performers (Charlton Heston, Rosemary Harris, Martha Scott) might have chucked the whole business and got up a production of *Coriolanus* or *The Constant Wife* or *something*.

The Tumbler was a determined verse play by Benn W. Levy, formerly given to tossing off engaging trifles on the order of *Springtime for Henry*. It was written in such obvious imitation of Christopher Fry that one whole speech in the first act ("I am a man, a sack of skin . . . three yards of winding viscera") might easily have been taken from *The Lady's Not for Burning* if Mr. Fry hadn't been looking and had been sufficiently untalented to write it that way.

I do think, though, that the evening did one thing for us. It put us in a position to compose an utterly infallible guide to the writing of conventional verse drama. The guide would include the following helpful hints:

(1) Begin in a barn. Verse plays must necessarily take place in a void, and a barn is about as good a void as you can get nowadays. A barn is also a place for storing fresh, growing things, fruits of the soil, which can be talked about. Barns

are also good for thunderstorms and, the hay being handy, for trysts.

(2) When the heroine comes into the barn she should be wearing a raincoat and have her hands in her pockets. Since nothing real is going to be talked about for quite a while, and therefore no gestures will be required, she will have some place to keep her hands.

(3) When the hero comes into the barn, he should make it clear at once that he is an imagist and on friendly terms with nature. He should, for instance, look up into the sky after a particularly loud clap of thunder and exclaim, "All right, my little bow-wow!"

(4) All characters should address one another in diminutives. The heroine thinks of the hero as her "little Prometheus," the hero thinks of the heroine as his "little bulldog," and we already know about the thunder.

(5) Literary quotes are good. When the hero gets around to explaining how he hurt his bandaged hand, it helps if he can say he hurt it "against a friend's jaw, a too, too solid jaw."

(6) Lines that can be read forward or backward are even better. The hero can remark that he doesn't know whether "the hill is mine, or I its." After taking a breath, he can add that he doesn't know whether he leads the sheep or they lead him.

(7) Certain words are unmistakably poetic. "Umbilical" is one of these, because it is so hard to get into a prose play. Others are "promontory," "entrails," "prefatory," "womb," and the use of "remembered" as an adjective ("I found myself walking the remembered fields").

(8) If, as the hero and heroine are beginning to coil their arms around one another, you can catch hold of an image, hang onto it. He: "Let your passion roar." She: "It roars, my darling." He: "How beautifully it roars."

(9) Use paradoxes, twice before act-curtains and once at bedtime. The answer to "Are you ill?" is "As well as the next

man, and very ill." This can shortly be topped by "You cried because you had no more to give than everything."

(10) Keep the musical comedy rights in mind. If someone can say, "Carry it, if you will, to the police and see your new love, true love hanged," the work of the lyricist is already half done.

Step on a Crack

One evening at the Ethel Barrymore, as the customers were being seated, I noticed a lady with one of those cotton-candy coiffures—it was like the sea rising from Venus, rather—and I instantly bridled on behalf of the poor soul sitting behind her. She has a nerve, I thought. How does she expect anyone to see? A short while later, though, I took it all back. I wished she were sitting in front of me.

With an unobstructed view of the stage, a man was immediately in trouble. In almost as much trouble, in fact, as the characters on stage. The nature of the characters need not detain us long. Daddy was a doctor and the rest of the family were pills.

Mother was perhaps the least tasty. She was very jealous of Daddy, who had a new young receptionist, and she kept lapping up vodka in the moonlight on the veranda, pausing to remark, "I'm bad company," which may have been the most straightforward piece of information we were given all evening.

Son Donald Madden, whose hair tended to bob on top of his head as he walked, was very fond of Mother in an agonized way, clinging to the vines at the side of the house whenever Daddy and Mother quarreled and moaning over his inability to resolve their unhappy situation. "I'm not dense enough to cast a shadow on events" is the way he put it, though I think he underestimated himself.

Certainly by the middle of the third act he was at least having an effect on people. At this point he had strapped receptionist Maggie McNamara to a post in the toolshed, gagged her mouth with a handkerchief, assembled a great supply of fourth-of-July fireworks about her feet, and was fiendishly setting fire to the Roman candles.

Mr. Madden was, really, very active—spinning on his feet as though his dueling instructor had just prinked him, flinging one hand to his ear during soliloquies and shifting his eyes to their far corners as though he were listening for the prompter, or perhaps for an offer of other work. Mr. Madden had once played more than 100 performances of *Hamlet,* and, as he spread his fingers out before him as though to ward off a ghostly universe, he was either still playing *Hamlet* or a lively game of basketball.

It was easy to see how he could have become confused in this instance. Author Bernard Evslin had a way with words, a wayward way. "You are eminently torturable, you have a low threshold of indignity," Mr. Madden said to Miss McNamara. "When are you going to rise from the hurly-burly of your couch and take a look out the window?" he said to best friend William Hickey, with whom he did not have a homosexual relationship. (The play was original in almost every way.) "Certain wallpaper is not beyond listening," he said to himself as the other characters fled him to make love, two by two on the beach, while he scratched his fingernails over George Jenkins' scenery.

Gary Merrill played the doctor, and though he was obliged to try to live up to his wife's description of him ("You can feel his voice running over your skin, he turns the light on in a woman") he gave a remarkably unembarrassed performance. It might even have been a good performance if he hadn't had to read lines like "You can trust me as though I were a stranger" and if we hadn't all become so distracted wondering what the A.M.A. was going to have to say about this curious emphasis on the tactile pleasures medical men get while ren-

dering presumably diagnostic services to their female pa-
tients.

If I have not dwelt at length upon pretty Miss McNamara,
it was because she was so fortunate: one whole scene with a
gag in her mouth, unable to speak a word.

With so many porches and so much moonlight, *Step on a
Crack* looked rather like a sick *Seventeen*. Perhaps it established one principle, however. It is perfectly all right for interesting people to be miserably unhappy for two and one-half
hours on stage. But there is no democracy in these matters.
Boring people can't get away with it.

Goodbye, Charlie

Perhaps one lesson that can be learned from George Axelrod's
Goodbye, Charlie is that no writer of casual light comedy
should ever stray too far from Schrafft's.

When Mr. Axelrod wrote his very merry and very successful first play, *The Seven Year Itch*, he was still cocking an eye
at the everyday foibles of ordinary folk. Ordinary, at least, in
the sense that they had jobs to go to, wives to betray, psychi-
atrists to shy away from, and nerves like anybody else. The
hero of that easy essay on the temporarily bachelored male
went to Schrafft's for a lonely dinner, was trying to cut down
on his smoking, and dreamed now and then of a fling with
some secretaries he had actually met.

If a few fairly fantastic things happened to him thereafter,
such as having the ceiling of his apartment ripped out by a
dazzling wench who was trying to get at him, we were glad to
go along for the ride because we knew what kind of car this
fellow drove, and what garage he kept it in, and where the
keys were. He was somebody you might have run into on the
5:23 to Stamford, if the 5:23 to Stamford was bothering to
run that day. (Even exurbia is somewhat rarefied to some
folks: but it is not on the moon.)

265

With a hit under his belt and a wad in his wallet and an open sesame to the enchanted fleshpots of Hollywood, Mr. Axelrod did not at once begin to investigate the moon. He began to investigate himself, his success, his strange new position in the theatrical scheme of things, his shifting and suddenly bizarre environment.

Because he is a man with a sharp eye and a candid tongue, he did not precisely succumb to the rapids that were swirling about him. He was decently wry about them. In his second produced play, *Will Success Spoil Rock Hunter?*, he directed a good, swift rabbit-punch at the fellow who has had exactly one Broadway smash: the fellow, he said, was a "playwrote." He also stared at the kidney-shaped swimming pools and the man-eating palm fronds of Hollywood and found them debilitating. For the purposes of his play, he is reported to have sized up an actual and well-known Hollywood agent, and to have brought him on stage in the person of the Devil.

The wit was still working. But it was turned inward. His best joke was not about a hundred recognizable males who might have been observed doing something foolish, and wearing their foolishness in common. It was about the George Axelrod who had once written *The Seven Year Itch*, and you had to know something of Mr. Axelrod's precarious status in the ranks of new playwrights (the status that comes from one big hit and defies you to write another) in order to savor it fully.

The jibes at Hollywood, and at satanically conniving agents, were no doubt sound enough jibes, as well. But instead of being written from the outside, with the outsider's perspective on all that is preposterous in the ways of an existing but unbelievable world (as *Once in a Lifetime* had done so long ago), it seemed to have been written from a curled-up position deep inside a low-slung canvas chair.

The references were local, the satire was shoptalk, the mood was the mood of a "California Confidential" which spoke, when it managed to get its tongue out of its cheek, mainly to those in the know.

With Mr. Axelrod's third comedy, *Goodbye, Charlie,* the removal from East Seventy-second Street to outer space had accelerated. The quipster's mind continued to function; incongruity could still tease his ear. His initial conceit—a funeral service for a sex-hound of whom nothing good could be said, not even in requiem—was in itself fresh and barbed, even if the author-director seemed unaware of the practical fact that an interminably prolonged silence must necessarily be followed by a laugh big enough and shattering enough to justify so much suspense.

But even within this mordantly jolly passage, we began to hear references to actresses who wear Peter Pan collars (if you had an inkling of just which actress he might possibly have been referring to, you snickered a little louder than if you hadn't). We began to notice Mr. Axelrod enjoying himself on his typewriter: there were syntactical jokes (Sydney Chaplin, mourning his dead pal, spoke of "his un-, and now never-to-be, fulfilled literary promise"), and while these did seem a comment on pretentious Hollywood jargon, they were too finicky and too special to explode on the stage.

Much more troublesome, however, was the nature of the basic gag on which the entire evening depended. It was not a gag with any roots in the average theatergoer's psyche.

It was a gag of satiety: the kind that *must* be concocted when all the good ones are exhausted; the kind that poolside companions strain toward when they know that their colleagues are hopelessly "hip," that a switch on a standard gag is going to be too soon anticipated, that the only likelihood of landing a laugh and impressing the professionals lies in going so far out that not even the master of the "gassers" can conceivably have thought of *this* one.

In this gag the dead playboy, Charlie, returned to earth transformed into a girl (Lauren Bacall, feet planted apart and long hair matted) to make advances to a horrified Sydney Chaplin and to learn how tough it is to be a woman unloved. The problems that followed—the unfamiliarity of the little girls' room, the reported visit to Elizabeth Arden's, the nervous embarrassment with which Mr. Chaplin recoiled from every affectionate gesture—were explored at some length, and with some literalness.

But they were not problems—not real problems, not comic problems, not even the intelligible problems of fantasy. What we saw on the stage was not Charlie but Miss Bacall, who looked enticing: we saw her advance upon Mr. Chaplin, who looked enticeable. And what, we asked, could all this backing away be about? It was necessary for the audience to supply some ambiguous sexual image (or some double sexual image) in order to remind itself that there was a concealed joke beyond the evidence of their eyes; and the moment they had so supplied it, the whole thing became unpalatable.

The fact that his players were exemplary did not keep Mr. Axelrod from landing, at last, on the moon. All that is lifelike, and hence all that is really earthy, in comedy had been left far behind.

It is possible that none of these remarks would apply if the author were essentially a writer of rarefied high comedy, of intellectual riposte and admirable bad manners—though they still might apply in the sense that even Oscar Wilde achieved his effects by turning something actual inside out, and here there was nothing actual to thumb a nose at. But Mr. Axelrod's best vein would seem to be something cozier, more domestic, closer to home: the worm in the apple, and the wild look in the eye of the man who is contemplating eating it, in a probable duplex where the doorbell might ring.

Revivals

It is surprising how often off-Broadway feels the urge to revisit the conventional theater of the years of our youth in abundant, and indiscriminate, detail. Mounting new productions of *White Cargo, Tobacco Road,* and *Rosalie* does, after all, suggest total recall.

As I understand it, *Tobacco Road* originally opened on Broadway to very poor reviews and then proceeded to run and run. Since it is clearly a play that thrives on bad notices, and since every effort should be made, whenever it appears, to prevent the whole thing from starting up all over again, I tried—in reviewing its reappearance—to say everything good about it I could.

I went out on a limb and said I liked the way Ellie May chewed her hair. Ellie May is the one with the harelip about which Jeeter Lester, her father, is so uncomplimentary. Jeeter can't see no dang use for that there lip because, after all, "you can't spit th'u it and you can't whistle th'u it," and he keeps wondering why the good Lord put it there. Ellie May doesn't wonder, though. She just pulls her hair down over it and starts to chew, and by golly—as they say in the television commercials—that's good chewin'.

I thought Grandma Lester had the best part. All Grandma has to do, while the others are massaging the pains in their stomachs and trying to get a peep at such bridal-night festivities as are going on, is crawl around in the dirt on all fours until she is safely under the corncrib. She is safe because there are no rats there; there are no rats because there is no corn there. These people are poor. They have no seed to plant, no food to eat, and—as I deduced in this instance from the condition of the actors' ankles and toes—no money for anything except Band-Aids. I was glad they could afford the Band-Aids. That Georgia back-country is rough.

I had no trouble at all finding a word of praise for the designer's tumble-down shacks (what was wonderful about them was that they didn't tumble down in spite of the traffic going in and out the windows) or for the faded sunlight the electrician had spilled so gently over the spectacle of friend Jeeter lifting his daughter's skirt or a couple of frustrated country kids grappling about in the dust at stage center. The actors grappled pretty graphically, too. I mean, they understood the play.

I have a thought about all this slithering and tussling that decorates *Tobacco Road*, though. I suppose *Tobacco Road* has something of a reputation for being vulgar. But the true vulgarity of the occasion does not consist in the pop-eyed leering that goes on across fence posts or in the ardor with which a revivalist preacher (female) "horses up" a male in the middle of a sermon.

What is genuinely coarse about Jack Kirkland's adaptation of the Erskine Caldwell novel is its pretense to seriousness. There are odd little documentary gestures here and there that seem to ask some sort of sympathy for the downtrodden, the underprivileged, the inbred, the unlucky. At the very same time the downtrodden and the unlucky are being held up to view for our ribald delectation as though they were the delicious last dregs of third-rate vaudeville.

Faced with this combination of specious sociology and generally tedious hokum one can only wonder which are worse: economic conditions in the South or theatrical conditions in the North.

There's one thing you've got to say for *White Cargo*. No homosexuals.

White Cargo belongs to a time when men were men and women were women and dialogue was dreadful. "Everybody in the tropics thinks about sex all the time—it's the damned heat!" roars an unshaven fellow whose shirt won't stay buttoned, offering what may be the least interesting explanation of an interesting subject I have ever come across.

I don't want to run down the heat. At the Players Theater, where this jewel of the twenties was given thoughtless revival, it was hot. Men mopped their brows. Natives in loincloths crept through the underbrush to peer into the distance (since their noses were now actually touching a blank backstage wall, the far distance wasn't very far). Glycerine poured in rivulets down many a hairy chest, and the company boasted no navels that were not gloriously on display.

Tondeleyo, the native girl, had the best navel, if it's criticism you're looking for. But I'm sure you'd rather hear more about the heat. It led to things. Every time somebody said, "Oh God, it's hot tonight," a row started, with the fellows throwing sofa cushions all over the place and stomping on important government papers, while a hard-breathing old-timer named Harry (not Handsome Harry, though I don't know why not) collared a cowering minister in a corner and shouted at him that "morals is a matter of longitude and lassitude." And that's not the end of it, we were given to understand. "It's worse in the rainy season," Harry said.

The second act was the rainy season, and he was right. Now Tondeleyo, who had begun by disrobing so far as the law allows, refused to get up off the floor because she was utterly mad for young Henry B. Walthall (he wasn't really Henry B. Walthall, but he looked like him, which was suitable considering the age of the play) and she wanted him to lower himself in the eyes of his white brethren by joining her in the underbrush, or at least on the floor. No one else wanted him to, because they were all solid citizens (U.S.A.) and they knew he'd go to seed if he messed around with this miscegenation business. ("That's the trouble with mixed blood, the primitive always predominates.")

Well, the lad was a fool, and he married this girl, and she sat around (on the floor) all day making noises like a cheetah

271

and spitting (on the floor, luckily). In due time, friend Harry got so angry with all the disintegration that was going on ("This damp rot is like a weed which we destroy without ever killing the root") that he decided to kill the root—Tondeleyo, that is—and he was kicking her in the stomach as I took my quiet leave.

I should mention, I guess, that the designer had provided so much splendid underbrush that it spilled far out beyond the normal playing area, with the result that deep, deep in the jungle you could see a bright red sign saying "Exit." It was by this exit, I presume, that the director had left, an early-evening telegram to the newspapers indicating that he had washed his hands of the whole thing. I should also mention that the action, originally located (I believe) in Africa, had been shifted to Brazil. And just when we need to put our best foot forward with South America, too.

A Central Park revival of the ancient musical *Rosalie* was rained out on its opening night but succeeded in unveiling itself an evening later, proving that what we needed was more rain.

We certainly didn't need *Rosalie*. The festivities began with three Air Force men huddled around a telephone desperately dialing the Department of Trivia at the Pentagon. They were trying to locate the mythical kingdom of Romanza, and they spelled it out: *R* for romance, *O* for oh baby, *M* for Marilyn Monroe (hearty slapping of knees), and so on. I might explain that this was a "modernized" version of *Rosalie* and that the names of Marilyn Monroe, Farouk, and such-like kept turning up at odd and unsuccessful intervals.

The minute this sketch was over we were whisked into a long pause. Then a bugle blew, forlornly. Then the stagehands cleared the scenery. Then the lights went up again. Then peasants.

The peasants danced, waving long handkerchiefs. When they were through, there was another pause. Hearing no applause, they went off. Henny Youngman came on. He was wearing an untidy admiral's uniform, he had his hands firmly planted on his hips, he wittily addressed a certain Captain Rabisco as "Nabisco," and he told jokes to the orchestra leader.

I had the feeling that some of these jokes were his own, not Guy Bolton's, not William Anthony McGuire's, not Groucho Marx's or Jack Benny's. For instance: "My wife got a mud pack and she looked fine for three days, then the mud fell off." It must be admitted that this particular sally did break up the orchestra, but the orchestra was in a pretty battered condition to begin with.

The joke over, Mr. Youngman raised his hand, gave the conductor a mighty downbeat by way of a musical cue, and a truly blessed silence ensued. I don't mean that Mr. Youngman didn't seem to be mouthing the words of a song. It was just that the microphones were so arranged that only the off-stage ones worked, and you had to wait for a singer to get through his number and scurry into the wings before you picked him up ("Get out of the way, get out of the way, I've got a costume change!"). This gave us an interesting insight into the fabled backstage world we've all heard so much about.

Once Mr. Youngman was off, Mimi Benzell was on. Miss Benzell was as pretty as a picture and it wasn't her fault that she was wearing a pink tunic with a black heart on it while ten chorus boys—in white tunics with red hearts—crossed rapiers over her head. At this point hero David Brooks entered in a pilot's cap, dropped to one knee, sang one chorus of a song, and was immediately lost at sea.

Other things happened. That nice Ruth McDevitt wandered into view, was given the snappy retort "Nuts!" to somebody's thoughtless query, and was to be seen swigging vast quantities of what I took to be gin at frequent intervals. Helen Wood is an attractive girl and a fetching dancer, and I liked her even if she did fall down.

On board the S.S. *Smoothie*—don't ask me how we got

there, I might tell you—a passel of beaming passengers played at badminton without being able to hit the feathered ball so much as once, and a boy and a girl bounced a beach ball without being able to catch it. (When last seen, the juvenile was chasing it into the wings in the general direction of Fifth Avenue.) For a first-act finale, the company lined up at the railing of the S.S. *Smoothie,* pointed its fingers into the air, and cried: "There she is—the lady with the torch!"

But why go on? As they said in the play: "Don't torture yourself, Rosalie."

To think that the Park authorities had been worrying about muggers, with a problem like this on their hands.

The Bard

Conventional Shakespeare is still with us, too.

As of late 1961, the most disturbing thing about the Festival which flies its flag at Stratford, Connecticut, was that it was becoming enormously proficient at everything it chose to do.

During its earlier three or four seasons one could always presume that the situation was fluid. A mistake was a mistake, a modest success could be taken as a feeler that might come to something, the whole process of trial and error was to be cheerfully accepted as a prelude to future glories. At last, however, the mixed ingredients seemed to be firming up, and they were firming up as meringue.

Whatever was now wrong was deliberately, conscientiously, imaginatively wrong. Before mentioning the matter of getting comedy out of bath towels while character humor was left to rot on the beach, a word is in order about the Festival's adoption of a considered speaking style.

When Katharine Hepburn, the Viola of *Twelfth Night,* arrived at that charming passage in which she suggests that if she were in love with Olivia she'd build herself a willow cabin near the lady's gate and call her name to the hills night and day, the actress wrenched her head to the upper gallery and made a reverberating halloo of each separate syllable. Before the thought was revealed, the tones had turned into neatly spaced echoes. As a result, the passage was all tone and no truth: though the words were heard, they all had the same color, which served to drown the moment in an articulate monotony.

Since Miss Hepburn was not alone in this enunciation suited only to hilltops, the technique had to be regarded as an intended point of style. Perversely, it made one yearn for the days of unintelligible Shakespeare. There once was a time in our theater when casual and even slovenly realistic readings were thought to bring the playwright up to date, and there was a certain consolation to be taken from the muddiness. If, say, one had taken a fourteen-year-old child to such a baffling experience, and the child had patently understood nothing that was said, it could always be explained to the bewildered beginner that Shakespeare could be delightful if he were only spoken clearly.

What the Stratford techniques achieved was to rob us of the apologetic explanation. Here the language was utterly, forcibly, endlessly clear—and the play was still dull. Now our youthful companion could only conclude, and with apparent fairness, that he had indeed grasped every word the man wrote and that what the man wrote was uninteresting. This, it seemed to me, spelled real trouble for all of us. Because the Connecticut attack did not begin by discovering a real and private personality for each of Shakespeare's glowing zanies, and then let each properly clear line-reading take its impetus and inspiration from a particular heart or a particular mind, the case was all but lost. If the people weren't people, what price the glistening diction?

275

But that was only a part of the story. Director Jack Landau, continuing the "souvenir-of-your-trip" policy that had gradually been arrived at over several years, was determined to make you remember your experience in terms of the knick-knacks you picked up. Some of these were foolishly attractive in themselves.

Having entered the handsome teakwood playhouse (you could photograph the outside but not the inside) you were bemused by the great crust of divinity fudge that greeted you. Rouben Ter-Arutunian had enscalloped the entire proscenium with mushrooming shapes that suggested the world had gone up in sea shells, the entire mass was as radiant as sunshine on snow, and you did feel as you had the first time an elderly aunt took you to your local equivalent of Disneyland.

You could see other sights and wonders. While one actor was delivering a soliloquy, you noticed two very pretty maidens darting in gossamer skirts across a gossamer balcony, giggling together and shushing one another and pretending to overhear. While Malvolio was reading the letter that leads him into making such an ass of himself, you observed Sir Toby Belch searching vainly for Fabian in the upstage shadows of a bathhouse. You feasted on delicate lace parasols being opened and shut, tea trays being shuffled from deck chair to deck chair, and Sir Toby's "canary" being poured out of a polished silver flask as you made mental note that you were present at what may prove to be the *only* production of *Twelfth Night* ever mounted at a Victorian seashore. And you could congratulate yourself on being able to say that you had *seen* Katharine Hepburn, who—in her close-cropped curls and with a tasseled sword at her seaman's belt—was incontestably something to see.

The fact that most of the samples mentioned here amounted to calculated distractions from the movement of the text was not the primary problem, though it did seem as though the director had made a very careful study of Shakespeare's play in order to see what else he might do. A text can be embellished and transplanted and given every sort of gloss so long as the gloss in some way revitalizes it. The thorn in the Stratford garden was that emphasis everywhere was not on Shakespeare but on Festival, and on Festival in the sense of a random, one-day-a-year journey into exotic byways. The pleasure was all in the launch and the lunch and the fresh country air, not ever in the written and acted substance that tended to interrupt the frolicsome outing. The production did not dare to rely on the play; with a tourist's passion for coming home with tales, it relied on "the funny things that happened" along the way. And so home to bed, tired and happy after an inconsequential day and a gay roadside stop for dinner.

The danger, to put it plainly, was that the American Shakespeare Festival seemed ready to settle down as a kind of cultural Howard Johnson's.

Similarly, the Connecticut production of *The Merchant of Venice* was a great big toasted marshmallow, crisp and golden to look at and quicksand-soft inside.

The surface was burnished till it dazzled. Against the copper-toned lighting that spilled through the sky-high Venetian blinds which served as a permanent setting, romantic people appeared in the boldest of reds, greens, and blinding whites. Platforms glided into view bearing the lightest and airiest of scrollwork gates. A curlicued boudoir for Portia suggested that Steinberg might have fashioned it in a single rolling line, without ever lifting pen from paper. High in the background, and spanning the stage, rose a spindly, buoyant bridge that floated as serenely aloft as Shakespeare's pleasantest phrases.

If only the actors had been able to cross that bridge when they came to it! Instead, they were constantly to be seen going wildly out of their way to climb it, pause on it, kiss on it, make pictures on it, and then come down again to play out the sequence in the same place from which they had so errantly departed.

The production as a whole resembled the love affair that was going on with the bridge. It was a studied, graceful Sunday-morning pastorale which carefully moved, skirts lifted high, all around the edges of the matter at hand, never quite daring to look it directly in the eye.

Katharine Hepburn's Portia was a giddy adolescent who had been reading far, far too many novels and had remembered the prettiest postures in all of them. Miss Hepburn, again ravishing to look at in her undernourished way, swept onto the stage in one or another Ellen Terry-type gown—roses clambering all over it—to dart and sweep and canter and, at last, fall in a pool of satin to the floor. When the Prince of Morocco romantically offered a knife with which to test his quality of blood, she seriously considered slitting his wrist to find out: she was that kind of girl, if there is such a kind. When Bassanio selected the right casket—the caskets were little gingerbread mountains held up to view by cross-legged menials sitting side by side—and then turned to Portia as though he might kiss her, Miss Hepburn jiggled up and down with the impatient ecstasy of a woman of six.

As for Morris Carnovsky's Shylock, there was dignity both in the person and in the performance; among other things, Mr. Carnovsky did not beg for sympathy, an approach which finally earned him somewhat more sympathy than most recent Shylocks have got. Pictorially, too, the actor was arresting: a rigid titan as he stalked up underground stairs into the court, at all times a menace whose malevolent features were curved into the hard, curled lines of a Greek mask. Vocally, he was unfailingly clear.

But the mention of voice-work brings us back to the problem of Connecticut's opulent, orotund, though not really musical style, a style it has since promised to do something about.

The moment Mr. Carnovsky drew his breath for the "Hath not a Jew eyes?" speech, the stage lights began to dim. The actor moved to stage center. He spoke neither to anyone on stage nor directly to us. Instead, virtually spotlighted, he delivered an operatic aria, a quote from the play instead of a cutting episode in it.

When Miss Hepburn arrived at the "quality of mercy" speech, another—and equally destructive—attack was used. This Portia, daunted no doubt by the audience's familiarity with what she was saying, so broke up the passage that she seemed literally to have forgotten it; in the end it sounded as though she were dictating a letter to a not terribly efficient secretary. But then the delivery was declamatory throughout, quite as though those tireless scholars had at last found out who William Shakespeare really was: William Jennings Bryan.

My own best memory of a summer evening in Connecticut centers on that fiend Iago. A no doubt unreliable legend has it that when the British actor Donald Wolfit—now Sir Donald Wolfit—first went into the provinces with *Othello* he cast a rather talented player as Iago, only to discover that Iago got all the notices. Moving to another repertory stop, he cast a somewhat less talented player as Iago; Iago still got all the notices. On an inspiration he decided to have the assistant stage manager play the crafty villain on the next leg of his tour; the assistant stage manager romped away with the reviews. A week later Wolfit was no longer playing Othello; he was playing Iago and purring over the nice things the press was saying about him. He could take a hint, that boy.

This is, to be sure, the tradition about *Othello*. The Moor is thought to be a good part, all right; but Iago scoops up all the cream. From the time I first saw a slinky confidant with a dagger at his belt (Fritz Leiber, was it?) glide up to his honorable but susceptible commander and begin whispering faint but fatal doubts into his ear, down to the time when José

279

Ferrer managed to pocket the play in the august presence of Paul Robeson, it's been a scoundrel's paradise. Things shouldn't work out this way, of course; the play achieves its full power only when the intellectual brilliance of Iago is set in perfect balance against the emotional agony and ultimate heartbreak of the Moor; but we are rarely offered so sublime and shattering a combination.

It is a curious circumstance that one of the few times I have ever seen an Othello who really seemed the storm center of the play, carrying the whirlwind with him and letting Iago buzz busily at the vulnerable edges, was in an off-Broadway production of some years ago featuring Earle Hyman. What is so curious about it is that Mr. Hyman was once again stabbing at the role in Connecticut and failing altogether to sustain an authority won earlier.

It was not easy to say why. Mr. Hyman appeared, for the moment, to be having a great deal of vocal trouble: the instant his voice was pitted against the incisive inflections of Alfred Drake (Iago, as if you hadn't guessed) the struggle for mastery was over: Iago was keen, Othello a blur. As Mr. Hyman hurled himself into the terrifying mental torment of his distrust of Desdemona, the interior thrashings brought forth garbled roars rather than plain, piercing statements. It was as though we were listening to the man by transatlantic phone: we knew he was suffering, but the static was intolerable.

If Alfred Drake's Iago threw the evening into its traditional imbalance, it was not because Mr. Drake had any such thievery in mind. If anything, he seemed eager to avoid showiness. Apart from a few unobjectionable flourishes—the vicious scratching of a quill pen across a table, for instance—he was essentially concerned with the odd and malignant mind of his man. This malignance was not wholly directed at the Moor; it was more nearly a contempt for the reasoning processes themselves, a sadistic pleasure taken in using the orderly workings of nature toward disorderly ends, a mocking determination to show all "truth" as intrinsically corrupt and only one inch removed from its opposite, the lie.

Mr. Drake's scoundrel was a scoundrel who took deep satisfaction in never being obvious, in never having to do more than let the bad habits of the world work for him. He was playing a game with vices that already existed; he needed only stir the broth lightly, speak politely the expected words, and hell's brew would begin to simmer under its own power. Even in defeat—as he stood, hands limp at his sides, head cocked as though still trying to puzzle things out—he was not so much a bad man caught as a keen unscrupulous mind baffled that a cog should have slipped. If Mr. Drake could not wholly explain Iago (who has?) he drew plainly and precisely the particular shape of his mind, the intellectual canker that nagged him into motion and then, to his astonishment, destroyed him.

Although contemporary Shakespeare has made few gains in Connecticut, the plays have fortunately found other friends. You can say what you like about the difficulties facing fresh young talent fluttering about the Broadway edges, about the stony indifference of New York audiences to genuine quality, about the cold and cash-minded opportunism of the average commercial producer. Whatever you say is apt to turn around and bite you. The trouble with all such laments is that they are almost never true.

The project least likely to succeed in recent years was the visionary effort to make free Shakespeare palatable to people who were wandering through the city parks at night. This was the notion of an under-financed young dreamer named Joseph Papp, who came equipped with a trailer-truck, some scenery that all but flapped in the evening breeze, a relatively unknown director named Stuart Vaughan, and a company of players who could risk a possible fiasco because they had nothing in the way of reputation to lose.

281

Everything was against the project. In the first place, it was free. If there is one law of the theater more absolute than another it is that you cannot convince an audience of the worth of any enterprise it has paid nothing to get into. (Try "papering" a house sometime: it is almost impossible to do, and the deadheads who do show up invariably display a contempt for the proceedings that would chill the blood of the most loathsome professional critic.)

In the second, third, and fourth places the performance was out of doors (everybody knows you can't concentrate on Queen Mab when all of TWA is roaring overhead), the inexperienced actors did not have diplomas from the Royal Academy of London (Americans can't mouth the stuff unless they have been dipped in, and cleansed by, an older tradition), and the initial charitable grants that had made the whole thing possible were bound to run out in the middle of *Two Gentlemen of Verona* one sultry evening and never be replaced. Mr. Papp was a heroic fellow with a hole in his head.

Now watch the ball closely. Out of the trembling doorways that constituted the insubstantial scenery came a flaring battery of torches that somehow or other seemed much more real, hurling fitful shadows at the rustling scenery, than they ever had indoors.

Behind them came players who did not require interpreters. The commonest experience we all have of Shakespeare—or of verse plays, generally—is that of trying desperately to listen on two levels. We try to grasp the sound of the unreeling words on the one hand, as though this were a mystical value in itself; on the other, we try rapidly and even frantically to translate the clattering cascade into some sort of emotional sense. Sound is a veil rather than a vehicle; meaning is deeply hidden and must be dug out, seconds or even minutes late; the twain do not meet much in our time.

They were so well met, during a performance of *Romeo and Juliet* in Central Park, that that low clown Peter suddenly turned from the most trying of anachronistic buffoons into the funniest and most intelligible of not very intelligent men. Better still (and for the first time among my own theatergoing adventures) Romeo was recognizable as a member of the species: wonderfully foolish in his adolescent swoon over Rosaline, just as wonderfully flabbergasted by the unexpected intensity of his feeling for Juliet. He did not stand under a balcony serenading his lady with consciously liquid rhymes and a look of elaborate pain on his face. He was exhilarated. He could hardly contain himself. He all but fell down with the delight of what he was experiencing. He was having a splendid time being in love, he obviously didn't give a hoot what all of this might lead to (an attitude that began to make sense of the rest of the play), and his protracted farewells had a front-porch-at-midnight feeling about them that quickly reminded you what a fool you made of yourself at that age. The other players, most of them unknown and most of them excellent, helped out by simply and vigorously saying what they meant.

Well, the quality was there. Did anybody come? Customers not only came—and stayed—but apparently mentioned it to their neighbors. The available space in Central Park wasn't big enough to take care of all the quick-witted folk who were hurrying in from the corners of the city by the time the scheduled performances were drawing to a close.

Of course, the money ran out—as it was bound to in the circumstances. Did anybody care? Today Mr. Papp has a permanent theater in the Park, in part the gift of a once grudging city, and though he still has difficulties they are small when compared to his audiences. The truth of the matter is that talent attracts everybody. Legends may live on, and the theater may remain the most unstable of all enterprises, but no whisper of quality ever goes entirely unheard.

There is a school of thought that says Shakespeare's comedies are no laughing matter. Director Tyrone Guthrie dismissed that school for the summer—if not forever—on a certain evening at Stratford, Ontario.

The problem that faced the spindly, the padded, and the cross-gartered clowns in the Canadian Festival's arrangement of *Twelfth Night* was to cut short the laughs in order to get all of the lines in by midnight.

Douglas Campbell, an immense and immensely dignified Sir Toby Belch apparently just escaped from a Franz Hals portrait, sailed like a not quite seaworthy ship onto the wide-open stage. He gargled a brief bit of French, and the airy pretension was funny. He seemed to curl his toes deep inside his high gray boots, and the effort at sedately drunken balance was inspiring to behold. He tried to shoulder a pillar aside as he made a haughty exit, he hurtled down an aisle with a hallooing Maria perched wildly on his shoulder, he joined his cronies in a precise, bawdy, and mocking little madrigal in honor of an outraged Malvolio. And everything he did had the taste and tang of good wine about it, so much so that the audience quickly grew tipsy.

Sir Toby's cronies were equally buoyant. Christopher Plummer opened his share of the revels by crashing tardily and clumsily through a rear exit in the steeply pitched auditorium. When he descended onto the stage—as a tittering Sir Andrew with a tip-tilted nose—the reign of reason was altogether over. Mr. Plummer's Sir Andrew was light of foot (he had an enormously fetching back-skip at his command), but his mind was a mind of lead. Snapping his mouth open and shut like a half-witted cod, listening to absolute nonsense with the intensity of a research scholar, peering vacantly over the shoulder of a man he was supposed to be hiding from, sagging as limply as his wilted stockings when he was challenged to a preposterous duel—in every feebly courageous gesture and in every wistfully woebegone line he was superb.

The clowns were not the whole of it. The moment these fetching and endlessly elegant players turned to the lunatic love story of the piece, a vein of caustic and crackling high comedy was uncovered. Frances Hyland, as an overly romantic Olivia who was still intelligent enough to read her own foolish mind, charmed the birds off the Stratford trees with the proud, yet charming, simplicity of her candid self-praise. Siobhan McKenna, a radiant Puss-in-Boots in the Cavalier costume designed for her, twisted her mouth into a curled-leaf smile, opened her enormous eyes, and somehow or other succeeded in suspending herself in a state of permanent rapture. Miss McKenna's rippling and buttered speech did not always inflect the lines for due emphasis; but it was pitched at a level of silken comedy that kept the frolic light and the atmosphere heady.

We have still not touched, however, on the evening's most striking point of style and director Guthrie's most daring innovation. Mr. Guthrie had noticed that beneath all real merriment there runs a strain of melancholy; laughter lives right next door to lunacy, and there is always a haunting danger that lunacy will decide to move in.

From the outset of the evening an undercurrent of ingrained sadness, of rueful longing for a time when gayety came easier, served as contrast and counterpoint to the abandoned horseplay. The antic ne'er-do-wells of the piece were having a whale of a time—because they had nothing else to do. Feste was an old man now, idly sewing with an absent needle that would somehow stitch things together again, rubbing his grizzled beard in perplexity whenever he was commanded to make a joke. When he sang "The Wind and the Rain," it sounded as plaintive and moving as a Jewish lament. When the drunken roisterers burned a candle at midnight and raised their voices in "O, Mistress Mine," there was more regret than ribaldry flickering on the cellar walls. When Sir Toby asked Malvolio if he didn't think there were going to be further cakes and ale, an upward strain in his voice suggested that yes, there were going to be more cakes and ale—but that these were going to be the last.

The conceit gave *Twelfth Night* a double richness. Hilarity, it said, will never be stilled. It cannot afford to let itself be. There is that slightly broken heart beneath it which must not be confessed.

AT RANDOM

LOVE AND HATE

THE SOCIETY I know is divided into two camps—people who love the theater, and people who hate the theater. It is possible to tell these people apart, and within a few minutes of meeting them. The people who hate the theater are the people who go to it. The people who love the theater, or announce most loudly that they do, are the people who don't.

You may not have noticed this, in your hurry, but it's true. Whenever you hear a fellow inveighing caustically and with some passion against the institution fathered by Aeschylus, he is always bellowing about a specific case. He is talking about a play he has seen. In the course of his harangue, furthermore, he is prepared to make comparisons between that particular play and three other particular plays he has seen within weeks before; he is ready to cite instances, compare performances in some detail, batter you down with what must be accepted as evidence. The source of his pain is rooted in space, and he can tell you precisely what playhouse you had better avoid in this year of diminished grace.

Consider the man or woman, on the other hand, who is almost moist-eyed in his (or her) devotion to drama. "I just love the theater," this enraptured soul murmurs, eyes focusing a little dreamily on a memory of bliss. The remark is always, and instantly, followed by another: "Of course, I don't get to go very often." The balance of the conversation is occupied by a thorough discussion of the reasons why this starved admirer of plays and players is never quite able to make it to Forty-fourth Street. The conversation can, quite naturally, take no other course, since there are no actual plays or players to be mentioned.

I know that the first and most obvious explanation for this perverse state of affairs is that the theater itself is in such a

289

poor way that it must inevitably breed hate in the people who risk attending it, and that genuine love is possible only in those who have been lucky enough to stay home.

I don't believe that explanation, no matter how confused I have become. I have noticed something about carpers generally. They care. The man who is most apoplectically outraged by the conduct of one or another fool in the State Department is usually the man who has followed the whole devious maneuver most minutely, a man who has the facts at his fingertips, fire in his heart, and an enormous fondness for a possible ideal. The cab driver who gives you the bitterest catalogue of the Yankees' clodhopper conduct is invariably the cab driver who loves the Yankees best. Chances are that whenever you talk (listen, really) to a fellow who is prepared to blister the air with his personally-felt injury, you are listening to someone who believes deeply not only in what he is saying but also in the thing he is saying it about. I'm inclined to include my friends who are fiercest in their tongue-lashings of the theater in this category. I doubt that they're hurting anything. If the stage is their whipping-boy, it is because they are determined to whip things up, to provide some of the contentious energy needed to keep a sometimes enfeebled but seriously beloved form alive.

Certainly the professed partisans aren't doing as much. So far as I can figure, they are huddling safely at home, self-appointed baby-sitters, musing mellowly on an enthralling institution they are determined to defend to the very last ditch, which is where they seem to have taken up their positions.

Love is not love which fails to alter when it alteration finds, Shakespeare and meter to the contrary. The swain who doesn't notice a line or a blemish on his fair one's face is a swain who hasn't been looking. And the swain who doesn't instantly demand, as loudly as he is able and as bluntly as he dare, that the object of his devotion do something about it is a swain who just plain doesn't care.

A HELPING HAND

SHALL WE all raise our hands and solemnly resolve to help
our harried and unstable theater? There is a perfectly clear
way of going about this, if we will only put our minds to it.
That the theater needs help, this instant, is beyond doubt:
altogether too many plays come to town looking slightly sheepish, as if to say, "Well, you're here now and it's too late to go
anywhere else tonight; couldn't you *try* to like us?", and so
much beguiling wistfulness leads critics into writing the kind
of notices that cause readers, earnestly advancing at cocktail
parties, to say, "I always read your reviews; is there anything
you think I might like?" Everybody knows the situation. I'm
not blabbing.

But has anybody done anything about it? I don't mean has
anybody done anything about the plays. Nothing can be done
about the plays; let's not be whimsical. Plays are written by
playwrights, not people; and playwrights belong to a gifted
species who must be given their heads and permitted to follow their secret hearts all the way to Wilmington, where they
will hastily try to make them a little less secret and so probably spoil everything just in time for the New York opening.
Nor is it any use demanding that the direction be firmer, the
acting finer, and the scenery thrown out. These are not practical attitudes: we can stamp our feet and ask for such things,
but that isn't going to produce them; it's just going to get everybody overheated.

The real question is what can we do, *ourselves*, to make our
few short hours in the playhouse seem shorter? Not only
shorter; perhaps brighter, more soothing, more gracious, even
heart-lifting. Aren't we all responding to a limp theater rather
limply, when we might be examining our consciences, discovering where *we* have failed, and adopting measures to insure
our gayety and contentment the next time we hazard the

291

trip? I realize I'm not being very specific. All right. How many here, for instance, are in the habit of taking the very elementary precaution of going to a bad movie the night before they see a Broadway play?

This isn't so impossible. With a little spying and a little leg-work, you can find a bad movie. You can not only find a movie bad enough to make the Old Vic's *Macbeth* look good, you may even uncover one capable of leading to the revival of *Rose Marie*. But the selection should not be hastily made. It is not enough that the film itself should have a cast of thousands, none of them actors; it should also be showing in a large house. A poor movie will attract relatively few customers; and in a large house you may come to feel lonely. This means that on the following evening your joy at returning to the society of men will know no bounds. You will leap into the lobby fray with unconcealed exhilaration. Here, once more, is the tang and thrust and crush of your fellows. Each gouge will have its glint of glory, each damaged instep its brotherly stamp. You will come away marveling at the wisdom of the architect who arranged these aisles: people can know what it is to be in touch here.

There are other do-it-yourself ways of enriching the theatrical experience. Have you ever tried not letting a cab driver get a word in edgewise? One extremely important reason why people are quickly bored by the sound of actors' voices is that they have been listening to the sound of the cab driver's voice all the way to the theater, and they don't really want to hear another word out of anyone for the rest of the evening. Suppose, though, you were to get the jump on the hackie as you crawled in the taxi door, barely including your destination in the rush of opinion, anecdote, reminiscence, gratuitous advice, and inventive profanity you were already showering all over him, and that you kept up the clatter until his ears folded forward, signing off only after you were safely on the sidewalk again, flipping him a small tip and calling out suggestions on how to spend it as you vanished beneath the marquee? Don't you think you'd be willing to sit back and let the actors talk, then? And wouldn't you feel wonderful, no matter what was happening on stage?

We are simply not taking our responsibilities seriously enough. Now I could go on and on with this, but I want to leave some room for free enterprise. Areas everybody can start working on are money and food. It is downright foolish to brood about the cost of theater tickets in an economy built upon deductible losses and galloping consumption. Surely the thing to do is to plan your theatergoing for a week in which you expect to beat somebody out of something—the government out of its just income tax, or, if it is a week when the schools are closed, the children out of their allowances—so that no matter how much you pay for the tickets you'll know you're really coming out ahead.

Planning your food for the week around the show you're going to see is imperative, though difficult to prescribe for on a mass basis. I myself have been made the subject of a brilliant piece of research, by one Susan M. Black, in a thoughtful journal known as *The New Yorker,* which made it incontrovertibly clear that I spent one entire fall describing actors and plays in terms of tantalizing edibles. In a most sympathetic and understanding diagnosis, Miss Black suggested that I was compensating for something, and was perhaps on a diet.

I was not on a diet, though for a long time I have been watching my weight. (When I say that I have been watching my weight, I mean just that: I don't do anything about it, I just watch it.) But Miss Black's intuition had not played her false. I had been conditioned in my theatergoing for all those months by an incident directly related to this matter of menu, and I knew, I knew it was going to come out. On the very first theater evening of that particular fall I had had dinner in a restaurant where I meant to regale myself with certain seasonal dishes which would soon be vanishing. I had ordered judiciously, lingered over a drink, waited no longer than a suitable interval, and had then been served a one-legged soft-shell crab. I swear it. Now these are the things that condition us far more than we know, and we do owe it to the theater to investigate them, weigh them, and counterirritate them.

Happy conditioning.

A HORSESHOE NAIL

MORE AND MORE OFTEN producers who run into too much trouble on the road are closing their shows right there, without letting those of us who live along Broadway get a look at them. If this sort of thing continues the residents of New Haven, Pittsburgh, and Toronto are going to know more about the state of contemporary drama, and particularly what is wrong with the state of contemporary drama, than those of us who inhabit the metropolis. Reviewers are either going to have to migrate or turn in their typewriters.

Sealed away in New York, of course, it is impossible to determine what has gone so wildly wrong with presumably promising shows that they elect to abandon their large investments rather than chance the blight of Broadway. Any dozen things may have gone wrong, and all at once; one can have nothing but sympathy for such casualties of the road, especially if one hasn't seen them. But I have called them "presumably promising" for a reason: these premature failures are generally graced by performers of some quality and/or mounted by producers of demonstrated intelligence. Somebody has liked them, and in most cases none of these somebodies can be described as a dolt.

What this suggests to me, at a surface scratch anyway, is that each such venture very likely contained a couple of lively, workable scenes, or one or two parts that were catnip to actors, or perhaps a shovelful of good lines—but that these

294

things existed independently of a story line simple enough and strong enough to see them home. The commonest trap of our time in the theater is the trap of quality where it doesn't count: quality in the upholstery, with no frame to rest on.

I suppose one's first reaction to this state of affairs, if it is indeed the state of affairs that prevails, is to scold the playwright for his bad engineering: why couldn't he have thought up a good idea in the first place and then made sure that all of its cogs and cotter pins were in the right places? My own reaction is one of increased sympathy. For the contemporary playwright is asked to undertake a virtually intolerable task: he is first asked to *invent* an entirely original narrative that will function with an efficiency unknown to Atlas rockets, and he is next asked to bring fresh insight and intense imaginative energy to each of its thousand details. He must pour the concrete and do the interior decorating, too.

This in spite of the fact that the greatest playwrights we know wouldn't have considered for a moment doing any such thing. Sophocles didn't waste manpower on plots: he started off with one he knew would work because it had already worked for so long. Shakespeare almost literally scanned the best-seller lists and lifted what seemed most sure-fire. Nor is it any use pointing out that these men wrote, luckily for them, at a time when audiences were not yet jaded and plots not yet overworked. Two thousand years after Sophocles, Racine came along and borrowed what Sophocles had borrowed, with presentable results.

Is this an academic cliché, irrelevant in the light of our present sophistication? Not necessarily. An audience doesn't ask a man where he has got his plot; it only asks what he sees in it. Imagination is in the *how* of things; the *what*, after all, has been going on forever.

It is possible, and it may even be sensible, to regard stories as primeval statements of the human condition, primeval and infinitely recurring. Creative work does not consist in altering the statement; it consists in understanding it. Indeed, the strain toward an altered statement, toward utter originality in reporting the facts of the human condition, generally drives a playwright toward the bizarre, the eccentric, the abnormal, and the just plain inexplicable. But that isn't the point here. By forcing the writer to shy away from what is plainly functional, if faintly familiar, in the way of structure, the effort at total originality may leave him without a roadbed along which his real virtues can speed. It may just possibly also leave him out of town, with his play in his hand.

One of the things we seem to need, along with a central ticket agency, is a plot bank. I'm almost serious, especially after having read P. G. Wodehouse's delightful collection of letters to a fellow writer, *Author! Author!* You see, one of the things Mr. Wodehouse and his friend exchanged over the years was plots. If Wodehouse happened to hit upon an idea he couldn't use, but that W. Townend might, he sent it to him, no strings attached; and vice versa. Actually, Mr. Wodehouse seems to have used only two or three of these hand-me-down inspirations in the course of producing forty-seven novels; he was a pretty good architect himself.

But the literary atmosphere of the moment is such that I'm sure almost any writer who reads of Mr. Wodehouse's willingness to help himself at the open hearth, even two or three times, will be scandalized. That's conscienceless, isn't it? And uncreative? Isn't it even a sin? *Where* is the man's integrity?

Integrity need not consist in originating the universe, all of it, all over again. It need not even consist in assuming the responsibility of inventing one new narrative shape. (No doubt this will happen again, sometime, in which case we should be delighted that one more shape has been added to the common store, not depressed that it has now been used up.) What should really cheer us in this repetitive world is the number of variations that have been born and can be born of the very same human cocoon.

Well, this is all speculation. But I feel fairly certain that some good things go down the drain for want of an old horse-shoe nail.

AT THE CIRCUS

A CONVENTION I am ready to dispense with is the one whereby a reviewer troops off to an entertainment in the company of as many of his small children as he has been able to get clean enough for the occasion, and then instead of telling you what *he* thought of the entertainment gives you a gem-by-gem rundown of his children's responses. This dastardly little trick is generally defended on the principle of "seeing it through fresh eyes," whereas all it really does is let the reviewer watch the girls go by for two and one-half hours without giving any real attention to his work and thereafter substitute for his work a collection of the limpest responses ever to be set in linotype. Children's responses are always limp, or did you know that? Take them to the circus, say, and all you'll ever get out of them, after the devil's own prodding, is, "Well, *I* liked it," or perhaps, after profound consideration on the part of the child and an almost unbearable struggle to arrive at the *mot juste*, "Cool."

Having had a bad week in the theater not long ago, I decided to go to the circus. As an afterthought, I took the children along, a gesture which had the entirely misleading but socially fortunate side-effect of causing the neighbors to murmur "Isn't he a good father?" as the group, caroling merrily, pulled out of the driveway, where we stopped, because the car doors weren't shut tightly. I also brought them home again, which is a far, far better thing I do. But I promise you faithfully: no word of what those children thought of the show is going to be recorded here. The information goes with me to my grave.

297

I am perfectly willing to tell you what I thought of it, or rather what I thought about while I was sitting, passive and bemused, in its comforting presence.

I thought about the theater, and particularly about the bad week I had been through, together with some earlier bad weeks that had all blurred into one another and now constituted, in some senses, a shadowy contrast to the very simple brilliance I was looking at.

The circus retains, in however primitive a way, one or two fundamental energies the contemporary stage is in some danger of letting slip or go slack. I am not going to repeat here my essay on the virtues of the arena, or again discuss the descent from barbaric ritual, or anything like that. The powers I have in mind are much closer to home. One of them is the energy of direct engagement.

There is a clown act, for instance, in the latest Ringling Brothers' roundup that is quite a good clown act by present-day standards, which are not altogether the standards I was brought up on. And what makes it a good act is that the thing you keep hoping to see happen actually does happen, and is not discreetly or safely bypassed. What you hope to see happen, as three or four zanies in white coveralls swing into the center ring carrying paint buckets filled to the brim with a sudsy substance approaching the consistency of whipped cream (each bucketful in a different, and dazzling, primary color), is for man to meet mess, but head-on. No slopping wildly this way and that, and missing. No *almost* immersion, protectively ducked. (You fear that this is going to be the case early in the act when one and all slither and slide across an oilcloth rink on which a pail full of pink has been spilled.) You want one whole bucket to land upside down on one unready head, in order to see what the real thing—the full slop and slosh—looks like. Luckily, the worst happens, and it happens five or six times. Gratification could scarcely go deeper.

In what way has the theater *not* been living up to its obligation to turn the promise into pandemonium and the possible into the actual? More and more plays (of all kinds) seem to me to be fearful of The Scene, the moment in which everything is changed, shiveringly, before our very eyes. More and more the essential action is explained to us, as an apology or a rationalization or a rehearsed story, in the psychological quiet of its aftermath. We have a tendency nowadays to flirt with the big event, to intimate its likelihood (at some unidentified vanishing-point off stage), to talk about it and to analyze it and to remember it and regret it, but to stay, always, two feet shy of it.

I suspect we *are* shy of it. If we write it, and don't write it well enough, we are going to come out cornball: the very thought of writing it makes us wonder if we aren't succumbing to the temptation of tastelessness, of melodrama, or of slapstick. After all, aren't the important elements of drama personal and psychological, and aren't they richer in the act of reflection than they are in the act of acting without reflection? Well, yes they are—provided something has happened that is worth reflecting on, and that all of the reflection is not mere brooding in a vacuum about a rumored contest which seems to be taking place, if it is taking place at all, four miles away. We are well supplied with plays which consider what should be done, or what has been done, but which nervously refuse us, in the end or in the beginning, the point of contact.

The circus also reminded me of how little we prize skill. We prize—in our acting as in our playwriting—sincerity, groping sensitivity, the well-meaning heart that may be beating irregularly but that is manifestly doing its beating in the right place.

The fact that these virtues, which are real enough, appear in a play that is utterly without precision in displaying them does not bother us much. We have half a suspicion that true merit must be untidy and that whatever is obviously adroit must also be in some way specious: would it be so adroit if it weren't trying to cover something up? We distrust technique, which is rather like distrusting well-built ladders.

But when one is noticing the unthinkable tensions in balance, the musculature in control, of fools engaged in such profitless enterprises as descending from the top of the tent on a wire, balancing feet in air on the fulcrum of a single finger, or hurtling out of a cannon to land—hopefully—on a rather narrow net, and when one is remembering the disciplines that have gone into such minor but desperate accomplishments, a vision begins to take shape: what if the same determined disciplines, the same concentration of energies toward supple and instant command of the situation, could be applied to the far more complex and more meaningful crafts of the theater?

Sincerity will get you nowhere on a high wire. Whether your heart is in the right place or not, your foot had better be. How pleasant, perhaps even how thrilling, the results might be if, on our stages, we could have both at once: true heart and sure foot. Is the stage really so much less precarious that it can afford to be so much less precise?

Thus, then, my thoughts while watching the circus. *I* liked it.

HANDMADE MERCHANDISE

THE PRICE of theater seats is high, to be sure. But I find myself deeply contented by a remark made not long ago by a stage manager who may prefer to remain anonymous. "Why shouldn't the theater cost more?" he exploded. "It's handmade merchandise in a machine-made world!"

There's a little something to chew on there, as we agonize over the production costs that won't go down and as we wonder how to swell the attendance figures that won't go up. Perhaps our merchandising is wrong. Perhaps we are trying to tell people that as soon as we get the shop efficiently organized, the payroll streamlined, and the price of tickets scaled to the competitive level featured by discount houses, we'll be in a precision-tooled position to offer goods off the assembly line exactly as all those television studios out in Hollywood do. The theater, too, can offer more for less money.

What if it can't? What if there's no reason on earth why it should? Instead of reassuring customers that we'll eventually find a means of producing plays as though they were so much malleable plastic, might we not be better off trying to persuade them that the theater is not plastic but sheer mercury and that the high cost of mercury is worth it?

This last image is pretty unstable, I know, because mercury isn't handmade. But the two do have some things in common: unpredictability of behavior, elusiveness to the touch, and a tendency to give folks the feeling that they are dealing with something that is at least half alive.

A good many people are inclined to groan over the fact that theater can't be preguaranteed, can't be run like a sensible business, can't be taken out of the lucky long-shot category. All of its elements are too unstable: scripts that refuse to play as well as they read, performers who play hob with rehearsals, accidents of time and place and those curious cloud formations over Philadelphia.

But it may be that this very uncertainty is a part of the inherent health of the theater. Because nothing is cut-and-dried, because nothing *can* be cut-and-dried or delivered as specified or printed forever just as it stands, there is some room left over—at every performance, including matinees—for a creative miracle to take place.

If nothing about the theater can be entirely foreseen, it is because everything about the theater is entirely personal. The two people standing on a stage are truly and somewhat helplessly there, just as they came from the hotel a few minutes ago. The actress has a cold and the actor, having slept well and noticed that his mirror glowed at the sight of him, is confident that he is on the verge of giving the greatest performance of all time. Between the actress' effort to rise above the cold and perhaps even above that strangely energetic actor, and the actor's effort to pare down his exuberance to the point where it will not run over into the orchestra pit, something exceedingly strange and unlooked-for and electrically interesting may happen. There are actual hands at work, they are in varying and even contending states of flexibility, and they may weave a different bit of needlepoint on the very day we chance to drop by.

The very fact that *we*, the audience, are in the theater today puts another set of hands to work. If one of us brings a cold along, he's going to affect the evening's reality, for good or for ill: mostly ill, no doubt, though a few sharp barks have been known to stir the seal-tamers on stage to unimagined flights of self-assertion. If a couple of us bring a highly susceptible set of responses along, laughing as Jack Benny is said to laugh at every other comedian's least sally, chances are we're going to see a performance of leapfrogging brilliance. We're certainly going to see the only performance of this particular shade and intensity—because it's the only performance that was ever affected by us, personally, privately, intimately.

Even the stagehands are present in person, a large part of the time, and the particular way in which one lowers a drop (late, medium-late, or early, or perhaps even on time) or the sunny expression one of them happens to be wearing as an actress passes him on the way into the set contributes to all that is unpredictable because it is happening in a place in space. I am sure that ushers have affected performances because they do affect customers' temperatures, up or down, as the party is assembling and an occasion that has never exactly taken place before is getting under way.

Now all of this is costly. Because an actress has promised to be where you are tonight, and not off making more money on a studio lot somewhere, a compensating hike in her salary is called for. Because a backdrop is going to be hauled up and down tonight and tomorrow night and eight times this week, with fresh energy spent every time it is touched instead of being spent only once and recorded on film, some minor-league Hercules is going to be paid eight times rather than once.

And because we have indicated that we would like to be invited to the ballgame, instead of watching it on television, an extra nick is taken out of the allowance the government has left us.

Or never mind that notion of a ballgame, and consider that theater is really a house party, where each guest is expected to bring a gift. In this day and age he *must* bring a gift, or else settle for staying outside and looking in the windows, as one does with television and movies. The fun must be put together freshly every single night, in our presence and with our cooperation. Should we say to the customer: if you want to be where the fun is, cough up? That's not very polite, I know, but it at least acknowledges one of the facts of contemporary life.

WITHDRAWAL SYMPTOMS

THE DEMANDS that Broadway has lately made upon playwrights are oppressive enough to be paralyzing. The playwright who would like to live to write another play, and see it produced, must write such a blockbuster this time out that money rolls in forever, and for everyone: backers, agents, actors, sign-painters. Nor is it enough for him to write a play capable of generating so much economic power. He must also compromise that play in advance—or so the rumor goes—by letting it be "packaged" for theater-party and recording-company appeal with name stars who may or may not be right for it, with a guaranteed director and a marketable title and some tidbit or other in the subject matter that will help to make a splashy billboard. Small wonder that the playwright is to be heard saying, with increasing frequency, that he'd like to get away for a time, perhaps for all time; small wonder that those who wish him well wish he could earn his living and ply his trade in a pleasanter environment.

Furthermore, his present environment would seem to be a failing environment regardless of what he does for it. The Broadway theater has been outspoken about its economic difficulties in recent years, giving rise to the suspicion that the situation may be so bad as to be beyond remedy. What if Broadway, for which so many sacrifices are made, is truly doomed to ever-increasing losses and hence ever-decreasing activity, or doomed to restrict itself to the production of big expense-account musicals? Hadn't all people who care about theater, or literature, or art, or quality of any kind better pull up stakes now, refuse to compete in a foundering commercial stockyard, and take themselves off to some quieter spot where nothing will be demanded of them but that they remain true to themselves?

At an educational conference meeting in New York the suggestion has been made that Broadway might well be headed for extinction, and perhaps good riddance, but that theater—quality theater—would find a far more stable and far more nourishing home for itself in the college and community theaters that have proliferated across the continent.

Among more deeply concerned urbanites, committed to New York, committed to intellect, committed to drama that will not be forced to pander, this same restiveness takes the form of looking with longing toward the tiny house, presumably off-Broadway, in which work of distinction may be done without any need to compete for dollars from the masses.

Coupled with the itch to find a small enough closet is the

demand for subsidy—whether from government sources or private foundations—so that the dollars from the masses will never be missed as the unruffled pursuit of quality continues. And the impulse toward withdrawal takes yet another, more fundamental form, which we shall discuss in a moment.

Now the dismay with which a serious artist reacts to the pressures of Broadway is understandable. The temptation to find himself a more secluded and sheltered spot in which he can give his whole energy to his work and squander none of it on bickering, bargaining, or blockbustering, is just as understandable. Sympathy is in order; so is respect.

But before anyone makes a strategic retreat into a happily hidden hole, ready to pull down the blind that conceals the entrance, he had best ask himself how deep the hole is, whether there are any other exits, how long he can hold out there, and whether or not there is light enough.

Consider the suggestion of the educators that the playwright bring his new plays to the quiet of the campus. No one need doubt or undervalue the preparatory work that has been done and is being done in an increasing number of campus and community playhouses. Immature writers have been given some opportunity to find out what it is about them that is, at the moment, immature. Actors have cut their eyeteeth on materials they may not get another opportunity to explore —the genuinely great plays of the past, for instance—in a subsequent ten or fifteen years of professional performing. Audiences have been instructed, and in some cases entertained. It is even possible, as educators like to contend, that fresh audiences are being recruited for the professional theater, though there is some evidence to suggest that where local enthusiasm is at its most intense it is also somewhat parochial, self-contained, and perhaps even a bit jealous. Cities in which community theaters flourish most happily do not necessarily become more receptive to touring companies, as many a sorry manager has found out.

305

Still, the contribution to the idea of living theater and to a sense of its long history is enormous. What must be remembered in the midst of honest praise is the fact that experiences of theater at the college and community level must inevitably remain tentative experiences because they are inevitably unfinished experiences.

It is the business of a university to deal with immature people in the hope of making them less so. The playwright whose play is performed under the best possible campus circumstances may very well be rewarded by occasional flashes of intuitive brilliance. On balance, however, he will have to try to judge his play—and the audience *will* judge his play—on the basis of ensemble work that is at best erratic and at worst inadequate. The physical production will almost certainly be technically flawless, and will have become so without haggling over union skills or costs; but the interior life of the play must stand short of the threshold because the personnel performing it are, by definition, short of that threshold. I do not see how universities can overcome a nonprofessional callowness without sacrificing their identities as universities, nor how a playwright can hope to grow riper by returning to the world of the quite defensibly green. The contribution of these theaters is a contribution to something else, to something beyond themselves that does not accept their self-imposed and eminently proper limitations.

Community theaters are a breed apart, of course, staffed as they are by adults. But the fact that the men and women performing these plays are mature does not make them professionally mature.

Apart from those few, and certainly intelligent, local playhouses that are beginning to import a nucleus of genuinely experienced players (from New York, as a rule, because it is in New York that they have acquired the experience that is sought), community theater is generally manned by ardent actors who work eight hours a day elsewhere and have further chores waiting for them at home. Nor should anyone pretend that in this demiparadise there are no pressures of a theatrical kind. The playwright exiling himself to a community theater will leave behind him the need for enormous grosses and for the enormous compromises of an artistic kind that are made in the interests of those grosses. He can forget about featherbedding and "ice" and stop-clauses. But not everything that is done to his play now will be done out of motives of esthetic purity: he will sometimes find himself casting an actress, cutting his play, and accepting a director for reasons quite as irrelevant as those he fled on Broadway.

But perhaps this is little more than a quibble. What is essentially unprofitable for the playwright in the no-return trek to the theater that is distributed across the face of the country is the simple fact that it is so distributed. Decentralization is fine for everything that does not live and grow by crossbreeding, that does not require a thousand contending influences and impulses in order to arrive at its own highest sophistication and natural complexity. But drama is a complex form, drawing into its web not only a number of separate skills that must be independently sophisticated but the hum and buzz, the concentric layers of emotion and meaning, that charge the national air and set off sparks in passing.

It is where the buzz is thickest and the crossing of intellectual and emotional currents is at its liveliest and most abrasive that drama's particular tensions and insights are distilled. In every sense drama is a dynamic rather than a reflective form, and it needs the tumble and contention of a nerve center, a vast crackling switchboard, in order to assimilate its sources of energy and to produce its electrical discharge.

It is thus no accident that all great drama has erupted in just such centers—Athens, Paris, London, Moscow, Dublin— or that contributing influences coming in from smaller centers have always required the metropolitan crucible to refine them. And if nothing so absorbent and so turbulent can be managed without penalties, it is only by wrestling with penalties that the texture of the work can grow rich enough.

There are those who accept the need for the metropolitan concentration in which all currents fuse (and who secretly do not think that the playwright is going on that threatened long journey to the outlands, anyway) but who are terrified that the penalties have now got so out of hand that the playwright will be corrupted not by what is vitally and profitably central but by what is falsely and peculiarly Broadway. These are the worried rebels who would have the theater tuck up its skirts and withdraw to small lodgings on side streets, where it might possibly live on a pension.

Off-Broadway is the retreat so prescribed. Here are small houses: not so many seats for the writer to fill. Here are lower costs: not so many dollars for him to underwrite. Here are specialized audiences rather than expense-account boors, people of quick sympathies and developed tastes who are willing to follow him where his private bent may take him. Let him retire from the fray and probe his soul in security.

I think there are three questions to be asked quickly. The first is: What sort of continuing freedom from economic pressure does off-Broadway offer? Obviously, its costs are lower than Broadway's: a play can be presented for between ten and twenty-five thousand dollars. Furthermore, it is open-armed and fecund: off-Broadway now mounts as many as one hundred productions a season. The price is right and the doors are ajar.

But there is a catch. Nearly all off-Broadway productions lose nearly all of their respective investments. At the end of one recent season the *Variety* summary of successes and failures among new off-Broadway ventures showed no successes, all failures. A more "representative" season might show four to six successes out of a hundred tries. The upshot? Taking the lower figure of ten thousand dollars as an average production cost, off-Broadway is capable of losing—and almost certain to lose—close to one million dollars a year.

The problem—which must sooner or later be faced as Broadway is now trying to face *its* problems—is compounded by the fact that when Broadway does discover a hit it returns vast sums of money to all of its participants and to the common kitty, whereas the less frequent off-Broadway "success" tends to yield infinitesimal profits: seating capacity is too small to take care of sudden, overwhelming interest. The result is that, even in a good season, off-Broadway loses a higher proportion of its total investment than Broadway does. The drain is more constant, the replenishment feebler. So far from offering our playwright a permanent trouble-free nest, off-Broadway promises him literally less security than the uptown jungle does. Looked at from an economic point of view alone, the small outlying house does not so much resemble a savings bank as a bankruptcy court.

Those who are most concerned for the playwright's integrity, and who have given most thought to the matter, are aware of this. Thus they are quick to couple with their demand that the playwright be free to work under easier circumstances in smaller laboratories a further demand that productions be subsidized, in whole or in part, by foundation and government monies. Why should not the million dollars to be lost each year be paid for by someone other than audiences?

The problems of subsidy are various and interesting. I do not see how anyone can question the need for, or the wisdom of, national funds for the establishment of permanent companies playing the permanent repertory—preserving for us those works that have already made their way in the marketplace and in the library and now truly deserve the shelter of our fully financed respect. But someone must soon raise a subtler issue. Is there a psychology attendant upon subsidy, and, if so, how does it function?

The commonest worry attached to subsidy is that either the

government or the private source will take to meddling, particularly with subject matter. This seems to me a remote danger: governments and foundations are generally forced to behave themselves by the weight of public opinion. But is nothing going to go on in the heads of those who are contending and competing for subsidies? If one hundred productions a year are to go to the executive carpet in an appeal for funds, will they not begin "packaging," too? The packaging will of course be somewhat different from Broadway's. But if the need is urgent and the situation competitive—as it surely must be unless we are to envision a society in which *all* theatrical effort is automatically subsidized without prior investigation or qualification—isn't it lamentably likely that a hopeful manager will begin by trying to put together the sort of director with the sort of play with the sort of subject matter that the committee is reported to like? I am not certain that I see an escape from human nature, any more than I see an escape from cost accounting, here.

But it is a third question that concerns me most. Let us suppose that some massive form of subsidy would indeed fill in off-Broadway's financial quicksand, and that the subsidy would generate no subjective conniving on the part of producer or playwright. The bills are paid and no honor is forfeit. The playwright is free to sit down and write one kind of play (whatever kind he wishes to write) for one kind of audience (the kind that wishes to see this sort of play) in a suitably small auditorium.

The step, when and if taken, might very well prove fatal. Good things are possible in small houses: granted. Limited audiences with limited preferences have discovered, and passed on to the rest of us, fine things: granted. But the attempt to sustain the procedure on a long-term basis, to bind the playwright to a handful of preinterested "regulars," is an invitation to roost in a cul-de-sac, and so wither.

It is not the playwright's task to satisfy a single audience that constitutes no more than a segment, and very possibly an unrepresentative segment, of the body social. His true task, his ultimate task, is to touch a rainbow of segments, a motley assembly of disparate minds, in such a way as to polarize them, fuse them, make them one in the excitement of many. This is the theater's most peculiar gift, the gift that detaches it from a dozen other art forms and helps define it. It is what makes the theater a public rather than a private rite, a coming-together rather than a diaspora. Until a dramatist has mastered the unbelievably difficult feat of speaking in all tongues at once, and in such a way that all who are listening to him will also come to feel that they understand one another, he has not begun to exercise the particular power that is most naturally his.

Such exercise must take place in the open, with all comers admitted; only after they are admitted can they be made to realize their homogeneity. To go off in a corner with the few friends one already has is not the best way to prepare the universal feast; it is the best way to form a cult.

But there is more to be said about the audience than this. Because the Broadway theater does open its arms to expense-account customers (though these customers tend to come in large numbers only in the early months of a run) and because pleasing such customers is equated with pandering, the playwright who would respect himself is urged to banish all thought of an audience—all thought of *any* audience—from his head while he is working. It is an awareness of potential customers that does the most insidious damage, he is told: he will inevitably falsify his meanings in an effort to placate, or even to reach, these people. He is to write as though he were writing for no one, honoring only his intentions and the perfection of the work.

It is extraordinarily difficult to take any other view of the matter at the present time, though unless we take some other view it is hard to see how any shred of professional theater

311

activity can survive. Obviously a writer must honor his intentions and not be deflected from them by thought of gain. Obviously the perfection of the work must remain uppermost in his mind: art consists in the achievement of such perfection. And just as obviously the notion of writing directly for the theater-party audience or the expense-account crowd— which often seem to be the only audiences available—is a demeaning notion which must end in the pandering we fear.

Yet it seems to me that this last invitation to withdrawal— the rejection of the audience as a vital factor in a playwright's practice—is the most chilling, most wrongheaded, of all. The nub of the difficulty lies, I think, in a false equation. It is currently assumed that any consideration of the presence of an audience in the theater must be a pandering consideration— that the moment a playwright takes his audience into account, in any way, he must necessarily bend and then break the integrity of his thought, the strictness of his purpose, the perfection of his vision.

Why must he? The only reason that could conceivably be given is that the audience always and everywhere is a gathering of the playwright's inferiors. If it is truly impossible to speak to this assembly without blunting intention and coarsening expression, then the assembly itself must be coarse, doltish, substandard. When we say that the writer's sole hope of achieving quality depends upon his maintaining an absolute indifference to the communal aspects of theater, what we are really saying is that the community in general is intellectually incapable of listening to the playwright at the playwright's level. To speak to them at all he must necessarily speak down.

Let us skip over the implications of snobbery here. It seems to me that the assumption we make so easily in fact overlooks two important possibilities. One is that the response an audience makes in the theater has nothing, or relatively little, to do with its intellectual quotient, its habits of speech or dress, its environmental origins, the kind of restaurant it came from, or the work it does by day.

What a playwright touches, when he succeeds in touching anything serious, is an intuitive shoot deep in the universal psyche that stirs at a level below one's facility with arithmetic and lifts to an exaltation high above it. I have seen men engrossed in *Oedipus Rex* who could never have passed a civil service examination. This is a commonness men have; it is a font of their understanding; it awaits tapping in everyone, even people on expense accounts. When it is tapped, it bypasses differences in cerebral equipment and background and rises transcendent as a shared knowledge which glows brighter than what used to be called book-learning. Because of the audience's power to respond from its bowels, it can be raised to any heights a playwright may have in mind, and can manage. Not to try to manage this feat, however, not to prod with a divining rod for the universal well, confines the playwright to the smallish company of his precise intellectual equals, whether these be high, middling, or lower than he thinks. He can only be saved from the prison of a clique by the enforced need to communicate at large.

Which brings us to the second possibility—that a playwright can speak to a large and varied body of people and still say exactly what he means to say. Why should we not conceive that a writer can be utterly honest with himself, please himself, satisfy himself, and then work very hard to find a way of pleasing a vast audience with what has already pleased him?

Is this possible? Of course: it is what the master writers have always done. Is it difficult? Of course: it was the process of overcoming the difficulty that made the master writers masters. Pandering is never a failure imposed by the audience; it is a failure of the playwright to finish his intolerable task.

His task is intolerable, but it is not beyond doing. A transla-

313

tion is involved, from the private language in which his thoughts have first come to him into a "poetic" formalization that will reach all minds at once; but the translation need not be inaccurate. When it is accurate, and when it is intelligible, the audience matures surprisingly.

Pandering stems from a weakness in the craftsman rather than in the body politic. We do not have to be told that it is wrong. There is also a sense in which a practiced playwright need no longer be directly conscious of an audience for whom the play is created. Lillian Hellman has said that she does not compose with invisible customers staring her in the face. I am sure she does not. But Miss Hellman has long since grown into her form; she moves about in it as a resident of long standing, tidying familiar furniture without quite noticing what she is doing. She has good habits that will take care of the housekeeping, and is now truly free to think only of her meanings.

The fact remains that every playwright who is truly a playwright either consciously or unconsciously composes his house so that people will come into it, and arranges the furnishings so that while these people are there they will behave in a certain way. "It took me a long time," Romain Gary remembers in *Promise at Dawn*, "to admit that the reader was entitled to a certain amount of consideration and that it was necessary to explain to him, as to every newcomer [in a hotel] the number of his room, the way the switches worked, to give him his key and indicate where he would find all the necessities."

But once this is learned it need no longer be in the forefront of any writer's mind. It is what he committed himself to long ago. A good conversationalist does not examine his conscience while he is telling a story. When he first began telling stories he noticed that there were certain ways of catching his listeners' attention and certain ways of holding it. Noticing, he practiced. Now he *is* a practiced raconteur, adept at what he does. Because he is adept, he is free to do it. He need only use his good habits and say what is on his mind. It is the storyteller who has never bothered to attend to the responses of those about him who fails: because he has not for a moment considered the people to whom he is talking, he lectures, he pontificates, he bores. The decision to work for an audience is, I would think, a decision taken long prior to the creation of any one mature piece of work; it is a fact of life faced during creative adolescence, a philosophy, a craft. To suggest that it be abandoned, or never acquired, or acquired in code for the members of a secret society, is to deny the nature of a vocation.

For the audience is not a stumbling, unlooked-for intruder. The audience is part of the playwright's form. The very "perfection" of the work in this instance requires that the work be playable in a public place with people present, and the work will be held more nearly perfect, more illuminating and more expressive, as it commands the attention of more people. Though customers bring dollars to the window, they are not dollar signs; they are persons.

Our general difficulty today is not that we do too much for the audience but that we do too little for it. The audience is literally capable of better than we have been giving it, wistfully waiting to be wakened again in its deepest recesses. Waiting, and aware of the little that is most often offered, it has grown restive, dissatisfied, finally absent in large numbers. Nor is it eager to be baited into returning by extravagantly superficial and essentially condescending appeals. It may still go, though less and less frequently, to shows that are all color and splash. But it does not go to these things because its taste is irretrievably low; it goes to them because its other experiences of theater are so empty. It does not really like being taken for a fool; and it knows when it is not respected.

This seems to me the true and ultimate root of our present impasse; after all, it is the boredom and the consequent absence of a larger audience that has brought into being the economic difficulties. So far from urging the playwright to dismiss the multitude, I would suggest to the playwright that he pay the audience the compliment of remembering it with respect and of struggling to please it at the very highest level of which *he* is capable—with those very same things that enchant him.

THE LADY IN THE RAIN

No MAN can keep up with all of the current magazines, but I do try to leaf *The New Yorker* the minute the mailman delivers it. Unless I do, I am forced to spend the rest of the week listening to the rest of the family quote me the cartoon captions, a fate just slightly worse than trying to keep the children quiet during the first four hours of *Ben Hur*. This way I can deflect my benefactors by quickly saying, "Oh, yes, I saw that one," or perhaps by reciting the caption right along with them. I am aware that this last gambit is possibly the meanest that mortal e'er devised, but it does help speed the conversation along to other matters. Of course, admitting to having seen a certain cartoon also makes you vulnerable: you may be asked to explain it, in which case you'd be better off back at *Ben Hur*.

But I digress. Leafing one issue of *The New Yorker* I came across an item that tantalized me:

A Shakespeare buff of our acquaintance reports that when he attended a performance of *King Lear* in Central Park, on a clear, starry night, he was distracted by a fidgety lady seated beside him. At the beginning of Lear's mad scene, which was accompanied by flashes of man-made lightning and stentorian claps of backstage thunder, the woman stared querulously at the sky, dug into her purse, extracted one of those collapsible plastic rain hats, and wore it through the remainder of the scene.

I suppose we could editorialize about all sorts of things on the basis of this minor incident: about the simple faith some childlike souls can bring to the theater, about the need to restore the theater to people who have been so long away from it that they are unable to distinguish between man-made thunder and the real thing, about the power of the theater to create a mesmerizing, and even confusing, illusion.

But it was something else that intrigued me in the behavior of the lady with the rain hat. She seems to have thought that real thunder and real lightning were playing about her. She seems to have been convinced that the weather was going to get worse rather than better, and that if she was not about to be felled by a bolt from the heavens in her seriously exposed position she was at the very least going to get wet. Calmly, and in the face of these things, she stuck it out.

I sometimes have the feeling that all of us who bother going to the theater in these slightly aging years of the twentieth century are pretty much in the lady's position. Certainly there is every sort of man-made thunder to discourage us.

The twentieth-century theater isn't much of a theater, we are constantly told. It certainly hasn't the dignity Aeschylus gave it, there isn't so much as a flicker of Shakespeare's brief candle anywhere in the dark, it hasn't even displayed the intelligence of a ten-year-old since Shaw died. There have been protracted periods in the history of the theater when creativity burned low and the institution had to scrape along as best it could on the commonplace; we are living in such a period, and don't we wish we'd been born into a time when at least Sheridan was around?

This general estimate of the theatrical atmosphere we breathe is probably sound enough, by the way. We know where we are: in an interregnum marked by uncertainty, restiveness, a sense of continuing defeat relieved only by erratic flashes of a most modest distinction. The great ages have gone and will no doubt come again, but not tonight. When these things are said, however, and said loudly, they often have an arrogant clap of command about them.

The message tends to read: You know that the contemporary theater is at best second-rate and probably not that, in which case your clear obligation as a responsible person is to abandon it altogether. If it is not good enough to admire unreservedly, it is simply not good enough to attend. Let it go; quality will somehow be born of its complete destruction.

The command, and the implied invitation to go elsewhere (where quality is), comes sometimes from people who have been to the theater and found the movies infinitely superior (thus *Last Year at Marienbad* becomes acceptable material for serious discussion, where Tennessee Williams does not). It comes sometimes from people who are rarely able to bring themselves to the theater, being preoccupied with novels which have the blessing of the academic community (thus two or three contemporary novelists are given sober and minute attention while Thornton Wilder's work for the theater must, in the nature of things, be smilingly dismissed). I must say that these alternative forms seem to me to continue to labor under problems of their own: I seem to find at least as much strained mannerism and unresolved style in films as I do cliché in the theater; and the novelists, even when they are interesting, are not so overpoweringly endowed as to make me loathe the theater more.

But the electrical storms that rage about the theater, and come close to deafening the theatergoer as he tries to listen to the play, are nevertheless real, born of real causes. The crash and the rumble pick up still further menace from the economic situation that is so widely, and worrisomely, advertised.

Even as we put foot into a playhouse these days we have the nervous feeling that the building may be atomized into a parking lot before we can get out of it again. We are going to lose more theaters without getting new ones; the walls are tumbling. We are going to lose all of the theater's backers the day after tomorrow, except for big musicals. The stage is not solvent; to its literary limpness must be added a progressive inability to support itself. Under all of this devastating clatter, true or false and mostly true, who would be well advised to buy one more ticket, or even to stick out this evening's performance?

I admire the lady in the rain hat. She has come for only one purpose: to see the play, whatever it may be. She cannot be dissuaded from her purpose, not even by threatening circumstances that seem to her actual: she likes where she is and what she is doing a shade more than her immediate comfort. She is being a bit stupid, of course: she doesn't really know, when all is said and done, whether the strange performance she has stayed for will please her. But as long as she stays, some actor or writer will try.